LETTERS FROM OUR MOTHER

C. Peter R. Gossels

Gossels, C. Peter R., author

Letters From Our Mother

ISBN 978-0-578-57096-9

e-ISBN 978-0-578-57106-5

CONTENTS

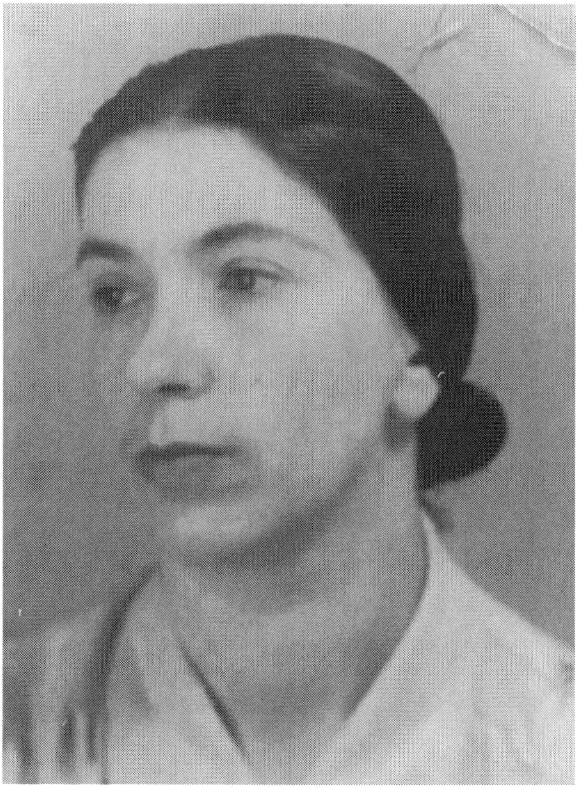

Charlotte "Lotte" Lewy Gossels

INTRODUCTION

Our mother, Charlotte, was lovingly known as Lotte. Before she was deported from Belin and murdered at Auschwitz on March 2, 1943, Lotte gave birth to me, Peter, in 1930, and my brother, Werner, in 1933. She divorced our father, Max, in 1936 when he could no longer support his family and raised her boys as a single mother.

In order to support her family, she started a business as a cosmetologist, who provided massages and spa type care for her clients. And when it became clear that there was no future in Nazi Germany for Werner and me, Lotte worked hard for an entire year to obtain French visas for us so that we might escape to a free country.

Lotte finally obtained those visas and saw us off on a train to France on July 3, 1939. And she followed us with a series of twenty-nine letters while we were in France doing our best to stay alive. We received her last letter dated November, 1941, after she learned that we had arrived in the United States. Those letters form the core of this book.

And I kept those letters as I grew up, went to school, served in the United States Army, married Nancy, helped her to raise three children, practiced law, served as President of my congregation, and as Moderator of the Town of Wayland.

Until one day last spring, I looked at my files and decided that the German letters that I had received from our mother more than 80 years ago should be translated and published to demonstrate to our family what a wonderful woman our mother was. They had seen our mother's picture which serves as the front piece of this book, but a picture does not, and can not, convey the remarkable qualities that Lotte Lewy demonstrated to her children and her entire family.

THE LEWY FAMILY

Charlotte Lewy was born on September 7, 1903 to Lina Lewy (born Lewy) and Isidor Lewy. Charlotte's father, Isidor, was born near Posen on May 19, 1859. Her mother was born on June 19, 1875 in Posen, which had been a part of Germany since 1815, but was returned to Poland after the First World War. Lina's parents were Julius Lewy, an insurance broker (born in 1840), and his wife, Johanna Jacobson (born in 1853), who apparently lived a comfortable life until Johanna died in 1903. Julius died in 1927.

When Lotte arrived at the Lewy home, she met her two-year old sister, Hildegard Margot Fanny (Hilde), who had been born on September 24, 1901.

We know nothing about Isidor's parents, but have obtained a copy of documents, thanks to Simon Lütgemeyer[1], indicating that Isidor owned property and a textile factory at 192 Brunnenstrasse in Berlin as of April 3, 1907, where he manufactured a variety of clothing. A phonebook of the period indicates that Isidor manufactured clothes on the second floor of 13 Burgstrasse.

In or about 1904-05, while he was living at Schleswiger Ufer 15 (later No. 7) with his family, Isidor purchased 35 Lippehner Strasse, a building with 42 apartments, in the newly developed section of Berlin, called Prenzlauer Berg. The street, which was renamed Kathe-Niederkirchner-Strasse by the East German government, runs between the Friedrichshain, a large park, and Greifswalder Strasse.

In 1909, Isidor, Lina and his daughters, Hilde (8) and Lotte (6), moved to 21 Levetzowstrasse.

---

[1] An architect now living in the apartment building formerly owned by the Lewy family, who painstakingly uncovered the history of the people who once lived there and dedicated the building to their memory.

Johanna and Julius Lewy

Isidor Lewy

— **R. Lewy,** Cravattenfbrk, C Bischofstr. 17. (Tel. I. 8299) Inh. Siegmund Lewy.
— Hugo, Direct. d. Act. Ges. vorm H. Gladenbeck, & Sohn, W. Motzstr. 69. I. (Tel. VIa 11176.)
— Paul, Director, SW. Großbeerenstr. 5. (Tel. VIa 11177.)
—, Bernhard, Drechsler, C Koblankstr. 17.
— ~~Isidor, Drechsler, C Gipsstr. 19 I.~~
— Isidor, Fabrk., N Brunnenstr. 192.
— ~~Solmar, Fabrkbes., N Oranienburgerstr. 87 pt.~~
f. Berliner Wallextract-u Fettwaaren-Fabrik rc.

~~Mendelssohnstr. 1 IV. (Tel. VII. 720.)~~ Inh ~~Bernh.~~ Lewy.
J. Lewy's Confection, Tricottaillen, Blousen, Jupons u. Kleidchen, C Burgstr. 13 II. (Tel. V. 3638.) Inh. Isidor Lewy.
~~M., Trödler,~~ N Auguststr. 27 pt.

The address connected to "I. Lewy Confection" in the phonebook was Burgstr. 13 - which I found in an area right opposite the former castle (and becoming Humboldt Museum), an area where lots of Jewish properties have been lost (still an empty field, formerly Marx-Engels-Forum):
http://aktives-museum.de/gmitte/public/details/index/644
There you can see the house (with a "Briefmarken" shop) where Isidor might have been (2nd floor).

Our grandfather's clothing factory was located
above the Briefmarken sign.

Fabrikgebäude
Brunnenstraße 192/193

Denkmalgerecht erneuerte Klinkerfassaden
Foto: Anne Lampen Architekten

Lageplan

Bundesministerium des Innern, für Bau und Heimat

Städtebaulicher Denkmalschutz

Das zwischen 1900 und 1910 errichtete Fabrikgebäude Brunnenstraße 192/193 befindet sich im Bereich der ehemaligen Kolonie Neu-Voigtland, aus deren Entstehungszeit die schmalen und tiefen Grundstücke und erhalten sind.

Es besteht aus zwei Quergebäuden sowie einem dreigeschossigen Seitenflügel als verbindendes Element.

Das in seinem Originalzustand noch weitgehend erhalten gebliebene Gebäude ist Zeugnis der Industriekultur des ehemals vorstädtischen Quartiers. Charakteristisch ist die zurückhaltend gestaltete Fassade aus Sichtmauerwerk, die durch verschiedenfarbige Bänder, Brüstungsfelder und abgetreppte Gesimse gegliedert ist. Besonderes Wahrzeichen ist der an einen Förderturm erinnernde historische Lastenaufzug am zweiten Quergebäude. Er prägt als technisches Denkmal die Zweckarchitektur des Fabrikgebäudes. Ungewöhnlich ist auch die außen liegende, eiserne Feuertreppenkonstruktion am Seitenflügel.

Das Gebäude ist nach denkmalpflegerischen Vorgaben sorgfältig instand gesetzt und modernisiert. Im Rahmen der Sanierung ist die historische Bausubstanz behutsam erneuert und den heutigen Nutzungsanforderungen entsprechend verändert und ergänzt worden. Im Inneren des Gebäudes sind großzügige lichtdurchflutete Gewerbelofts entstanden, die auch zum Wohnen geeignet sind. Offene Grundrisse erlauben eine flexible Anpassung an individuelle Wünsche der Nutzer. Die Einheiten mit jeweils einer integrierte Küchenzeile und einem Sanitärblock können nach Bedarf unterteilt oder zusammengelegt werden.

Daten

- **Baujahr/Entstehung:** um 1905
- **Eigentümer:** privat
- **Geförderte Maßnahmen:** Instandsetzung der baulichen Hülle
- **Architekten:**
  Architekturbüro Karl-Heinz und Thomas Roy
  Gutzmannstraße 17
  14165 Berlin
- **Fertigstellung:** 2003

Our grandfather's clothing factory was located in the building shown above

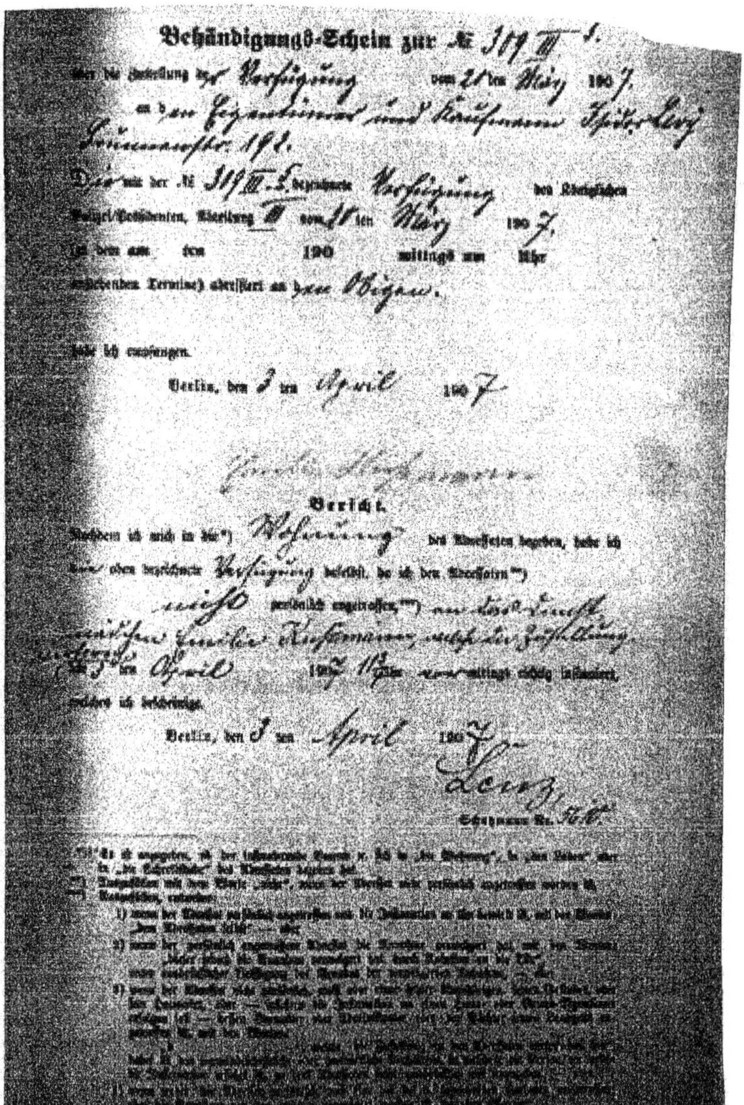

Behändigungs-Schein zur № 319 III

Berlin, den 3ten April 1907

Bericht.

Berlin, den 3ten April 1907

Schutzmann Nr.

Official document concerning Isidor Lewy dated March 20, 1907

BERLIN, Käthe-Niederkirchner- Ecke Bötzowstr.

The Lewys were part of a large, extended family: Lina's brother, Erich, a dentist, who lived in Mannheim with his wife, Eleanor "Lorle" Rosenberg after they married in 1921. Her sister, Martha, married Charles Stern, M.D. and lived in Hartford, Connecticut. Isidor had six brothers, including Ludwig from Chemnitz, who had three children, Lucy, Leo and Benno. Betty Lewy, the daughter of Isidor's brother, Herman, was particularly close to the family. But Lina was, in many ways, the center of the family; a balabusta you might say.

We know nothing about the schooling of the Lewy sisters, but we don't believe that they had the benefit of anything like a college education. Hilde never married, but Lotte met a man named Max Gossels and married him in 1929.

Max was born in Berlin on February 5, 1901, to Gottfried, a tailor who had been born in Emden on May 9, 1874, and his wife, Francisca Israel. While matriculating at the Köllnisches Gymnasium in Berlin, Max had driven wagons filled with potatoes to the German front during the First World War. In 1923, Max completed his final examination in law and economics with honors at the University of Berlin. In 1926, Max served as a judge until he was appointed to serve as a magistratsrat of a section of the City of Berlin in 1927. In that capacity, Max supervised the building and administration of housing and development projects, veterans' and other welfare programs as well as the administration of various hospitals in his district of the City. In 1928, Max was appointed a functionary for life at the age of 27.

The newly married couple soon found and rented an apartment at 20 Tile Wardenberg Strasse in the Wedding section of Berlin, not far from the River Spree.

When I, their first child was born on August 11, 1930, Lotte and Max could not agree on what to name me. So they compromised: My first name, Claus, was dictated by Max; Lotte gave me my second name, Peter, and they agreed that Rolf would stand for my Hebrew name, Reuven.

The wedding of my uncle, Erich Lewy, and Eleonore (Lorle) Rosenberg in 1921 attended by members of our family.

1 David **Rosenberg**	11
2 Regine **Rosenberg** nee **Wallach**	12 Charlotte Lewy ?
3 Julius **Lewy** (1840-1927)	13
4 Lina **Lewy** geb.(1875-1942)	14 Jenny Krauss
5 Franz **Schloss** (1884-1941)	15
6 Elsa **Rosenberg** (marr. **Schloss**) (1892-1945)	16
7 Martha **Stern** > Stearn nee **Lewy**	17 Charles **Stern** > **Stearn**
8	18 Juelle **Sonders** (friend of Lorle)
9 Eleonore *Lorle* **Lewy** nee **Rosenberg (1897-1989)**	19
10 Erich Lewy (1885-1971) [in USA >Lewis]	20 Simon **Lewy**

Hilde, Erich and Lotte Lewy (1921?)

Hilde, Benno and Lotte Lewy

Lotte, Hilde and Lucy Lewy

Hilde Lewy

Lotte Lewy

Max Gossels

RESUME

Name: Max Gossels

Address: c/o C. Peter R. Gossels
Sullivan & Worcester
185 Devonshire Street
Boston 10, Massachusetts

Telephone: HU 2-3215

Born: February 5, 1901; Berlin, Germany.

Family: Married; Two sons: one an engineer with General Electric, the other an attorney practicing at the above address.

Formal Education

1. Kollnisches Gymnasium, Berlin: 1908-1920.

2. University of Berlin: 1920-1923

   a. Fields of Concentration
      1) Public Law (Administrative, Constitutional, and Comparative International Law).
      2) Roman Law.
      3) Welfare Legislation and Administration.
      4) Economics.

   b. Examination - 1923
      Completed the final examinations in the faculties of law and economics with honors, and was thereupon appointed Referendarius.

3. Referendarius: 1923-1926

   a. Study and Experience
      Served as law clerk to attorneys, the Office of the Prosecutor, and assistant to a number of judges in various courts.

   b. Examination - 1926
      Passed the Assessor examination in the Ministry of Justice Magna cum Laude; was thereupon appointed an Assessor.

Experience

1. Banks and Financial Institutions - 1923
   I worked part time for the bank of Guttentag and Goldschmidt in Berlin and helped in currency arbitrage at the Berlin Stock Exchange and was appointed head of the Research Department of the Berlin office of the bank, Buchholz and Co., Danzig.

2. Judge - 1926

Served for nearly a year as judge in the Amtsgericht Berlin.

3. Magistratsrat - 1927 - 1933

In my capacity as Magistratsrat of the City of Berlin, I was principally concerned with the Department of Social Welfare and supervised:

a. The building and administration of housing and redevelopment projects.

b. Veterans' and other welfare programs.

c. The administration of the various hospitals in my district.

Was appointed functionary for life in 1928. Recalled as ober-Magistratsrat in 1946, and retired.

4. Teaching

a. Lectured at the Administrative Seminary of Berlin (1930-1933)
   1) Civil law
   2) Public law
   3) Social welfare legislation and administration.

b. Lectured at the Judische Volkshochschule (1933-1934) on the same subjects.

5. Publication

a. Articles in various professional journals including "Das Grundeigentum".

b. Articles on legal problems for various newspapers including the "Vossische Zeitung", the "Berliner Tageblatt" and "Gemeindeblatt",

6. Business

a. 1930-1932- Consultant to various German manufacturing companies especially textile concerns.

b. 1941-1942- Legal consultant in Lapalisse (Allier) France.

c. 1942-1959- Business consultant and accountant to a number of Venezuelan enterprises.

-2-

d. 1942-1959- Participation with Venezuelan lawyers in problems of civil and corporate law.

e. 1946-1959- Officer and Director of a number of Venezuelan corporations including
   1) Laboratorio Farmacologico Venezolano
   2) Terapeutica, S.A.
   3) Mago, Cia. Anon.
   4) Comest

7. Miscellaneous

   a. 1932-1933-"Demokratischer Klub," Berlin, Germany.

   b. 1933-1934- Head of the "Judische Wirtschaftshilfe", an organization that gave legal and financial assistance to "non-aryans".

   c. 1933-1939- Acted as attorney, representing "non-aryans" before the German authorities, including the Gestapo.

Languages

1. Fluent in German, Spanish, French, and English
2. Know Latin, Greek, Italian and Dutch.

Specialties

1. Roman Law.
2. Comparative Law.
3. International Commercial Law.
4. Social Welfare legislation and Administration.
5. Political Theory.

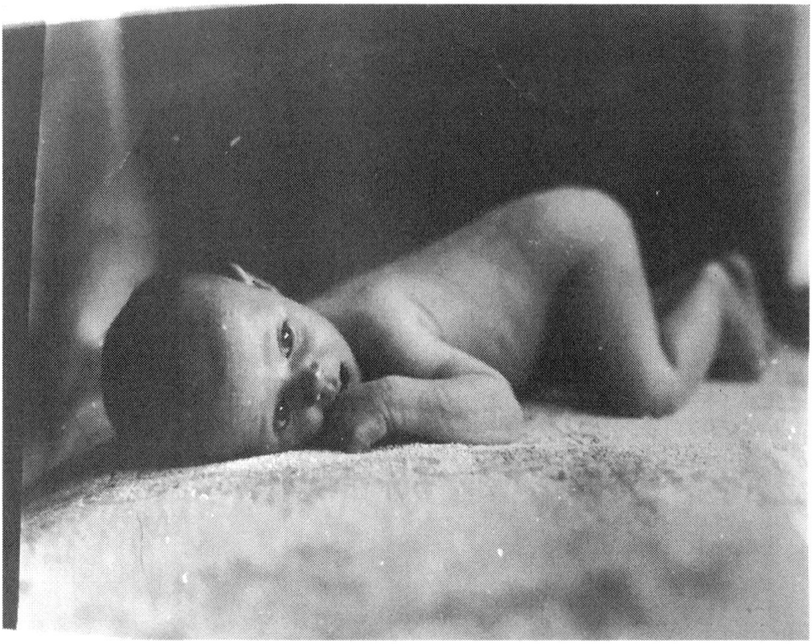

Claus Peter Rolf Gossels

While Max continued to work as a Magistratsrat and lectured at the Administrative Seminary of Berlin, the Weimar Republic gradually collapsed under pressure from the Nazis and the Communists.

On January 30, 1933, President Paul von Hindenburg named Adolph Hitler as Chancellor of Germany.

On July 23, 1933, Lotte and Max rejoiced as their second child was born. They named him Werner Franz Julian.

Within months after Hitler and the Nazis took power in Germany, all Jewish officials, including Max, lost their government jobs and teaching positions. Max became head of the Jüdische Wirtschaftshilfe, an organization that gave legal and financial assistance to Jews in need. Max also acted as attorney for Jews before the German authorities, including the Gestapo, and lectured at the Jüdische Volkshochschule on civil law, public law and social welfare legislation and administration.

As Max lost the principal sources of his income, his marriage to Lotte became more and more strained. Isidor tried to help by hiring Max to manage his building. Isidor also hired Max's father, Gottfried, but Lotte and Max engaged in intensive quarrels about their finances after their children went to bed.

Isidor died on May 5, 1936. His remains are in Section 7 of the Weissensee Cemetery (Row 28, No. 3) in Berlin. Lotte and Max divorced in 1936, and Lotte moved to the family home at 35 Lippehner Strasse with my brother and me to live with her mother, Lina, and her sister, Hilde. Although they were divorced, Lotte and Max remained on friendly terms with each other and Max would come to the apartment of Betty Lewy, Herman's daughter, around the corner at 28 Bötzowstrasse every Wednesday to visit with Werner and me.

Lina Lewy

Lina and Isidor Lewy relaxing in the Tiergarten.

Isidor Lewy on his balcony (1936?)

Hermann Wasserlauf
Verl.
Bln.-Schöneberg Kufsteiner Str. 12
Berlin NO 55 Pieskower Weg 14

Alfred Kirsch
Hanny Kirsch, geb. Schnell
VERMÄHLTE
Trauung: Sonntag, den 10. Mai, Synagoge Oranienburger Str., 3½ Uhr

Statt Karten
Für die uns anläßlich unserer Vermählung erwiesene Aufmerksamkeit allen Verwandten u. Bekannten herzlichen Dank.
Gerhard Wolff
Paula Wolff
geb. Treitel

VERMÄHLTE
5. Mai 1936 Mommsenstr. 42

Die glückliche Geburt unseres Töchterchens zeigen hocherfreut an
Alfons Alexander und Frau Anni, geb. Levi
Berlin 3. Mai 1936, Turiner Str. 46

Die glückliche Geburt eines gesunden Jungen zeigen hocherfreut an
Árpád Vigdorovits und Frau Babara geb. Fekele
Lajos Louis
Berlin N 41, Fehrbelliner Straße 81

Trauung e Synagoge Oranienburger Straße, 6.30 Uhr

Anläßlich meines am 11. Mai stattfindenden 10jährigen Geschäftsbestehens sage ich meiner werten Kundschaft, auch allen Freunden und Bekannten, meinen herzlichen Dank.
Mechel Magiermann, Schuhmacher.
Berlin NW, Tile-Wardenberg-Str. 29.

„Dichterherzog"
Ihr moderner Festdichter!
Flensburger Str. 22, C 9 Tierg. 2500

Festdichtungen von RM 5.— an
Erna Cohn
Barbarossastr. 46
B 6 3456 (nachm.)

Festdichtungen erstklassig, billig
Spiegel
Badensche Straße 42.
H 7 Wilmersd. 0737.

Am 1. Mai verschied nach kurzem, schwerem Leiden unsere innigstgeliebte Mutter, Schwiegermutter, Großmutter und Schwester, Frau
Clara Wolffenstein
geb. Blum
im 72. Lebensjahr.
Wer die Verstorbene kannte, wird unseren Schmerz verstehen.
Im Namen der Hinterbliebenen
Alfred Wolffheim u. Frau Herta geb. Wolffenstein
Fritz Wolffenstein u. Frau Rosa geb. Langmann
Werner u. Steffi Wolffheim
Charlottenburg 9, Bayernallee 47.
Die Beisetzung hat auf Wunsch der Verstorbenen in aller Stille stattgefunden.

Am 1. Mai entschlief sanft nach langer, schwerer Krankheit mein innigstgeliebter Mann, unser zärtlicher, gütiger Vater und Schwiegervater, der Buchhändler
Arthur Schlesinger
im 70. Lebensjahre.
In tiefer Trauer
Martha Schlesinger geb. Schildberger,
Hans und Sophie Bernhard geb. Schlesinger,
Ilse Schlesinger.
Berlin, Passauer Str. 24.
Die Beisetzung hat bereits stattgefunden.

Mein geliebter Mann, unser guter treusorgender Vater
Isidor Lewy
ist nach schwerem Leiden kurz vor Vollendung seines 77. Lebensjahres von uns gegangen.
In tiefer Trauer
Lina Lewy geb. Lewy,
Hilde Lewy,
Charlotte Gossels geb. Lewy,
Max Gossels, Mag.-Rat i. R.,
2 Enkelkinder.
Berlin, den 5. Mai 1936, Lippehner Str. 35,
Tile-Wardenberg-Str. 20.
Die Beerdigung hat bereits stattgefunden.

Am 30. April verschied unerwartet infolge eines Herzschlages meine heißgeliebte, treue Lebensgefährtin, unsere liebe Schwester, Schwägerin, Tante und Freundin
Else Kaliski
geb. Kronenberg
im 56. Lebensjahr.
Im Namen der Hinterbliebenen
Georg Kaliski
Berlin, 4. Mai 1936
W 30, Barbarossastr. 40.
Die Beisetzung hat bereits stattgefunden.

Dresden-Weißer Hirsch „Turmeck".
Die Beisetzung hat bereits stattgefunden.

Am 6. Mai verschied plötzlich und unerwartet nach kurzem Krankenlager meine liebe Frau, Schwester, Tante und Schwägerin
Hulda Cassel
geb. Lewin
(früher Wronke)
im 71. Lebensjahre.
Im Namen der Trauernden
Bernhard Cassel.
Die Beerdigung findet am Sonntag, dem 10. Mai, 9 Uhr (Neue Halle), statt. — Beileidsbesuche dankend verbeten.

Am 6. Mai entschlief sanft unsere liebe Schwester, Schwägerin und Tante
Auguste Halpert
geb. Guttmann
im 75. Lebensjahr.
Im Namen der Hinterbliebenen
Hulda Guttmann.
Bln.-Schöneberg, Eisenacher Str. 78.
Beisetzung: Sonntag, den 10. Mai, 11 Uhr, Alte Halle.

Nach kurzem, schweren Leiden entschlief am 3. Mai unser lieber Vater und Schwiegervater
Albert Joel
im 76. Lebensjahr.
Erich u. Manuela Nelly Rehfeldt geb. Joel.
Berlin NW 87, Claudiusstr. 4.
Die Beisetzung hat bereits in aller Stille stattgefunden.

Herzlichen Dank für alle Beweise der Teilnahme beim Hinscheiden meiner geliebten Schwester, Frau
Ada Lewin
geb. Ehrenberg.
Im Namen aller Hinterbliebenen
Margarete Blach geb. Ehrenberg.
Afrikanische Str. 141.

Nach kurzem, schweren
schied heute unser li
mein herzensguter Lebe
Leo Schw
im 67. Lebensjahr.
Berlin — Haynau, den
In tiefer Tra
Die Hi
Beerdigung: Sonntag,
12 Uhr, Weißensee, Al

Nach schwerem Leiden
29. April unser lieber
Onkel
Fritz Selig
im 57. Lebensjahre.
Charlottenburg, Droysen
Paul Seligsohn,
Dora Heße geb.
Die Beerdigung hat b
gefunden.

Am 30. April entschlief
Leiden mein inniggeli
unser herzensguter Vat
Hans Ung
In tiefer
Else Unger geb
und Ki
Die Einäscherung hat
gefunden. — Für alle
Teilnahme herzlichsten

Für alle Beweise der L
teilnahme beim Heimg
lieben, unvergeßlichen
vaters, Urgroßvaters,
Onkels
Abraham Stu
(früher Kolmar i.
sprechen wir hiermit
lichsten Dank aus.
Die trauernden Hin

Trauerspenden - Frische Bl
CARL BERNSTEIN W 50, Tauentzienstr. 9,

Isidor's death notice

During the first year after Lotte's return to 35 Lippehner Strasse, the family lived comfortably: Hilde worked, Lotte took care of us and Lina served as host to many visitors, including her nephew, Benno Lewy, and her niece, Lucy Lewy, who would emigrate to the United States. They even had a maid who came to cook and clean every day.

Although I reached school age in 1936, Lotte decided to hold me back until I turned 7, when Jewish children were no longer admitted to the public schools. As a result, I began my education at the Private Volksschule der Jüdische Gemeinde, which was conducted at the Rykestrasse Synagogue, a short walk from Lippehner Strasse.

The family observed most of the Jewish holidays and sometimes attended services at the Rykestrasse Synagogue and occasionally at the Oranienburg Synagogue.

As the pressure on the Jewish community grew, Lina's brother, Dr. Erich Lewy, his wife, Eleanor (Lorle), and his daughter, Gerda, came to Berlin from Mannheim in 1938 and stayed with the family until their boat for the United States was ready to sail from Hamburg. And Marian Stern, Lina's niece, came from Hartford, Connecticut, and visited with the family while she was seeing physicians in Berlin to treat her eyesight. But the pressure became more intense in 1938: Nazi SA troopers often marched through the streets to the beat of their drum. Jews could no longer sit on benches in the public parks: they had to sit on the few benches painted yellow. Lotte had to rescue Werner and me from a group of Hitler youth with hunting knives on their belt, who had surrounded and threatened us as we were walking home from the Friedrichshain. The destruction of synagogues, Jewish businesses and the arrest of Jewish men all over Germany on Kristallnacht, November 9, 1938, tightened the screws even further.

Werner

Werner and Peter on Aunt Betty Lewy's balcony at Boetzowstrasse 28

Werner and Peter

Peter and Werner

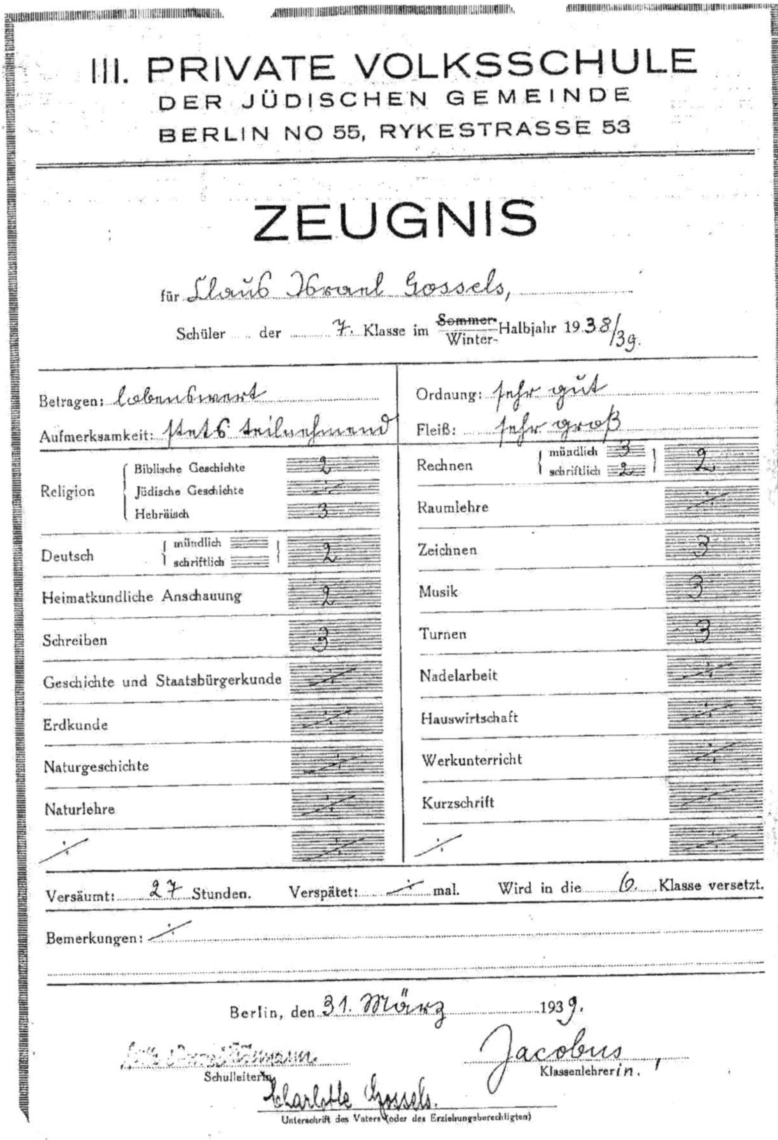

III. PRIVATE VOLKSSCHULE
DER JÜDISCHEN GEMEINDE
BERLIN NO 55, RYKESTRASSE 53

ZEUGNIS

für Klaus Israel Gossels,

Schüler der 7. Klasse im ~~Sommer-~~ Winter-Halbjahr 1938/39.

Betragen: lobenswert		Ordnung: sehr gut	
Aufmerksamkeit: stets teilnehmend		Fleiß: sehr groß	
Religion – Biblische Geschichte	2	Rechnen (mündlich 3, schriftlich 2)	2
Religion – Jüdische Geschichte	–/–	Raumlehre	–/–
Religion – Hebräisch	3	Zeichnen	3
Deutsch (mündlich, schriftlich)	2	Musik	3
Heimatkundliche Anschauung	2	Turnen	3
Schreiben	3	Nadelarbeit	–/–
Geschichte und Staatsbürgerkunde	–/–	Hauswirtschaft	–/–
Erdkunde	–/–	Werkunterricht	–/–
Naturgeschichte	–/–	Kurzschrift	–/–
Naturlehre	–/–	–/–	–/–
–/–	–/–		

Versäumt: 27 Stunden. Verspätet: –/– mal. Wird in die 6. Klasse versetzt.

Bemerkungen: –/–

Berlin, den 31. März 1939.

[illegible] Schulleiterin

Jacobus, Klassenlehrerin.

Charlotte Gossels.
Unterschrift des Vaters (oder des Erziehungsberechtigten)

Peter's report card from school in 1938/1939

Edith Schindler, our good friend, who was murdered at Auschwitz.

1939 brought a whirlwind of events: the family had to let their maid go, because Jews were no longer allowed to employ Aryan (non-Jewish) people. In order to generate income, Lotte purchased and installed a used barber's chair in the dining room and began offering her massage services to the public in the Judisches Nachrichtenblatt. She created her own cosmetics and often traveled to the homes of her customers to treat them. While Lotte was working, Werner and I would often visit the neighbors, Marta Klein, and her sister, Ursula Klein, across the hall, to sit on their porch and watch the people go by. The Klein apartment was particularly interesting, because it was still lit by gas, instead of electricity.

While all this was going on, Lotte worked hard almost every day to find a way to send us to safety abroad. In March, 1939, the Gestapo informed Max that he would be arrested in three days, unless he left the country. After meeting with the family, Max fled Germany for Antwerp, Belgium on April 2, 1939.

On April 24, 1939, Lotte signed a document, which conferred custody of Werner and me on the Comite Israelite pour Les Enfants Venant d'Allemagne et de l'Europe Centrale located in Paris, which was apparently funded by the Rothschild family.

On or about March 20, 1939, Lina was forced to sell 35 Lippehnerstrasse to one, Charlotte Klaus, a Nazi, for 127,000 marks, much less than the building was worth, because Jews were no longer allowed to own real estate. I was present as an 8 year-old and never forgot that transaction. Lina was forced to renovate the entire building with the proceeds of the sale and the balance was placed in a Sperrkonto (savings account) in Lina's name, from which she was allowed to withdraw only a small sum each month. On Monday, July 3, 1939, Lotte took Werner and me to a railroad station in Berlin in the company with our grandfather, Gottfried Gossels. She gave me a Hagada, put us on a train with 37 other Jewish children and never saw us again.

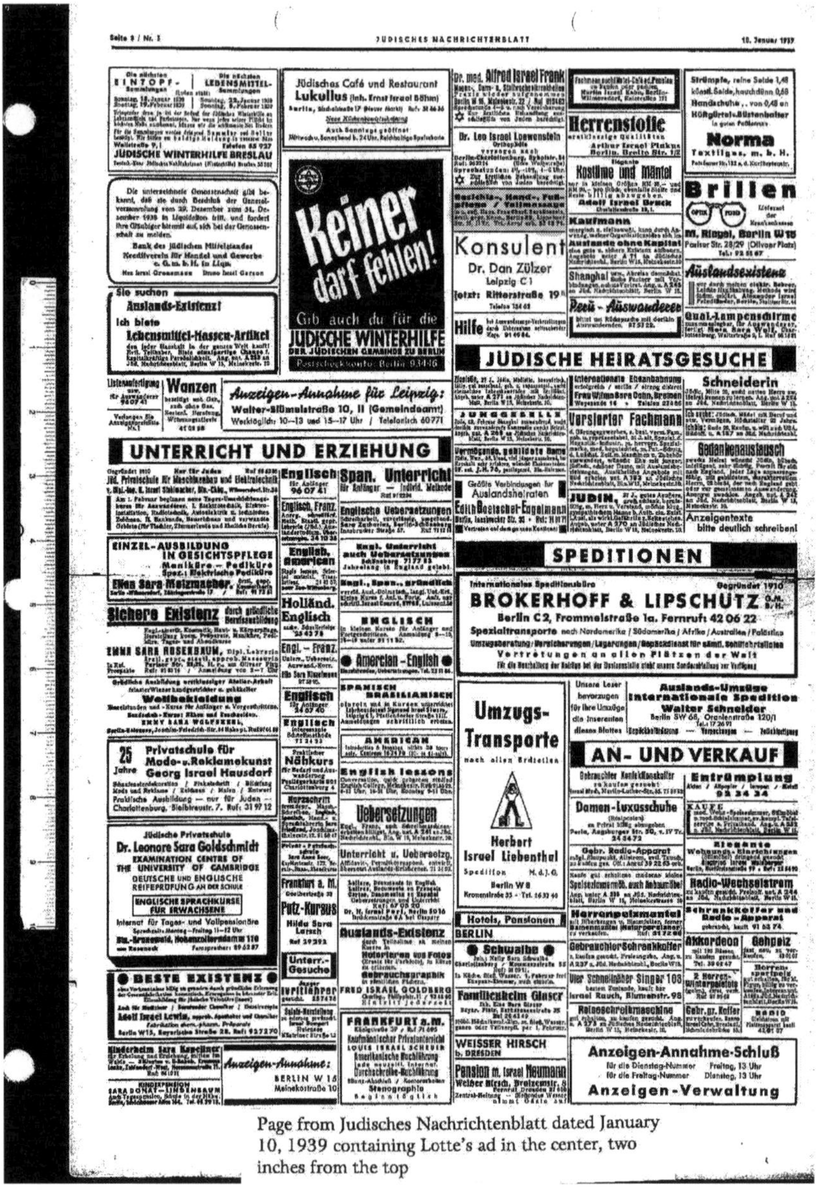

Seite 3 / Nr. 3 JÜDISCHES NACHRICHTENBLATT 10. Januar 1939

EINTOPF-Sammlungen / LEBENSMITTEL-Sammlungen

JÜDISCHE WINTERHILFE BRESLAU

Jüdisches Café und Restaurant Lukullus (Inh. Ernst Israel Böhm)

Dr. med. Alfred Israel Frank

Herrenstoffe

Strümpfe, reine Seide 1,48 ... Norma Textilien

Brillen

Keiner darf fehlen!

Gib auch du für die JÜDISCHE WINTERHILFE

DER JÜDISCHEN GEMEINDE ZU BERLIN

Postscheckkonto: Berlin 93446

Kostüme und Mäntel

Konsulent Dr. Dan Zülzer Leipzig C 1

Shanghai

Auslandsexistenz

Sie suchen Auslands-Existenz!

Ich biete Lebensmittel-Massen-Artikel

Wanzen

Anzeigen-Annahme für Leipzig: Walter-Blümelstraße 10, II (Gemeindeamt) Werktäglich: 10—13 und 15—17 Uhr / Telefonisch 60771

JÜDISCHE HEIRATSGESUCHE

Schneiderin

Versierter Fachmann

Größte Verbindungen für Auslandsheiraten

JUDIN

Anzeigentexte bitte deutlich schreiben!

UNTERRICHT UND ERZIEHUNG

Englisch 96 07 41

Span. Unterricht

Englische Uebersetzungen

EINZEL-AUSBILDUNG IN GESICHTSPFLEGE Maniküre — Pediküre

English. American

SPEDITIONEN

BROKERHOFF & LIPSCHUTZ G.m.b.H.

Berlin C2, Frommelstraße 1a. Fernruf: 42 06 22

Sichere Existenz

Holländ. Englisch

ENGLISCH

Engl. — Franz.

American — English

Weißbekleidung

Englisch

SPANISCH BRASILIANISCH

Umzugs-Transporte nach allen Erdteilen

Auslands-Umzüge Internationale Spedition Walter Schneider Berlin SW 68, Oranienstraße 120/1

25 Jahre Privatschule für Mode- u. Reklamekunst Georg Israel Hausdorf

Nähkurs

AMERICAN

English lessons

AN- UND VERKAUF

Entrümpelung

Damen-Luxusschuhe

Jüdische Privatschule Dr. Leonore Sara Goldschmidt

EXAMINATION CENTRE OF THE UNIVERSITY OF CAMBRIDGE

DEUTSCHE UND ENGLISCHE REIFEPRÜFUNG AN DER SCHULE

ENGLISCHE SPRACHKURSE FÜR ERWACHSENE

Uebersetzungen

Unterricht u. Uebersetzg.

Herbert Israel Liebenthal Spedition

Radio-Wechselstrom

Frankfurt a. M.

Putz-Kursus

Auslands-Existenz

Hotels, Pensionen BERLIN

Schwalbe

Akkordeon

Pelzmäntel

BESTE EXISTENZ

Familienheim Glaser

WEISSER HIRSCH b. DRESDEN

Pension

Anzeigen-Annahme: BERLIN W 15 Meinekestraße 10

FRANKFURT a.M.

Anzeigen-Annahme-Schluß

für die Dienstag-Nummer Freitag, 13 Uhr

für die Freitag-Nummer Dienstag, 13 Uhr

Anzeigen-Verwaltung

Page from Judisches Nachrichtenblatt dated January 10, 1939 containing Lotte's ad in the center, two inches from the top

Page from Judisches Nachrichtenblatt dated January 10, 1939

Containing Lotte's ad (highlighted).

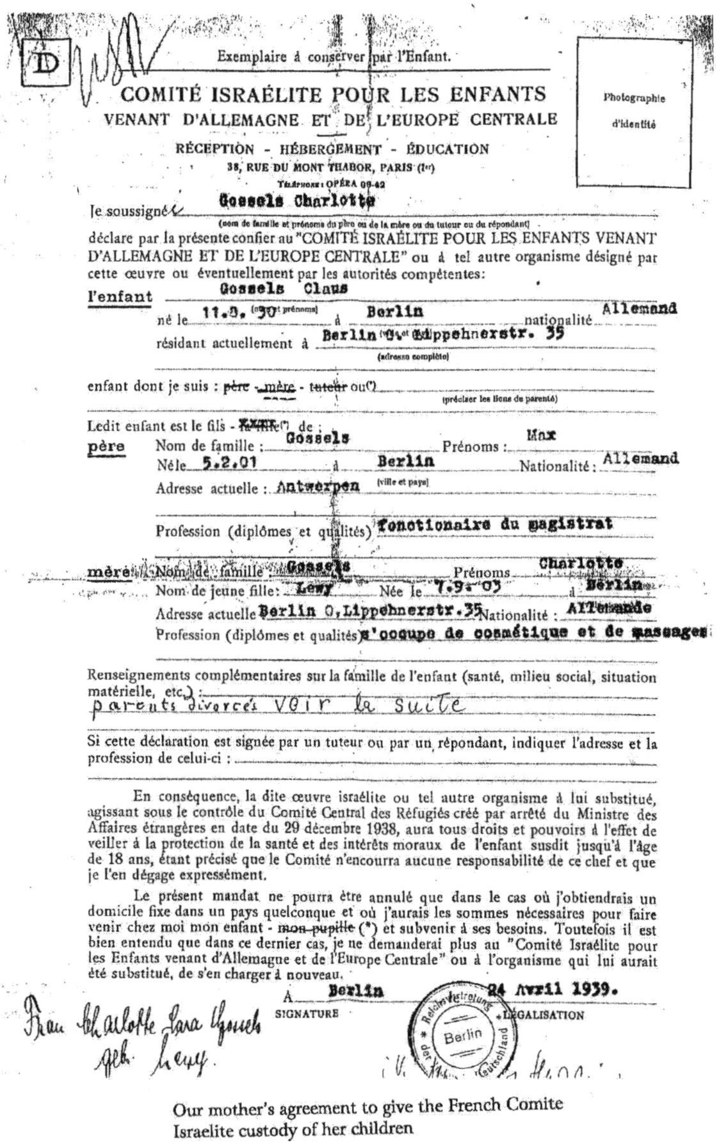

D

Exemplaire à conserver par l'Enfant.

COMITÉ ISRAÉLITE POUR LES ENFANTS
VENANT D'ALLEMAGNE ET DE L'EUROPE CENTRALE

RÉCEPTION - HÉBERGEMENT - ÉDUCATION
38, RUE DU MONT THABOR, PARIS (1er)
TÉLÉPHONE: OPÉRA 09-42

Photographie d'identité

Je soussigné(e) Gossels Charlotte
(nom de famille et prénoms du père ou de la mère ou du tuteur ou du répondant)
déclare par la présente confier au "COMITÉ ISRAÉLITE POUR LES ENFANTS VENANT D'ALLEMAGNE ET DE L'EUROPE CENTRALE" ou à tel autre organisme désigné par cette œuvre ou éventuellement par les autorités compétentes:

l'enfant Gossels Claus
né le 11.3.30 à Berlin nationalité Allemand
résidant actuellement à Berlin O, Lippehnerstr. 35 (adresse complète)

enfant dont je suis : ~~père~~ - mère - ~~tuteur~~ ou(*) (préciser les liens de parenté)

Ledit enfant est le fils - ~~fille~~(*) de :
père Nom de famille : Gossels Prénoms : Max
Né le 5.2.01 à Berlin Nationalité : Allemand
Adresse actuelle : Antwerpen (ville et pays)
Profession (diplômes et qualités) fonctionaire du magistrat

mère Nom de famille : Gossels Prénoms : Charlotte
Nom de jeune fille : Lewy Née le 7.9.03 à Berlin
Adresse actuelle Berlin O, Lippehnerstr. 35 Nationalité : Allemande
Profession (diplômes et qualités) s'occupe de cosmétique et de massages

Renseignements complémentaires sur la famille de l'enfant (santé, milieu social, situation matérielle, etc.) :
parents divorcés voir la suite

Si cette déclaration est signée par un tuteur ou par un répondant, indiquer l'adresse et la profession de celui-ci :

En conséquence, la dite œuvre israélite ou tel autre organisme à lui substitué, agissant sous le contrôle du Comité Central des Réfugiés créé par arrêté du Ministre des Affaires étrangères en date du 29 décembre 1938, aura tous droits et pouvoirs à l'effet de veiller à la protection de la santé et des intérêts moraux de l'enfant susdit jusqu'à l'âge de 18 ans, étant précisé que le Comité n'encourra aucune responsabilité de ce chef et que je l'en dégage expressément.

Le présent mandat ne pourra être annulé que dans le cas où j'obtiendrais un domicile fixe dans un pays quelconque et où j'aurais les sommes nécessaires pour faire venir chez moi mon enfant - ~~mon pupille~~ (*) et subvenir à ses besoins. Toutefois il est bien entendu que dans ce dernier cas, je ne demanderai plus au "Comité Israélite pour les Enfants venant d'Allemagne et de l'Europe Centrale" ou à l'organisme qui lui aurait été substitué, de s'en charger à nouveau.

A Berlin 24 Avril 1939.

SIGNATURE LÉGALISATION

Frau Charlotte Sara Gossels geb. Lewy.

Berlin

Our mother's agreement to give the French Comite Israelite custody of her children

Our mother's agreement to give the French Comite Israelite custody of her children.

D

Exemplaire à conserver par l'Enfant.

COMITÉ ISRAÉLITE POUR LES ENFANTS
VENANT D'ALLEMAGNE ET DE L'EUROPE CENTRALE

RÉCEPTION - HÉBERGEMENT - ÉDUCATION
38, RUE DU MONT THABOR, PARIS (Ier)
TÉLÉPHONE : OPÉRA 99-42

Photographie d'identité

Je soussigné(e) Gossels Charlotte
(nom de famille et prénoms du père ou de la mère ou du tuteur ou du répondant)

déclare par la présente confier au "COMITÉ ISRAÉLITE POUR LES ENFANTS VENANT D'ALLEMAGNE ET DE L'EUROPE CENTRALE" ou à tel autre organisme désigné par cette œuvre ou éventuellement par les autorités compétentes:

l'enfant Gossels Werner (nom et prénoms)
né le 23.7.33 à Berlin nationalité Allemand
résidant actuellement à Berlin 0. Lippehnerstr. 35 (adresse complète)

enfant dont je suis : ~~père~~ - mère - ~~tuteur~~ ou(*) --- (préciser les liens de parenté)

Ledit enfant est le fils ~~la fille~~ de

père Nom de famille : Gossels Prénoms : Max
Né le 9.2.01 à Berlin Nationalité : Allemand
Adresse actuelle : Antwerpen (ville et pays)
Profession (diplômes et qualités) fonctionnaire du magistrat

mère Nom de famille : Gossels Prénoms : Charlotte
Nom de jeune fille : Lewy Née le 7.IX.03 à Berlin (ville et pays)
Adresse actuelle : Berlin, Lippehnerstr. 35. Nationalité :
Profession (diplômes et qualités) s'occupe de cosmétique et de massage

Renseignements complémentaires sur la famille de l'enfant (santé, milieu social, situation matérielle, etc.) :
parents divorcés

Si cette déclaration est signée par un tuteur ou par un répondant, indiquer l'adresse et la profession de celui-ci :

En conséquence, la dite œuvre israélite ou tel autre organisme à lui substitué, agissant sous le contrôle du Comité Central des Réfugiés créé par arrêté du Ministre des Affaires étrangères en date du 29 décembre 1938, aura tous droits et pouvoirs à l'effet de veiller à la protection de la santé et des intérêts moraux de l'enfant susdit jusqu'à l'âge de 18 ans, étant précisé que le Comité n'encourra aucune responsabilité de ce chef et que je l'en dégage expressément.

Le présent mandat ne pourra être annulé que dans le cas où j'obtiendrais un domicile fixe dans un pays quelconque et où j'aurais les sommes nécessaires pour faire venir chez moi mon enfant - ~~mon pupille~~ (*) et subvenir à ses besoins. Toutefois il est bien entendu que dans ce dernier cas, je ne demanderai plus au "Comité Israélite pour les Enfants venant d'Allemagne et de l'Europe Centrale" ou à l'organisme qui lui aurait été substitué, de s'en charger à nouveau.

A Berlin, le 24 Avril 1939.

SIGNATURE LÉGALISATION

Frau Charlotte Sara Gossels
geb. Lewy.

Reichsvertretung der Juden in Deutschland * Berlin *

Sara Hellmann

Formule d'identité établie par les soins du Comité Central des Réfugiés, 129 rue de l'Université, Paris (VIIe)

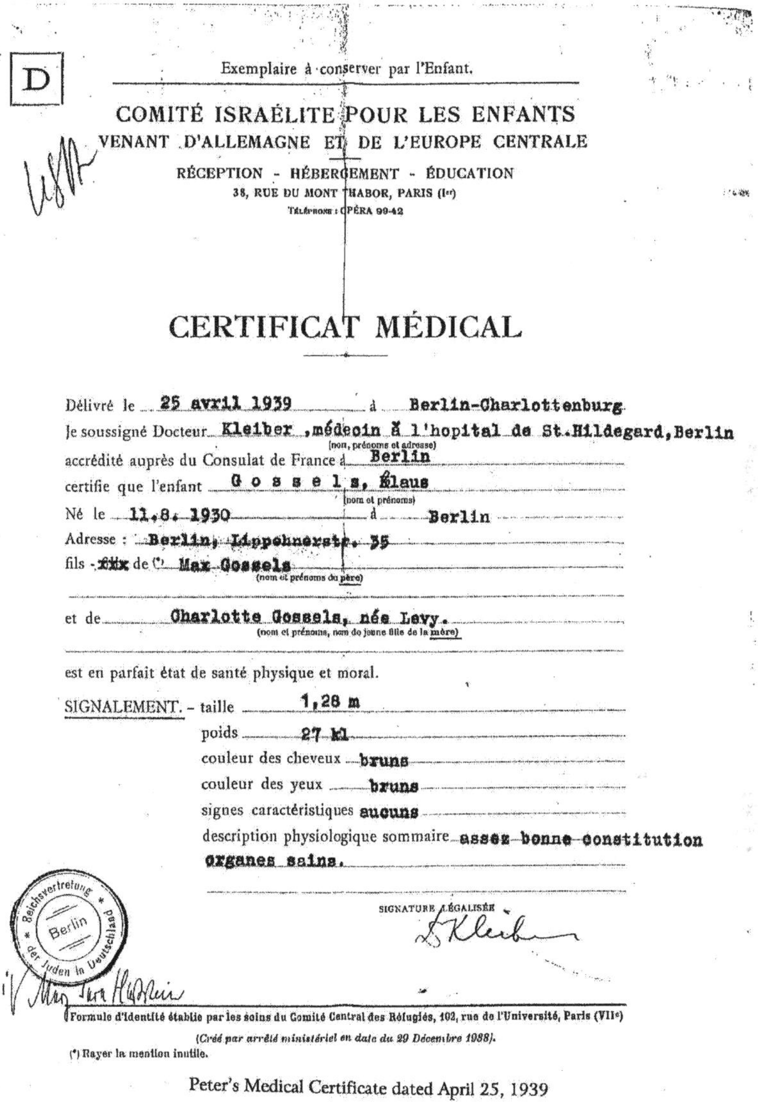

D

Exemplaire à conserver par l'Enfant.

COMITÉ ISRAÉLITE POUR LES ENFANTS
VENANT D'ALLEMAGNE ET DE L'EUROPE CENTRALE

RÉCEPTION - HÉBERGEMENT - ÉDUCATION
38, RUE DU MONT THABOR, PARIS (Ier)
TÉLÉPHONE : OPÉRA 99-42

CERTIFICAT MÉDICAL

Délivré le 25 avril 1939 à Berlin-Charlottenburg
Je soussigné Docteur Kleiber, médecin à l'hopital de St.Hildegard, Berlin
(nom, prénoms et adresse)
accrédité auprès du Consulat de France à Berlin
certifie que l'enfant G o s s e l s, Klaus
(nom et prénoms)
Né le 11.8.1930 à Berlin
Adresse : Berlin, Lippehnerstr. 35
fils - ~~fille~~ de (*) Max Gossels
(nom et prénoms du père)

et de Charlotte Gossels, née Levy.
(nom et prénoms, nom de jeune fille de la mère)

est en parfait état de santé physique et moral.

SIGNALEMENT. - taille 1,28 m
poids 27 Kl
couleur des cheveux bruns
couleur des yeux bruns
signes caractéristiques aucuns
description physiologique sommaire assez bonne constitution organes sains.

Reichsvertretung der Juden in Deutschland * Berlin *

SIGNATURE LÉGALISÉE

Formule d'identité établie par les soins du Comité Central des Réfugiés, 102, rue de l'Université, Paris (VIIe)
(Créé par arrêté ministériel en date du 29 Décembre 1938).
(*) Rayer la mention inutile.

Peter's Medical Certificate dated April 25, 1939

Peter's Medical Certificate dated April 25, 1939.

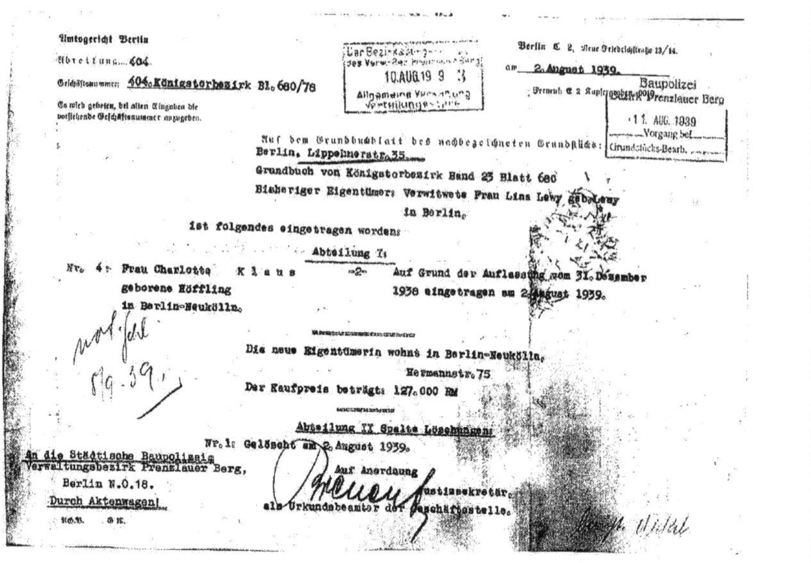

Amtsgericht Berlin

Abteilung 404

Geschäftsnummer: 404. Königstorbezirk Bl. 680/78

Es wird gebeten, bei allen Eingaben die vorstehende Geschäftsnummer anzugeben.

10.AUG.19 9

Berlin C 2, Neue Friedrichstraße 13/14.

am 2. August 1939.

Baupolizei Bezirk Prenzlauer Berg

11. AUG. 1939

Vorgang bei Grundstücks-Bearb.

Auf dem Grundbuchblatt des nachbezeichneten Grundstücks:
Berlin, Lippehnerstr. 35.
Grundbuch von Königstorbezirk Band 23 Blatt 680
Bisheriger Eigentümer: Verwitwete Frau Lina Lewy geb. Lewy
in Berlin.

ist folgendes eingetragen worden:

Abteilung I:

Nr. 4: Frau Charlotte Klaus geborene Höffling in Berlin-Neukölln. -2- Auf Grund der Auflassung vom 31. Dezember 1938 eingetragen am 2. August 1939.

Die neue Eigentümerin wohnt in Berlin-Neukölln,
Hermannstr. 75

Der Kaufpreis beträgt: 127.000 RM

Abteilung II Spalte Löschungen:

Nr. 1: Gelöscht am 2. August 1939.

An die Städtische Baupolizei
Verwaltungsbezirk Prenzlauer Berg,
Berlin N.O.18.
Durch Aktenwagen!

Auf Anordnung
Justizsekretär,
als Urkundsbeamter der Geschäftsstelle.

Document concerning Lena's forced sale of 35 Lippehnerstrasse.

Lotte gave the Hagada to her children when they left Berlin.

Claus Gossels.
Lippehnerstr. 35.II

סדר
הגדה של פסח

Erzählung
von dem
Auszuge Israels
aus
Ägypten
an den
beiden ersten Peßach-Abenden.

Nach einer Übersetzung von
W. Heidenheim

Berlin
Verlag: C. Boas Nachf.
Druck: Deese & Hauschild, Berlin N. 54

THE BOYS ARRIVE IN FRANCE

Werner, who had not yet reached six years of age, was the youngest of the group, who were traveling through the night to freedom in France. The oldest was 16. After arriving in Paris on July 4, 1939, we were put on a bus and driven to the Chateau de Quincy in Quincy sous Senart, a small town about twenty miles southeast of Paris. A very short film showing the arrival of the group may be seen on the website of the U.S. Holocaust Museum. The Chateau, a very large mansion set on several acres, was owned by Hubert de Monbrison, a French count, who had made his estate available to a boarding school for refugees from the Communist revolution in Russia while he was married to Irina Palovna Paleya, a niece of Nicholas II, the last Russian Czar.

He had also served as host to some refugees from the Spanish Civil War and a few Jewish refugees from Germany. Hubert de Monbrison's life is more fully described online.

We do not know why the Count decided to shut down the school for the Russian refugees and to serve as host to the German Jewish children from Berlin. Christian, his son, believes that Dr. Gaston Levy, the Monbrison's pediatrician who also worked at the Chateau and served on the Board of OSE (Oeuvres de Secours aux Enfants), may have persuaded him to serve as host of the group that included Werner and me. But recent research by Laura Hobson Faure, Ph.D., suggests that the Count's second wife, Renee, who was Jewish, worked in the same building as Louise Weiss, the head of the Comite Israelite, which had custody of the German children and may have persuaded the Count to shelter the German children.

Lotte wasted no time and sent her first letter to her rascals, as she called us, in response to a letter she had received from me. But as her undated August, 1939 birthday letter to me reveals, the Lewys had to move into the two front rooms and rent out the remaining rooms of the apartment to relatives of Lina. As a result, Lina, Lotte and Hilde had to sleep in the living room.

We survived thanks to the heroic efforts of our mother, who succeeded in obtaining French visas for us and for entrusting us to the care of the Comite Israelite Pour les Enfants Venant D'Allemagne et de L'Europe Centrale (the Comite) located in Paris.

Several counselors under the auspices of the Comite managed the Chateau and the boys who had arrived that day from Berlin. After the Chateau was requisitioned by the German military in the Fall of 1940, the boys were scattered and cared for by the American Friends Service Committee (Quakers) and a Jewish orphanage in Paris. In January 1941, Werner and I were sent to Chabannes, a small village in the Creuse, which is part of the town of Saint Pierre de Fursac, where we were housed in a large house, known as the Chateau de Chabannes, with about one hundred other refugees under the auspices of the Oeuvre de Secours aux Enfants (OSE). "The Children of Chabannes", Lisa Gossels' Emmy Award-winning film, tells the story better than we can on paper.

On September 1, 1939, the German Army invaded Poland, thereby initiating the Second World War. As a result, mail service between France and Germany became problematic.

Sometime in September, 1939, a picture was taken of all the children at Quincy.

Chateau de Quincy sous Senart.

Peter's sketch of the Chateau de Quincy when he was 10 years old.

The younger group at Quincy sous Senart 1939

First Row: Henry Hoppenstandt, Ralph Moratz, Werner Gossels, Peter Gossels, Wolodya Grajonza (later known as Bill Graham)

Second Row: Karll Heinz Wolfberg, Norbert Bikalis, Sammy Stuck, Edwin Cosman, Herbert Oberniker

Third Row: Werner Goldschmidt, Gerhard Glass, Henri Kreft, Arno Marcuse, Egon Zwirn, Berthold Friedlander

Behind: Mlle. Ramonde Sauviac in charge (with Marthe Ovard) – today Mme. Fanouillere

Wolodya Grajonza changed his name to Bill Graham when he arrived in the New York, saw combat in North Korea and became an impresario and rock concert promoter from 1960 to 1991, when he died in a helicopter crash.

Norbert Bikalis came to the United States after escaping to Switzerland and went on to become a distinguished polymer scientist. He worked in Paris as representative of the National Science Foundation.

The middle group at Quincy sous Senart 1939

Standing: Siegfried Knop, Gert Alexander, Pierre Marcus, Hans Stern, Adi Kimmefeld

Center: Henri Rettig

Seated: Horst Cahn, Ivan Rose, Horst Wolff, Sally Oberniker

Hans Stern came to the United States, married and became the father of Keith Stern, a distinguished congregational rabbi at Temple Beth Avodah in Newton, Massachusetts.

The older group at Quincy sous Senart 1939

First Row: Arno Waczinski, Eric Goldfarb, Stephan Lewy, Gerard Rosenzweig

Second Row: Harry, Wolfgang Blumenreich, Jura, Gunther Blatt (?)

Third Row: Bernd Warschauer, Walter Hertzig, Egon Heysemann, Claude Zimmermann, Jacob Jaub (?)

Gerard Rosenzweig somehow survived several Nazi concentration camps, emigrated to the United States and changed his name to Jerry Gerard, became a successful businessman in California and the father of Stephen K. Gerard, M.D.

The Spanish girls at Quincy sous Senart in August 1939

Consuelo, Maty, Mercedes, Pilar, Nieves with Egon Heysemann, Gerard Rosenzweig, Heinz Rettig, Stephan Lewy, Wolfgang Blumenreich

OUR MOTHER'S LETTERS BEGIN

Lotte's first letter to her children

Berlin, July 6, 1939

My two beloved Strolches [rascals]!

I was so very happy when just now, in the evening mail, your letter arrived. I am glad that you have seen so many beautiful things and hope that both of you are well and that you feel quite at home there. What are you doing, my dear Schnäuzelchen. Do play always play with the other children and don't act like you did at Kapellners; and you, dearest Peterle, please watch out for him and take good care of him; you know that Mutti cannot be with you now, and therefore, you Peter darling, must care for your little Werni and must always help him!!

I will also have your suitcases sent, so that you soon may wear your beautiful, light summer clothes. Your pictures turned out nice. It is very quiet here, because you are not here.

Now, be well today, my two darlings. Write a long letter sometimes soon of how you are spending the day there, how many children you are, and about everything that you are doing.

Many sweet kisses and greetings for both of you,

Love
your Mutti.

Oma, Tante Hilde, Onkel Fanti, Klara are saying hello.

Berlin, d. 6. Juli 1939.

Meine zwei geliebten-Strolchels!

Ich war ja so glücklich, als eben mit der Abendpost Euer Brief ankam. Ich freue mich, daß Ihr soviel Schönes gesehen habt und hoffe, Ihr seid beide gesund und fühlt Euch dort schon ganz wie zu Hause. Was macht denn Du, mein liebes Schnauzelchen? Spiele nur immer schön mit allen anderen Kindern zusammen und mach es nicht so wie bei Kapellner; und Du, liebstes Peterle, bitte paß auf ihn auf und Kümmere Dich sehr um ihn, Ihr wißt, Mutti kann jetzt nicht bei Euch sein, und da mußt Du, Liebling Peter, für Deinen kleinen Werni sorgen und ihm immer helfen!!

Ich werde nun auch gleich Eure Koffer schicken lassen, sodaß Ihr bald schöne leichte Sommersachen anziehen könnt. Eure Bilder sind nett geworden. Hier ist es jetzt sehr ruhig, weil Ihr fort seid.

Nun, lebt für heute wohl, meine zwei Lieblinge. Schreibt bald mal einen langen Brief, wie Ihr dort den Tag verlebt, wieviel Kinder Ihr seid, und über alles, was Ihr macht.

Viele liebe Küßchen und Grüße für Euch Beide zusammen, in Liebe

Eure Mutti.

Oma, Tante Hilde, Onkel Fanti, Klara, lassen grüßen.

Berlin Voss, July 9, 1939
Lippehnerstr. 35 II

Beloved Boys!

Today I am sending you the keys to the suitcase containing the things that were approved only after you left. You know the situation! I just now sent the suitcase to your address. Soon you should have everything there. You surely have settled in by now and have found nice playmates. Is it also so hot there as it is here and are you spending a lot of time outdoors? Tomorrow it will be one whole week that you are away. Your flowers are still standing on my night table, and when I enter the green room I am greeted by your smiling faces on my night table. Edith brought me your letter to read. How are things with you with writing and stamps for your letters? How often are you allowed to write and does the home give you stamps or must I send you an international reply coupon? Maybe you, Peterle, can find out and then let me know.

Thousand kisses to both of you

Your
Mutti

Berlin NO 55 d. 9. Juli 1939
Lippehnerstr. 35 II

Geliebte Jungens!

Heute schicke ich Euch die Schlüssel zu dem
Koffer, in dem die erst nachträglich genehmigten Sachen liegen. Ihr wißt doch Bescheid. Den Koffer habe
ich eben an Eure Adresse abgeschickt. Nun werdet
Ihr ja bald alle Sachen dort haben. Ihr habt
Euch nun bestimmt schon eingelebt und habt
schon nette Spielgefährten gefunden. Ist es bei Euch
auch so heiß wie hier, und seid Ihr viel in
der Luft? Morgen seid Ihr nun schon eine ganz
Woche fort. Eure Blümchen stehen noch immer
auf meinem Nachttisch, und wenn ich in
unser grünes Zimmer komme lacht Ihr zwei
mir von meinem Nachttisch entgegen. Edith
brachte mir Euren Brief zum Lesen. Wie ist
das bei Euch mit Schreiben und Briefmarken
für Eure Briefe? Wie oft dürft Ihr schreiben,
und bekommt Ihr dort im Heim die Marken
dazu, oder muß ich Euch einen internationale
Antwortschein schicken? Vielleicht fragst Du, Peterle
einmal danach und schreibst mir dann Antwort. Tausend Küßchen Euch beiden

Eure Mutti.

11 July, 1939

Werner and I are doing well. We are in a chateau. (A pipe in our cellar burst and it is now under water.) Werner and Ralph [Moratz] are going to school now. Congratulations on your birthday. Greetings and kisses.

Your Peter

2 Dec, 1939
(Sent on 5 Dec, 1939)

My dear ones!

We are happy that you are in good health. Are you going to school as well, Peter? Write again as soon as possible. How is Werner learning?

Heartfelt greetings and kisses.

Your Mutti

61 a

COMITÉ INTERNATIONAL DE LA CROIX-ROUGE

Palais du Conseil Général

GENÈVE (Suisse)

CM 69
28278
–5 DEC. 1939

DEMANDEUR

Nom GOSSELS

Prénom Claus

Rue Chateau de Quincy

Localité QUINCY SOUS SENART

Département Seine et Oise

Pays France

Message à transmettre au destinataire (25 mots au maximum, nouvelles de caractère strictement personnel et familial :

Mir u. Werner geht es gut. – Wir sind im Schloß (Rohrbruch: unser Keller unter Wasser.) Werner u. Ralph gehen jetzt in die Schule. Gratuliere zum Geburtstag. Grüße u. Küsse dein Peter.

Date : 7-11-39

DESTINATAIRE

Nom GOSSELS

Prénom Ch.

Rue Lippehnerstr. 35

Localité BERLIN N.O. 55

Province

Pays

RÉPONSE AU VERSO.

Prière d'écrire très lisiblement.

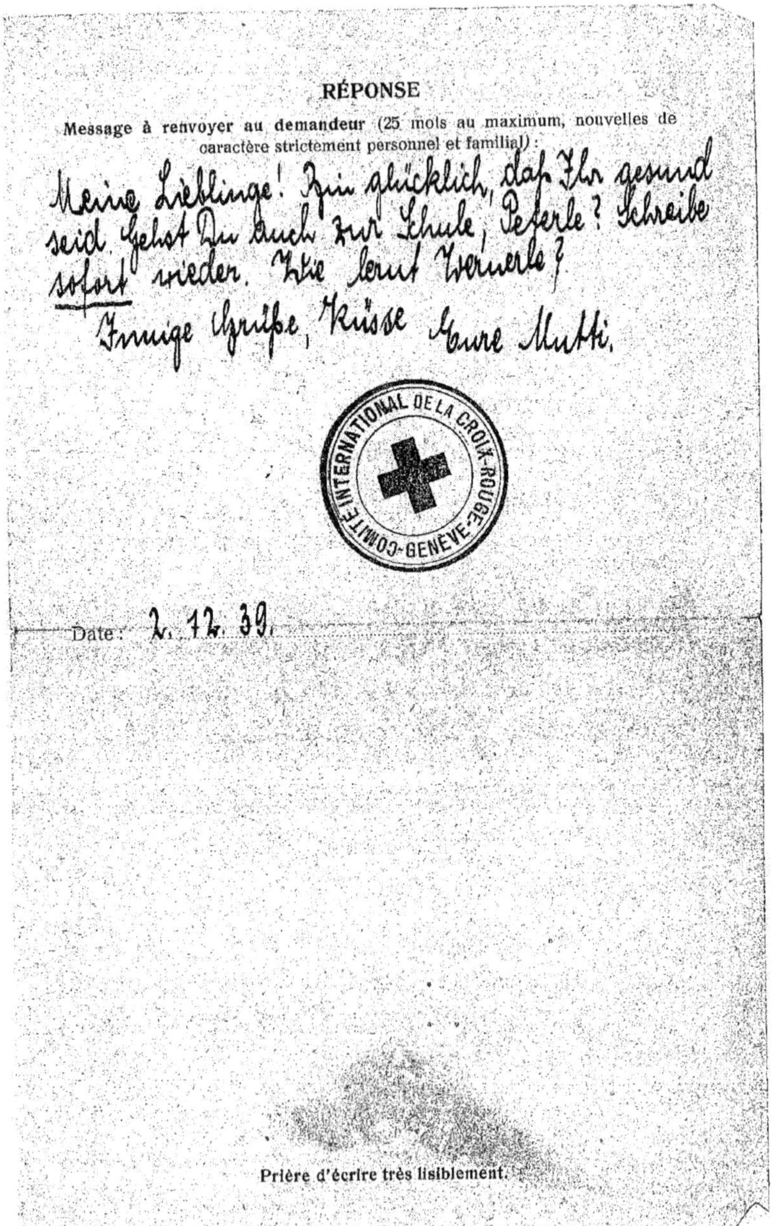

RÉPONSE

Message à renvoyer au demandeur (25 mots au maximum, nouvelles de caractère strictement personnel et familial) :

Meine Lieblinge! Bin glücklich, daß Ihr gesund seid. Gehst Du auch zur Schule, Peterle? Schreibe **sofort** wieder. Wie lernt Wernerle?

Innige Grüße, Küsse Eure Mutti.

COMITÉ INTERNATIONAL DE LA CROIX-ROUGE GENÈVE

Date : 2. 12. 39.

Prière d'écrire très lisiblement.

Berlin, July 20, 1939
Lippehnerstr. 35 II [?]

My beloved two boys!

I was very happy about your detailed letter and everybody, who loves you both, will get to read it. Tante Pach and Klein were the first to read it and they are glad that you like it there a lot. You, dear Peterle, seem to have totally forgotten these two aunts; they, who always have been so good to you? You should really send some greetings to them sometimes, therefore don't forget to do so in your next letter, you hear? What is going on with you, my little Schnäuzerle? Do you have to stay in bed and are you sick? It will quickly get better, darling; Mutti thinks of you a lot, my dear little one. Be well-behaved and listen to everything the adults tell you, then you will be able to jump around with the other children very soon again. And on Sunday our Wernchen will have his 6th birthday and then he also will be a quite big boy who will go to school soon and study hard. Mutti has sent a few bars of chocolate and Pomräuschen [?], which he loves so much to eat. Please write whether it has arrived and whether you like the taste. I wish you, my dear little Buberl [boy], that you will always be well in your new year of life and that you will be a very well-behaved, diligent and competent boy who brings joy to all. Do the other children know that it is your birthday? Have lots of fun and be glad that you have it so good. – You, Peter darling, please always write so detailed; you know that Mutti wants to know everything her two darlings are doing, otherwise she is restless; you do understand me, don't you? It is good that you do gymnastics and sport and that you must help all around, that is healthy and good for the future. Are you, my little Strolch Peterle, also obedient? Please write to me, when you can, whether you have received the key and the suitcase. I had to send the suitcase to Paris-North, because Quincy does not have a railroad station and I have written to the Committee in Paris to send the suitcase on to you; and what is the matter with the other things from Tante Merry [?]. Please tell me when you can. Also, please, write soon about what ails Werni, whether it's getting better and whether he is also as cheerful as you are. Do you spend a lot of time together and how is he being kept busy?

Edith was here and I fetched the pictures of you. Gert has not been here since. Which pictures do you want, darling?

Now I want to stop chatting with you both for today. Heartfelt greetings and kisses to both of you – I wish you, my little one, a speedy recovery.

Love
your Mutti.

Write again really soon! Everyone, Tante Kirchhoff, Pachs, Fantelen, Tante Betty, Hilde, Oma, Klara send thousand greetings.

Berlin, den 20. Juli 1939.
Lippehnerstr. 35. I.

Meine geliebten zwei Jungen!

Mit Eurem ausführlichen Brief habe ich mich sehr gefreut, und alle, die Euch Zwei gern haben, werden ihn lesen. Tante Pach und Klein bekamen ihn zuerst zum Lesen und sie freuen sich, daß es Euch so gut gefällt. Du, liebes Peterle, hast wohl diese beiden Tanten, die doch immer so gut zu Euch waren, ganz vergessen? Du mußt sie doch auch mal grüßen lassen, also, vergiß das nicht in Deinem nächsten Brief, hörst Du? Was ist denn mit Dir, mein kleines Schnauzerle? Mußt Du zu Bett liegen und bist krank? Es wird schnell wieder besser werden, Liebling; Mutti denkt viel an Dich. Du mein liebes Kleines sei nur sehr artig und höre auf alles, was die Großen Dir sagen, dann wirst Du auch sehr bald wieder mit den anderen Kindern herumspringen können. Und Sonntag hat unser Wernchen seinen 6. Geburtstag, und ist dann auch schon ein ganz großer Junge, der bald in die Schule gehen und fleißig lernen wird. Mutti hat ein paar Tafeln Schokolade und Pomeränzchen, die Du doch so gern ißt, an Euch abgeschickt. Schreibt doch bitte, ob es angekommen ist und ob es schmeckt. Ich wünsche Dir, mein liebes kleines Bubele, daß Du in Deinem neuen Lebensjahr immer ganz gesund sein sollst, und daß Du ein sehr artiger, fleißiger und tüchtiger Junge wirst, der allen Freude macht. Wissen denn die anderen Kinder, daß Du Geburtstag hast? Feiert recht vergnügt und freut Euch, daß Ihr es so schön habt. – Du, Liebling Peter, schreibe, bitte, immer so ausführlich; Du weißt, Mutti muß alles wissen, was ihre zwei Lieblinge machen, sie hat doch sonst kein Ruhe, Du verstehst mich ja schon, nicht wahr? Es ist fein, daß Ihr dort Gymnastik und Sport treibt und überall helfen müßt, das ist gesund und gut für immer. Bist Du, kleiner Strolch Peterle, auch immer gehorsam? Dann schreibe mir doch mal, ob Du die Schlüssel und den Koffer bekommen hast. Ich mußte den Koffer nach Paris-Nord schicken, weil Quincy keine Bahnstation hat und ich habe an das Comité in Paris geschrieben, es soll den Koffer an Euch weiter schicken; und was ist mit den anderen Sachen von Tante Herry? Bitte schreibe mir mal darüber. Ebenso schreibe bald, was Werni fehlt, ob es wieder besser ist, und ob er auch so vergnügt ist wie Du. Bist Du denn viel mit ihm zusammen, und wie wird er beschäftigt?

Edith war hier und hat sich Bilder von Euch geholt, Gert war noch nicht wieder hier. Was für Bilder willst Du haben, Liebling?

Nun will ich für heute Schluß machen mit meiner Plauderei mit Euch Beiden. Ich grüße Euch herzlichst und küsse

Euch Beide – Dir, mein Kleines, recht schnelle gute Besserung. Für Liebe Eure Mutti.

Schreibe sehr schnell wieder! Alle, Tante Rinele, Paula, Tantchen, Tante Betty, Tante Anna, Klara Stiefen grüßen Euch tausendmal.

Berlin, July 27, 1939

Dear Boys!

Yesterday evening I received your detailed letter, dear Peterle and we are all delighted about your so detailed description of your life there. I am happy that Wernchen is feeling better again. Does he eat better there than here or does he still have his cheeks full and does not want to chew? Please write about this soon and whether he also plays with the other children. You, dear Peterle, seem to feel quite at home already, as I can tell by your letter. It is very nice that you are out in the garden a lot and are allowed to help. That makes one healthy and strong. It's very good that the birthday of our little one was celebrated so nicely and that the sweets arrived on time. Have all the suitcases arrived by now? Please give me a full report, because otherwise I must contact the Committee in Paris. I am enclosing 3 pictures. – Edith and Gert were here recently and received some money from Oma to write a card to you. Absolutely everybody here is thinking of you and all are reading your letter, dear Peterle. – The weather here is not very good either, it's either too cool or too hot with many thunderstorms. Last Saturday and Sunday I visited a customer who has a little house in the country near Berlin with a beautiful fruit- and vegetable garden – and a chicken coop with many grown chicken and sweet little chicken children. I was allowed to help picking cherries and strawberries and in the morning the freshly laid eggs were collected from the chicken coop and consumed at noon. I could run around all day in my bathing suit and rest in the reclining chair. Since Monday morning I am here again and am busy all the time, as you well know. Today or tomorrow I will read your letter to Tante Martha Kirchhoff; she always inquires about you both and sends her heartfelt greeting. Do not forget to send her greetings in your next letter, or Peterle, when you are allowed, why don't you write a card to her and Pachs. - I have filled out and immediately returned the two forms. Are you learning French already or are you speaking German exclusively? When does school start? Mutti is so curious and must know everything.

Now, dear boys, stay well today; I cannot enclose a reply voucher because I can only get it on Monday and I do not want you to wait too long for a reply. Write real soon again. (You still have a reply voucher from me!) Tell me everything and answer all questions.

To both of you heartfelt greetings and kisses from

your
Mutti

Please give the enclosed letter to Miss Jacoby.

Berlin, den 27. Juli 1939.

Geliebte Jungs!

Gestern abend erhielt ich Deinen ausführlichen Brief, liebes Peterle, und wir alle freuten uns über Deine so genauen Schilderungen Eures dortigen Lebens. Ich bin froh, daß es Wernchen wieder besser geht. Ißt er dort besser als hier, oder hat er immer noch die Backen voll und will nicht kauen? Schreibe mir doch mal darüber, und ob er auch mit den anderen Kindern spielt. Du, liebes Peterle, fühlst Dich ja schon ganz zu Hause, wie ich das aus Deinem Brief herauslese. Es ist sehr fein, daß Ihr dort viel im Garten seid und mithelfen dürft, davon wird man gesund und kräftig. Ich freue mich, daß unser Kleiner seinen Geburtstag dort so fein gefeiert bekommen hat, und daß die Süßigkeiten pünktlich eingetroffen sind. - Sind denn die Koffer nun schon alle da? Bitte, schreibe darüber genauen Bescheid, da ich mich sonst an das Comité in Paris wenden muß. Die 3 Bilder lege ich hier bei. - Edith und Gert waren neulich hier und bekamen von Oma Geld, um an Euch eine Karte zu schreiben. Alle, alle denken an Euch und lesen Deine Briefe, liebes Peterle. - Das Wetter ist jetzt hier auch nicht sehr schön, entweder ist es sehr kühl oder zu heiß mit viel Gewitter. Letzten

Sonnabend und Sonntag war ich bei einem Kunden, der in der Nähe von Berlin auf dem Lande ein Häuschen hat mit einem schönen Obst- und Gemüsegarten -- und einem Hühnerstall mit vielen großen Hühnern und süßen kleinen Hühner-Kindern. Ich durfte helfen, Kirschen und Erdbeeren pflücken und morgens wurden die frisch gelegten Eier aus dem Hühnerstall geholt und mittags verzehrt. Ich konnte dort den ganzen Tag im Badeanzug herumlaufen und mich im Liegestuhl ausruhen. Seit Montag früh bin ich wieder hier und habe immer zu tun, wie Ihr ja wißt. Heute oder morgen will ich Tante Martha Kirchhoff einmal Eure Briefe vorlesen; sie fragt immer nach Euch beiden und läßt Euch herzlich grüßen. Vergeßt nicht, in Eurem nächsten Brief sie grüßen zu lassen, oder Peterle, wenn Du darfst, schreib doch mal an sie und Pachs eine Karte. - Die beiden Formulare habe ich ausgefüllt und sofort zurückgeschickt. Lernt Ihr schon französisch, oder sprecht Ihr nur deutsch? Und wann fängt die Schule an? Mutti ist so neugierig, und muß alles wissen.

Nun, liebe Jungs, lebt wohl für heute; einen Rückschein kann ich nicht beifügen, weil ich ihn nur am Montag bekomme und Ihr sollt nicht solange auf Antwort warten. Schreibt sehr bald wieder (Ihr habt doch noch eine Antwortkarte von mir da!) über alles und beantwortet mir alle Fragen.

Euch beiden innige Grüße und Küsse von
Eurer Mutti.

Inliegenden Brief gib bitte an Frl. Jacoby.

Berlin, August 1st, 1939

Dear Peter and Werner!

I may not have written to you yet but I have read all the letters that you wrote to your Mutti with great care. I am happy that you are doing well and that you are eagerly lending a hand. As I can see from your last card it is even hotter where you are than it is here. Is Quincy sous Senart really a part of Paris? Seine et Oise is after all the name of a specific Departement in France. When I was a prisoner of war I was also once in a French town called Quincy, but that one was near Douai, near the Belgian border. So now you are also learning French; and maybe you will soon be writing to us in French, too? – What would you, dear Peter, like me to get you for your birthday? I had wanted to send Werner something too, but your Mutti was saying, I should first find out if the package that she had sent to Werner has arrived. – On Werner's birthday – it fell on a Sunday here (where you are too, right?) – we, that is your Mutti and I, went to Biesdorf, a village near Berlin, 8 stops east of Alexanderplatz. We were visiting a friend of your Mutti's who has a house there that is surrounded by a garden in which cherry, plum and other fruit trees grow. Mostly the cherries were now ripe; we ate some of them directly from the tree, others from a plate and others as a soup. The gooseberries too were growing from the shrub directly into our mouths. We took a lot of sunbaths on a lounge chaise. Unfortunately only one chaise was available so we took turns lying on it each of us 15 minutes at a time. But when it was my turn, your Mutti never wanted to yield. She was only wearing a bathing suit and was getting sunburn. She is standing next to me at this moment and is saying that it was not her who never wanted to leave the lounge chaise but I. Since you were not there I had to carry your Mutti on my back around the yard (in an elephant trot). Your Mutti prepared the meals. One day we had rumsteak (I'm not sure if I spelled this word correctly), the next day eggs with bacon. They had a lot of eggs out there in general. There were 8 chickens and each of them lays an egg every day. Mr. L., the owner, came every 15 minutes running out of the chicken coop, triumphantly holding a newly laid egg in his hand. I have to close now because your mother needs the typewriter. I'm sending you kind greetings,

Your Onkel
Fanti

[DRAWINGS]
This is what our house in Biesdorf looked like.

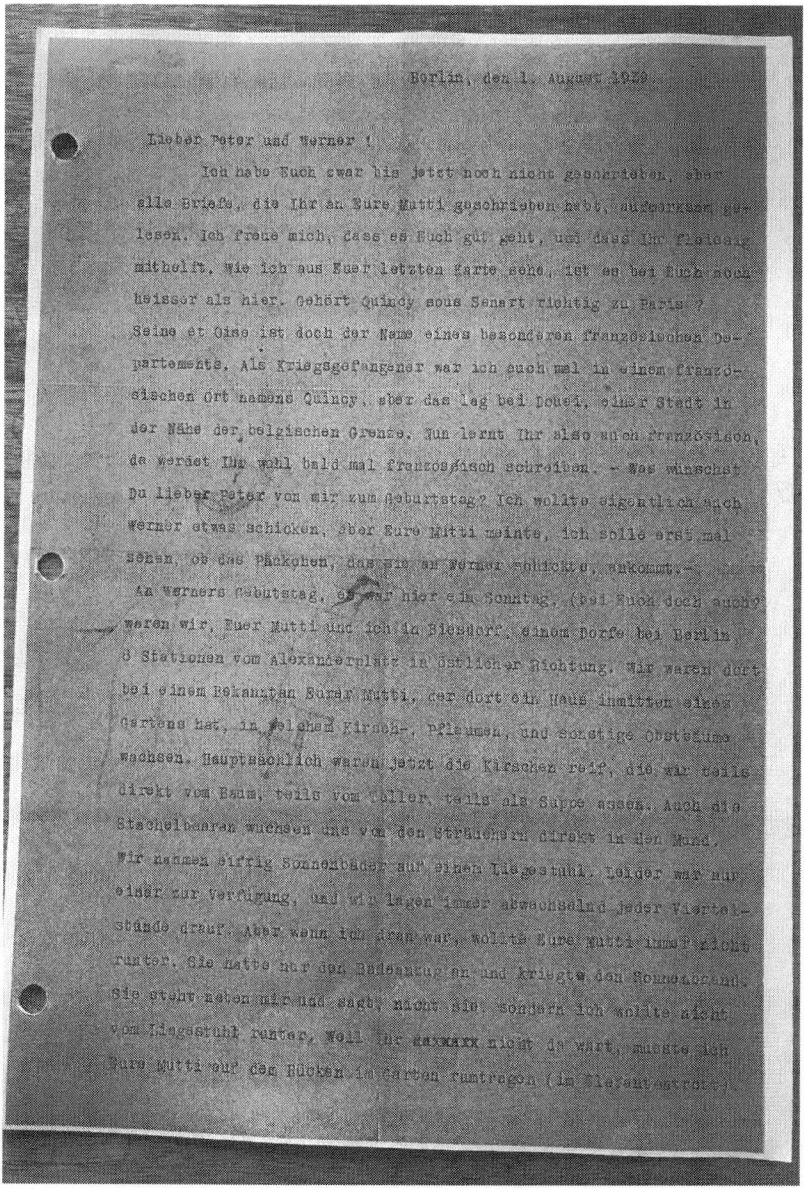

Berlin, den 1. August 1939.

Lieber Peter und Werner !

Ich habe Euch zwar bis jetzt noch nicht geschrieben, aber alle Briefe, die Ihr an Eure Mutti geschrieben habt, aufmerksam gelesen. Ich freue mich, dass es Euch gut geht, und dass Ihr fleissig mithelft. Wie ich aus Euer letzten Karte sehe, ist es bei Euch noch heisser als hier. Gehört Quincy sous Senart richtig zu Paris ? Seine et Oise ist doch der Name eines besonderen französischen Departements. Als Kriegsgefangener war ich auch mal in einem französischen Ort namens Quincy, aber das lag bei Douai, einer Stadt in der Nähe der belgischen Grenze. Nun lernt Ihr also auch französisch, da werdet Ihr wohl bald mal französisch schreiben. - Was wünschst Du lieber Peter von mir zum Geburtstag? Ich wollte eigentlich auch Werner etwas schicken, aber Eure Mutti meinte, ich solle erst mal sehen, ob das Päckchen, das sie an Werner schickte, ankommt.-

An Werners Gebutstag, es war hier ein Sonntag, (bei Euch doch auch?) waren wir, Euer Mutti und ich in Biesdorf, einem Dorfe bei Berlin, 8 Stationen vom Alexanderplatz in östlicher Richtung. Wir waren dort bei einem Bekanntan Eurer Mutti, der dort ein Haus inmitten eines Gartens hat, in welchem Kirsch-, Pflaumen, und sonstige Obstbäume wachsen. Hauptsächlich waren jetzt die Kirschen reif, die wir teils direkt vom Baum, teils vom Teller, teils als Suppe assen. Auch die Stachelbeeren wuchsen uns von den Sträuchern direkt in den Mund. Wir nahmen eifrig Sonnenbäder auf einem Liegestuhl. Leider war nur einer zur Verfügung, und wir lagen immer abwechselnd jeder Viertelstunde drauf. Aber wenn ich dran war, wollte Eure Mutti immer nicht runter. Sie hatte nur den Badeanzug an und kriegte den Sonnenbrand. Sie steht neben mir und sagt, nicht sie, sondern ich wollte nicht vom Liegestuhl runter. Weil Ihr xxxxxx nicht da wart, musste ich Eure Mutti auf dem Rücken im Garten rumtragen (im Elefantentrott).

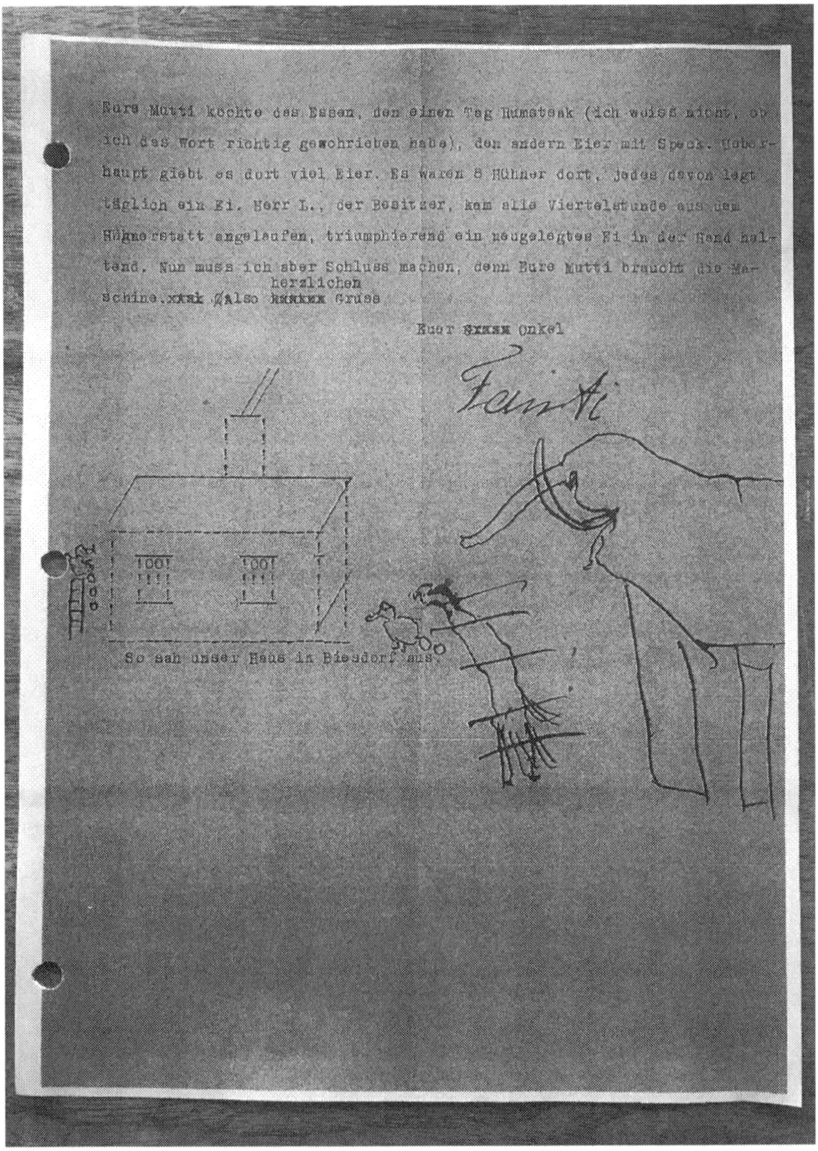

Eure Mutti kochte das Essen, den einen Tag Rumsteak (ich weiss nicht, ob ich das Wort richtig gewchrieben habe), den andern Eier mit Speck. Ueberhaupt giebt es dort viel Eier. Es waren 8 Hühner dort, jedes davon legt täglich ein Ei. Herr L., der Besitzer, kam alle Viertelstunde aus dem Hühnerstall angelaufen, triumphierend ein neugelegtes Ei in der Hand haltend. Nun muss ich aber Schluss machen, denn Eure Mutti braucht die Maschine. xxxx Also xxxxxx herzlichen Grüsse

Euer xxxxx Onkel

Fanti

So sah unser Haus in Biesdorf aus.

Berlin, August 11th, 1939

Dear Peter and Werner!

I am very happy that you are doing so well and that you will now soon be going to Paris. I do hope though that you will write in detail what you have seen there. Today, we unfortunately will have to be celebrating your birthday, dear Peter, without you! Your Mutti put the big bouquet of flowers which she would have otherwise given to you in person, next to your picture which is on the dresser that is now in the treatment room of your Mutti's, as well as the big green mirror and the children's table where your Mutti now keeps her chocolate and cigarettes. We had been meaning to go to the synagogue tonight in honor of your birthday but it is too hot for that (after it's been raining quite a lot these past few days), and so we will just be heading over to Weiss' for dinner, across the street from the Kulturbund-Theater as you know. On Monday, August 14th my sister and her husband, Onkel Fritz will travel with the seltzer machine, to Samoa (which is behind Australia) and then I will be here all by myself without any relatives. Recently, I had asked you, Peter, what you would like for your birthday but you have not yet written it to me. However, your Mutti says, that it will be useless anyway to send you something because you guys are now getting an allowance. You have not yet written whether you are continuing to study Hebrew over there, and what you do on the Sabbath - why don't you tell us about that some time. – Do you know Egon Zwirn, who left together with you? I see his father time and again at the Jewish Community and he was telling me today that he received an enthusiastic letter from his boy. Well, for today I am out of new things to tell you so I'm sending you my kind regards

Your Onkel Fanti

(see reverse)

8/15
Dear kids,

I still have the letter because I only received the reply form, which I will enclose, today. I am at the post office and do not have access to a typewriter, hopefully you can read my handwriting. My writing is very hard to read. I also did not know your address by heart so I just got it from Egon Zwirn's father. – Last night my relatives left for Samoa. The trip will last about two and a half months. So once again kind regards

Fanti

Berlin, den 11. August 1939.

Lieber Peter und Werner !

Es freut mich sehr, dass es Euch so gut geht, und dass Ihr jetzt auch bald nach Paris fahren werdet. Ich hoffe aber, dass Ihr dann auch genau schreibt, was Ihr dort gesehn habt. Heute müssen wir leider Deinen Geburtstag, lieber Peter, ohne Dich feiern. Deine Mutti hat den grossen Blumenstrauss, den sie Dir sonst persönlich überreicht hätte, neben Dein Photo gestellt, das auf den Kommode steht, die jetzt im Behandlungszimmer Eurer Mutti steht, desgleichen der grosse grüne Spiegel und das Kindertischchen, in welchem Eure Mutti jetzt ihre Chokolade und Zigaretten aufbewahrt. Heute Abend wollten wir eigentlich zur Feier des Geburtstages in die Synagoge gehen, aber es ist zu heiss dazu (nachdem es die letzten Tage viel geregnet hat), und so werden wir nur abends zu Weiss essen gehen, Du weisst, gegenüber vom Kulturbund-Theater. Montag, den 14. August reisen meine Schwester und deren Mann, der Onkel Fritz mit dem Selterwasserapparat, nach Samoa (das liegt noch hinter Australien) ab, und ich bin dann hier ganz allein, ohne alle Verwandten. Ich hatte Dich, o,Peter, neulich abgefragt, was Du Dir zum Geburtstag wünschst, aber Du hast es mir noch noch gar nicht geschrieben. Aber Deine Mutti sagt, es hat auch gar keinen Zweck, dass ich Dir was schicke, ~~[illegible]~~ ~~[illegible]~~ da Ihr jetzt Taschengeld bekommt. Du hast noch gar nicht geschrieben, ob Ihr dort auch weiter Hebräisch lernt, und was Ihr am Sabbath macht, berichte doch mal etwas darüber.- Kennst Du auch den Egon Zwirn, der zusammen Euch gefahren ist ? Ich sehe seinen Vater alle Tage bei der Jüdischen Gemeinde, er sagte mir heute, er habe von seinem Jungen einen begeisterten Brief bekommen. So, für heute weiss ich nichts mehr Neues zu schreiben, so seid denn alle beide vielmals und Herzlich gegrüsst von

Eurem Onkel

Tante

wenden!

15.8.

Liebe Kinder!

Ich habe den Brief immer noch, weil ich heute erst den Antwort-schein kriege, den ich beilege. Ich bin auf der Post und habe keine Schreibmaschine, hoffentlich könnt Ihr meine Schrift lesen. Ich schreibe so undeutlich. Ich wußte auch Eure Adresse nicht auswendig, die sagte mir eben der Vater von Egon Zwirn. – Gestern Abend sind meine Verwandten nach Samoa abgefahren. Die Reise dauert ungefähr zwei und einen halben Monat. Also nochmals

herzliche Grüße

Tanti.

Berlin, August __, 1939

Dearest Peterlein,

My letter of today is directed entirely to you personally, my beloved birthday boy! Mutti wishes only the very best for you, as you yourself already know. Most of all, stay healthy, always be very hardworking and listen well to what the adults tell and teach you to become a capable, decent human being. All the people who are taking great care in your education will be happy because of you. Do not simply pass over my words, but quietly read them over several times and think about whether Mutti is right. After all, you are now a big, reasonable boy with whom one can discuss serious things once in a while! And also Peterle, you must promise me that you will treat Wernchen nicer and not always scream and scold him. You know, even when you were here, I often spoke to you that, if ever I could not be with you anymore, you, being the older brother, should always protect and be good to Wernerchen, who after all is the youngest. And you should try to treat him like Mutti would. You do know that he is rather soft and cuddly, even when he is sometimes stubborn, he needs a lot of love. You know, he is still a little kid and playful and still too little to understand everything and to do everything right. Therefore, you being the older brother, must always give in and must never fight with him, but must be calm and treat him with love and explain everything quietly instead of screaming at him.

I was very happy to receive the card in which you answered all my questions. Gert Blumenthal stopped in today and asked why you are not writing to him. You still do have a reply voucher from him; why don't you send it to him with a few nice lines; Tante Martha would also like a card from you some time. Gert's address is Berlin 55, Bötzow Strasse 16 c/o Lewinski –

By the way, to whom did you give your tricycle? I wanted to sell it and it is no longer in the cabinet. Gert does not have it either. Please let me know!

Lots of changes here too and both of you would be astonished if you were here. Our two bedrooms are now rented to Oma's relatives and the three of us live only in the front rooms now. The salon is now our common bedroom. All this brought a lot of work and unrest into the house; the white chest of drawers and your little play table is now in my workroom in the front. Everything is very tight here now as you can imagine, but otherwise I am well and that's the main thing.

Mrs. Jacoby wrote to me that you, beloved Peterle, are helping her dust so diligently and that you, my dearest Wernchen, sweep the stairs so nicely all the time. I am glad that you do your work so neatly and that Mrs. Jacoby is satisfied with you. It is very nice that you, Werni have so many friends, in particular your little girlfriend. I know so well that you like little children; are you always nice to Ivette too?

So, Mutti must now go into the kitchen and get busy; therefore we want to say goodbye for today. Have fun celebrating your 9th birthday, beloved boy; I will also celebrate the day here and think of you. Say hello for me to all your friends and Madame Jacoby. I am sending you yourself my most loving thoughts and thousands of kisses to you and Wernerle both.

Your Mutti

Jlm., d. August 1939.

Liebstes Peterlein,

mein heutiger Brief gilt ganz persönlich Dir, mein geliebter Geburtstags-Junge! Daß Mutti für Dich nur das Allerbeste wünscht, das weißt Du ja selbst. Bleib gesund vor allen Dingen, sei immer sehr fleißig und paß gut auf was die Großen Dir sagen und Dich lehren, damit Du ein tüchtiger, ordentlicher Mensch wirst, und damit auch all die Menschen, die soviel Mühe mit Deiner Erziehung haben, sich über Dich freuen können. Lies über meine Worte nicht so leicht hinweg, sondern lies sie ruhig mehrere Male durch und denke einmal darüber nach, ob Mutti nicht Recht hat; Du bist doch jetzt schon ein großer, vernünftiger Junge, mit dem man schon mal ein ernstes Wort reden kann! Und dann Peterle, mußt Du mir versprechen, daß Du zum Wernchen lieber bist und nicht immer mit ihm schreist und schimpfst. Du weißt, schon hier habe ich oft mit Dir darüber gesprochen, wenn ich erst nicht mehr bei Euch sein könnte, müßtest Du als älterer Bruder Wernerchen, der doch der Jüngste ist, immer beschützen und gut zu ihm sein, und Dich bemühen, ihm die Mutti zu ersetzen. Du weißt doch, er ist so weich und schmiegsam wenn er auch mal eigensinnig ist, und braucht soviel Liebe.

Du weißt wohl, er ist wohl noch so ein kleines Schäfchen und verspielt und ist doch noch zu klein, um alles zu verstehen und richtig zu machen. Darum mußt Du als der große Bruder immer nachgeben und nie mit ihm zanken, sondern ruhig und lieb mit ihm sein und, statt ihn anzuschreien, ihm alles in Ruhe erklären.

Über Deine Karte, in der Du mir alle Fragen beantwortet hast, habe ich mich sehr gefreut. – Heute war Gert Blumenthal hier und fragte, warum Du ihm nicht schreibst. Du hast doch noch eine Antwortkarte von ihm da, schicke sie doch an ihn ab mit ein paar netten Zeilen, ebenso möchte Tante Martha auch mal eine Karte von Dir haben. Gert's Adresse ist jetzig N.O. 55, Zelterstr. 16 b / Lewinski. – Wem hast Du eigentlich das Dreirad geschenkt? Ich wollte es verkaufen, und es ist nicht mehr in der Kabuse. Gert hat es auch nicht. Schreibe mir, bitte, darüber!

Hier hat sich auch vieles geändert, und Ihr zwei würdet staunen, wenn Ihr hier wärt. Unsere beiden Schlafzimmer sind an Verwandte von Oma vermietet, und wir drei leben jetzt nur noch in den Vorderzimmern. Im Salon ist jetzt unser gemeinsames Schlafzimmer. Das alles hat wieder viel Arbeit und Unruhe ins Haus gebracht, die weiße Kommode und zwei Spieltischchen habe ich jetzt vorn in meinem Arbeitszimmer. Es ist nun alles sehr eng hier, das könnt Ihr Euch ja denken, aber sonst bin ich gesund, und das ist die Hauptsache.

Frau Jacoby schrieb mir, daß Du, geliebtes Peterle, so fleißig beim
Staubwischen hilfst, und Du, mein liebstes Wernchen immer
so schön die Treppen fegst. Ich freue mich, daß Ihr Eure
Arbeit so ordentlich macht, und daß Frau Jacoby mit
Euch zufrieden ist. Es ist schön, daß Du, Werni, soviel
Freunde hast und besonders Deine kleine Freundin. Ich
weiß ja, Du hast kleine Kinder so gern; bist Du auch
immer nett zu Yvette?

So, Mutti muß jetzt in die Küche gehen und
fleißig sein; darum wollen wir uns für heute verab-
schieden. Feiere Deinen 9. Geburtstag recht schön, geliebter Junge, ich werde den Tag auch hier feiern und
an Dich denken. Grüße alle Deine Freunde, ~~Wernerchen~~ und
Madame Jacoby, von mir und sei Du selbst innigst
gegrüßt und mit Wernerle zusammen tausendmal
geküßt von

Deiner Mutti.

Berlin, August 27, 1939

Beloved children!

Early today your card of the 25th arrived, dear Peterle. I am glad that you had such a nice excursion to Paris and have seen so many beautiful and fine things there. Was Werni also along and, by the way, how is he doing? You are not mentioning anything about him. Is he also studying French already? So Peterle, listen: when you write to me, you must always put my letter next to yours and answer all the questions that I want to know. Do you understand? I am always writing you long letters and you do not answer any of my questions. From now on, Peterle, you will do it this way, right?! By the way, did you receive the packages I sent for your birthday and moreover, I sent you a package from Tante Martha earlier. Tante Martha wants to know whether you have received hers. So, tell me, whom did you actually give your tricycle? Have you heard anything from Vati? Are you writing to him once in a while? And, by the way, what is his address? He has not written to me for quite some time. When you have his address, please let me know. What did you do on your birthday? Is Madame Jacoby still with you or is the other governess there already? Please write to me about this and the name of your governess. Then I will sometimes write to her too. – We have the best summer weather here right now and lots of heat and I hope that it is nice and warm also where you are and you can be in the air a lot. How are you spending Friday evenings? Are you learning Hebrew?

Now, dear Peterle, write to me right away and answer all my questions, and most specifically whether Werni is well and whether he is having fun as he cannot yet write by himself. I am enclosing an envelope and a reply voucher.

I must sign off for today for I have lots to do. Stay well, my two beloved boys. I embrace and kiss you both in love

your Mutti
Best wishes
Onkel Fonti

Pachs, Tante Martha, Oma, Tante Hilde, Tante Betty, Onkel Lanforg [?], Tante Else say hello.

Berlin, d. 27. 8. 39.

Geliebte Kinder!

Heute früh kam Deine Karte vom 25. liebes Peterle, hier an. Ich freue mich, daß Ihr einen so feinen Ausflug nach Paris gemacht habt und dort soviel Schönes und Feines gesehen habt. War Werni auch mit und wie geht es ihm denn eigentlich; Du schreibst über ihn garnichts. Hat er auch schon Französisch? Dann Peterle, paß mal auf: Wenn Du an mich schickst, mußt Du Dir beim Schreiben immer meinen Brief daneben legen und mir alle Fragen beantworten, die ich gern wissen möchte. Verstehst Du? Ich schreib Dir immer lange Briefe, und Du antwortest mir auf gar keine Frage. Gell wahr, Peterle, Du wirst das nun immer so machen! Hast Du eigentlich die Päckchen von mir zum Geburtstag bekommen, und dann habe ich Euch von Tante Martha noch vorher auch ein Päckchen geschickt. Tante Martha möchte wissen, ob Ihr es bekommen habt. Dann sag mir mal, wem hast Du eigentlich das Dreirad geschenkt? Hast Du mal etwas vom Vati gehört? Schreibst Du an ihn auch mal? Und wie ist eigentlich seine Adresse? Er hat mir schon lange nicht geschrieben. Wenn Du seine Adresse hast, schreibe sie mir doch. Was habt Ihr an Deinem Geburtstag gemacht? Ist Madame Jacoby noch bei

Euch, oder ist die andere Erzieherin schon da? Schreibe mir doch mal darüber, und wie Eure Erzieherin heißt. Ich will dann auch mal an sie schreiben. Hier ist jetzt das schönste Sommerwetter mit großer Hitze, und ich hoffe, daß es bei Euch auch so schön warm ist, sodaß Ihr viel in der Luft sein könnt. Wie verbringt Ihr die Freitag-Abende? Lernt Ihr auch Hebräisch?

Nun, liebes Peterle, schreibe mir sofort Antwort auf alle meine Fragen, ganz besonders auch, ob Werni gesund ist und ob er vergnügt ist, weil er doch noch nicht selbst schreiben kann. Ich lege ein Kuvert und Antwortbelein bei.

Für heute muß ich Schluß machen, da ich zu tun habe. Lebt wohl, meine zwei geliebten Jungen, ich umarme und küsse Euch herzlich in Liebe

Eure Mutti.

Viele Grüße

Onkel Tante.

Papa, Tante Martha, Oma, Tante Hilde, Tante Betty, Onkel Laufarz, Tante Else lassen grüßen.

Berlin 55, September 19, 1939
Lippehnerstr. 35

Beloved Peterle, beloved Wernerle,

We have not heard from one another for quite a while and I hope that you two are safe and sound. All of us, Oma, Tante Hilde, Betty, Onkel Lanforg, Tante Else, Pachs and all your friends and acquaintances who love you are also feeling well and talk about you all the time.

Please Peterle write immediately when you receive this letter whether both of you are healthy and whether you are still in Quincy and tell me everything that you have to say. Are you hearing from Vati occasionally?

However, you cannot address the envelope to me, but you should write the letter to me and on the envelope you write the following address:

Mrs. Löwy

Amsterdam/Holland, Daniel Willinkplein 13.

Moreover, you must also enclose a reply voucher, in order that the lady in Holland can forward your letter to me. I am sending this letter to you the very same way. There is no other way right now. Please show this letter to your governess, she will understand how this is meant and will certainly help you. School will start soon now and Wernerle may possibly attend already? Do you already have a picture of you? Please send me one when you can.

Also, beloved boys, write immediately so that I have a sign of life from you.

Heartfelt wishes and kisses to you both

Love
your Mutti

I suppose in time there will be the opportunity to reimburse the postage.

Berlin N.O. 55, den 19.9.39.
Lippehnerstr. 35.

Geliebtes Peterle, geliebtes Wernerle,

wir haben solange nichts von einander gehört und ich hoffe, daß Ihr beide gesund und munter seid. Wir alle, Oma, Tante Hilde, Betty, Onkel Lanforg, Tante Else, Pächs und alle Eure Freunde und Bekannten die Euch lieb haben, sind auch gesund und sprechen immer von Euch.

Bitte, liebes Peterle, schreibe mir sofort, wenn Du diesen Brief bekommen hast, ob Ihr beide gesund seid, und ob Ihr noch in Quincy seid, und alles, was Dir zu erzählen hast. Hörst Du mal was vom Vati?

Du kannst ~~den Brief~~ das Couvert aber nicht an mich adressieren, sondern Du schreibst den Brief an mich und schreibst auf das Kuvert folgende Adresse:

Frau Löwy
Amsterdam/Holland, Daniel Willinkplein 13.

außerdem mußt Du einen Antwortschein beilegen, damit die Dame in Holland Deinen Brief an mich weiter schicken kann. Ich schicke diesen Brief auch auf diesem Wege an Euch, anders geht das vorläufig nicht. Zeige doch diesen Brief Eurer Er=

sicherlich sie wird verstehen, wie alles gemeint ist, und Dir bestimmt helfen. Ibun fängt gewiß bald die Schule an und Wernerle macht wohl nun auch schon mit? Habt Ihr schon eine Photographie von Euch, wenn Du kannst, schicke doch mal ein Bild.

Also geliebte Jungen, schreibt sofort daß Ich bald ein Lebenszeichen von Euch habe.

Seid beide innigst gegrüßt und geküßt.

In Liebe

Eure Mutti.

✓ Es wird sich ja im Laufe der Zeit eine Gelegenheit finden, die Portoauslagen zu ersetzen.

Berlin Voss, September 28, 1939
Lippehnerstr. 35 II [?]

Mrs. Charlotte Gossels

My beloved Peterle and Wernerchen,

It has been long that we heard from one another. Last week I wrote to you via Holland, but you have not yet responded to this letter. Later Vati wrote to me from Antwerp that he already has written so many letters from Antwerp to you. Haven't you received any? We here are all healthy. Where are the two of you? Are you still in Quincy or do you have another address now? – Well, dear Peterle, when you receive this letter, please write immediately and tell me whether both of you are well, what your address is and whatever else you may have to say. How is Wernerchen, our little one? Is he going to school already?

Please address the envelope with the letter that you will be writing to me to:

An das Rote Kreuz, Genf (Schweiz)

and, if you can, enclose a reply voucher in order that the Red Cross can forward the letter to me.

Show this letter to your governess and ask her for me to help you and to explain what I have written to you.

I hope that you, my two dear children, will receive this letter and that you both are healthy and are having fun.

Heartfelt greetings and kisses

Love
Mutti

I am asking the Red Cross in Geneva to forward this letter to

Claus and Werner Gossels
Château de Quincy, Annese Garçons,
Quincy-suis-Sérrat (S. et O.) France

Sincerely
Mrs. Charlotte Gossels

Frau Charlotte Gossels.

Berlin NO55, den 28. September 1939.
Lippehnerstr. 35.II.

Meine geliebten beiden Peterle und Wernerchen,
solange haben wir nichts von einander gehört.
Vorige Woche schrieb ich über Holland an Euch, aber Ihr habt bisher auch auf diesen Brief nicht geantwortet. Dann schrieb Vati mir aus Antwerpen, er hätte schon soviel Briefe von dortaus an Euch geschickt. Habt Ihr nichts bekommen?
Wir sind hier alle gesund. Wo seid Ihr zwei? Noch in Quincy, oder habt Ihr jetzt eine andere Adresse? –
Also, liebes Peterle, wenn Du diesen Brief bekommst, dann schreibe mir sofort, ob Ihr beide gesund seid, wie Eure Adresse ist, und was Du sonst alles zu erzählen hast.
Was macht denn das Wernerchen, unser „Kleines"? Geht er schon zur Schule?
Auf das Kuvert, in dem Du den Brief an mich schickst, schreibst Du:
An das Rote Kreuz, Genf (Schweiz),
und legst, wenn Du kannst einen Antwortschein bei, damit das „Rote Kreuz" den Brief an mich weiterschickt.
Zeige diesen Brief Eurer Erzieherin und bitte Sie in meinem Namen, sie solle Dir helfen und alles erklären, was ich Dir geschrieben habe.

Ich hoffe, daß Ihr, meine zwei geliebten Kinder, diesen Brief bekommen werdet, und daß Ihr beide gesund und lustig seid.

Ich grüße und küsse Euch innigst
in Liebe
Eure Mutti.

Ich bitte das Rote Kreuz in Genf, diesen Brief an
Claus und Werner Gossels
Château de Quincy, Annexe Garçons,
Quincy-sous-Sénart (S. et O.), France,
weiterzuleiten.

Ergebenst
Frau Charlotte Gossels.

Berlin, October 26, 1939

Dear Vati, my two beloved boys!

I was delighted this morning when the mailman brought me your card with the interesting report. Many thanks for the prompt handling. Edith brought me your letter today that you, dear Peterle, wrote to your class in early August in which you described your impressions of the trip in such detail. I enjoyed reading your so comprehensive letter, because in the letter you sent me some time ago you did not report in such detail. Gert Blumenthal was here a few days ago and inquired about you two; he asked me for a picture of you. I also met Lillian recently; she too sends her best. Every single one of your playmates and friends, and all adults who knew and love you, come by and ask for you. Sometimes people whom you knew stop me in the middle of the street and ask what you are up to, you little Racker [rascals]. You can see that no one has forgotten you and all want to hear good news about you. That you, my little one, are now a "big schoolboy" makes me particularly happy. I was thinking that you would be starting school just about now. It won't take long now that Wernerle can add greetings for Mutti now and then, right? I am sure that you like learning a lot, because Peterle and Edith have already taught you quite a bit of writing and arithmetic! And you, dear Peterle, how are you doing in school, are you making good progress or is learning not so easy there and are the teachers stricter? Are you only attending home school or must you walk or ride to school? Mutti is so curious and would like to know everything precisely. Have you learned to swim, Peterle, or are you bathing in cold water only? And how are things with Wernchen? I am happy that you are healthy and like it there. I have written to you so many times, but you have not responded. Is Mrs. Jacoby still there? If she is, please give her my best and tell her that I thank her very much for all the care she is giving you. I myself am healthy and am working in the restaurant (preparing dinner, etc.) and in my "store," when there is something to do, something that you two are already interested in also. I often think of the morning hours with you, my beloved

Strolche, when you climbed into my bed, one on each side and the tussle started. And I am thinking of our chats when you, my dear and good Peterle sneaked into my bed in the dark and nestled to me and we talked until my little Pepi almost fell asleep. - Yes, everything has changed now. Our green room and Oma's bedroom are both rented to relatives. The three of us are sleeping together in the Salon. Your play table has become my work table. You always like to watch when Mutti set up the preparations. Mutti has stored all items for her cosmetics in your white chest of drawers. Your picture always stands on the chest and I am always thinking of you, even when I work. I wish I could visit you someday and look around - - but that is impossible. Tante Pach and Tante Klein feel quite abandoned since you are no longer here; they are thinking of you all the time and send their love and kisses. – Could you, dear Peterle, send a picture of both of you or have you not been photographed yet? How does our Wernerle look with his schoolbag? Has he learned to eat right or does he still forgo chicken for cheese sandwiches with *Steinbuscher* and *"Stolper Jungchen?"*[?]

Now, dear Peterle, please write a few lines to me as soon as you are allowed; you know how much Mutti thinks of you and how she is delighted with every letter from both of you.

Now I am saying good-bye to my two darlings for today; we will chat another time. In my thoughts I am holding you both in my arms and kiss you a thousand times with love and tenderness

Your Mutti

For you, dear Vati sends many thanks and greetings once again.
[illegible]

Peterle, please let Gert Alexander add a few lines for his parents to your next letter to; but don't forget this!

Thousand greetings from Oma, Tante Hilde, Betty, Onkel Lanforg, Fanti, Tante Else, Tante Martha.

Berlin, d. 26. Oktober 1939.

Lieber Vati; meine beiden geliebten Jungen!

Beglückt war ich heute früh, als der Br[illegible]
mir Deine Karte mit dem interessanten Bericht brachte. Vielen
herzlichen Dank für die prompte Erledigung. Heute brachte mir
Edith Deinen Brief, den Du, liebes Peterle Anfang August an
die Klasse geschrieben hast, und in dem Du Deine Eind[illegible]
über die Reise so genau geschildert hast. Es machte mir Freude,
Deinen so ausführlichen Brief durchzulesen, denn an mich hast
Du damals garnicht alles so genau berichtet. Gert Blumenthal
war auch vor einigen Tagen hier und fragte nach Euch beiden;
er bat mich um ein Bild von Euch. Auch Lilian traf ich
vor kurzer Zeit; sie läßt Euch beide auch vielmals grüßen.
Alle, alle Eure Gespielen und Freunde, und auch alle Großen,
die Euch kannten und lieb hatten, kommen und fragen
nach Euch. Manchmal werde ich mitten auf der Straße von
fremden Leuten, die Ihr wohl kanntet, angesprochen und
gefragt, was Ihr beiden, kleinen Racker macht. Ihr seht
also, niemand hat Euch vergessen, und jeder möchte etwas Gutes über Euch hören. Daß Du, mein Kleinster
nun auch schon ein „großer Schuljunge" bist, freut mich
ganz besonders. Ich dachte es mir gleich, daß Du jetzt
schon mit der Schule beginnen würdest. Nun wird es
nicht mehr lange dauern, und das Wernerle kann dann
auch schon mal einen Gruß an die Mutti anschreiben
nicht wahr? Bestimmt macht Dir das Lernen viel Spaß,

denn Du hast doch bei Peterle und Edith schon eine ganze Menge Schreiben und Rechnen gelernt! Und, wie geht's Dir in der Schule, liebes Peterle, machst Du gute Fortschritte oder lernst Du dort nicht so leicht und sind die Lehrer strenger? Habt Ihr im Heim Schule, oder müßt Ihr hingehen oder fahren? Mutti ist so neugierig und möchte alles ganz genau wissen. Hast Du, Peterle, Schwimmen gelernt, oder habt Ihr nur kalt gebadet? Und wie ist das mit Besuchen? Ich freue mich, daß Ihr gesund seid und es Euch gefällt. Ich habe schon so oft an Euch geschrieben, aber Ihr habt mir nicht geantwortet. Ist Frau Jacoby noch da? Wenn ja, dann, bitte, grüßt Sie herzlich von mir und ich lasse Ihr vielmals für alle Mühe, die sie sich mit Euch gibt, danken. Ich selbst bin gesund und arbeite in der Wirtschaft (Mittagkochen) und in meinem „Laden", wenn es dort etwas zu tun gibt, was Euch zwei ja nun auch schon interessiert. Oft denke ich an die Morgenstunden mit Euch beiden geliebten kleinen Strolchen, wenn von jeder Seite eins in mein Bett gestiegen kam und dann die Balgerei losging, und an unsere Plauderstündchen, liebes, gutes Peterle, wenn Du abends im Dunkeln in mein Bett geschlichen kamst, Dich an mich schmiegtest und wir zusammen plauderten, bis mein kleiner Pepi fast einschlief. – Ja, es ist jetzt alles anders geworden. Unser gutes Zimmer und Omas Schlafzimmer sind beide an Verwandte vermietet. Wir Drei schlafen zusammen vorn im Salon. Euer Spieltischchen

2

ist mein Arbeitstisch geworden, wenn Mutti Präparate macht, wobei Ihr immer so gern zusaht, und in Eurer weißen Kommode hat Mutti alle Sachen für ihre Kosmetik untergebracht. Auf der Kommode steht Euer Bild, und so denke ich immer an Euch, auch wenn ich arbeite. Ich wünschte, ich könnte Euch einmal besuchen und mir alles ansehen -- aber das geht ja nicht. Tante Pach und Tante Klein fühlen sich ganz verlassen, seitdem Ihr nicht mehr hier seid, sie denken immerzu an Euch und schicken Euch viele Grüße und Küßchen. Kannst Du, liebes Peterle, nicht mal ein Bild von Euch einschicken, oder seid Ihr bisher nicht photographiert worden? Wie sieht denn nur unser Wernerle mit der Schulmappe aus? Hat er nun richtig essen gelernt oder verzichtet er immer noch auf Hühnchen für Käsebrot mit Steinbuscher und „Stolper Jungchen"?

Nun, liebes Peterle, schreibe doch, sobald Du darfst, ein paar Zeilen an mich. Du weißt, wieviel Mutti an Euch denkt und wie sehr sie sich mit jedem Brief von Euch freut.

Nun sage ich Euch, meine zwei Lieblinge, für heute lebewohl; ein andermal plaudern wir wieder miteinander. Ich schließe Euch beide in Gedanken in meine Arme und küsse Euch tausendmal

in Liebe und Innigkeit

Eure Mutti.

Bitte Peterle, laß doch Gert Alexander an Deinen nächsten Brief ein paar Zeilen für seine Eltern anschreiben, aber vergiß es nicht! Innige Grüße von Oma, Tante Hilde, Onkel Hamburg, Tante, Tante Elsa, Tante Martha.

Für l. Vati nochmals vielen Dank und Gruß.

Translator's note: this letter is written in *Kurrent* script

Dear Peter, even when you have apparently forgotten me, I am thinking often of you and Werner and am always delighted when I hear something about you. When I want to talk to you, I hold your picture and look at it for a long time, but regretfully, you do not provide an answer. I hope that you are very healthy and remain so. It is good that Werner also goes to school now and you, being the big brother, can help with his assignments (but not [illegible]). You surely have a lot of friends already with whom you play. Write as often as possible to your dear mother. She is so delighted to hear from you.

Now, dear children, stay healthy. Heartfelt greetings from you old aunt

Pach

Tante Klein also sends her greetings.

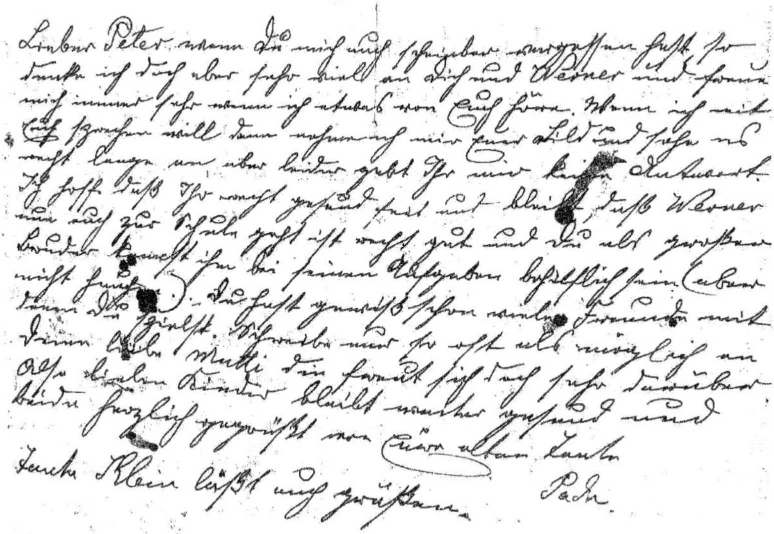

Lieber Peter wenn Du mich auch scheinbar vergessen hast so denke ich doch aber sehr viel an Dich und Werner und freue mich immer sehr wenn ich etwas von Euch höre. Wenn ich mit Euch sprechen will dann nehme ich mir Euer Bild und sehe es mir lange an aber leider gebt Ihr mir keine Antwort. Ich hoffe dass Ihr recht gesund seid und bleibt, dass Werner nun auch zur Schule geht ist recht gut und Du als grosser Bruder kannst ihm bei seinen Aufgaben behilflich sein (aber nicht zanken). Du hast gewiss schon viele Freunde mit denen Du spielst. Schreibe mir so oft als möglich an Deine liebe Mutti die freut sich doch sehr darüber. Also lieben Kinder bleibt weiter gesund und seid herzlich gegrüßt von Euer alten Tante

Tante Klein lässt auch grüssen.

Pada

8 Dec. 1939

My two beloved boys!

Vati forwarded your letter of November 12th to me and I am very glad that you, dear Peterle, have learned so much already that you can already write an entire letter. I believe that just a few months from now, Pepi will be quite perfect!? Is Wernchen also learning so much in his children's school? When you write again, why don't you let him write a greeting, or at least his name. Mutti would love so much to see Werner's handwriting. Mutti is happy together with you, that you like being in the Schloss and that you have such fine food. Edith too was very happy to receive your birthday letter. A smile was beaming all over her face when she brought it to me to read. She answered right away on the same letter, and you will certainly receive it in a few weeks. Gert comes practically every week and visits me. His class will have a performance for Channukah and he has a rather significant role to play. On December 30th will be his bar mitzvah in the [illegible] street. His foster parents will leave here on the 15th and Gert will go in the Auerbach [Orphanage]. He is really a very nice and affectionate boy, whom I like very much. He sends the very best to you both and wishes you well. How are you celebrating Channukah? Don't the older boys kindle the Channukah menorah and are you all singing together? Or do you do nothing? – Every evening Mutti lights your little menorah, Peterle, and then she thinks back of how every night her Peterle kindled another light until all the lights were lighted and then she hears the two lovely voices of her Peterle and Wernerle singing the Channukah song. Do you still remember when we all sat together and the Channukah man came and brought something for everyone? Wherever you went during those days, to Mutti's, to Aunt Martha's and everywhere, he left something for you! Yes, Mutti is very sad because she is so alone, but she is glad that you are doing so well!

Now, dear Peterle, I have a request for you. Always be obedient toward adults and be clean and tidy with your clothing and all the jobs assigned to you, regardless whether they are school or home assignments. You know even here I had to admonish you because you were messy and untidy. Mutti cannot be with you now and help you when you did something wrong. Now you must think of everything alone and because you are still too little to do everything right, you must obey every word when your teachers tell you something! They want only the best for you and just like they reprimand and punish you, when you are disobedient, they will also praise and reward you, when you obey and are clean and tidy. Please say hello for me to Mrs. Howard and tell her that I am very grateful for her report to Vati.

I can well imagine that the two of you must learn a lot now, but you, Peterle, will nevertheless have some time again to write a detailed letter, right?

Be well for now, my two beloved boys. Hugs and kisses with love

from your Mutti

8. XII. 39.

Meine beiden geliebten Jungen!

Durch Vati erhielt ich Euren Brief vom 12. Nov., und ich freue mich sehr, daß Du, liebes Peterle, schon soviel gelernt hast, daß Du schon einen ganzen Brief schreiben kannst. Ich glaube, ein paar Monate weiter, ist der Pepi schon ganz perfekt?! Lernt Wernerlein in seiner Kinderschule auch soviel? Laß ihn doch, wenn Du wieder mal schreibst, einen Gruß oder wenigstens seinen Namen anschreiben. Mutti möchte doch zu gern einmal Wernis Handschrift sehen. Mutti freut sich mit Euch, daß es Euch in dem Schloß so gut gefällt, und daß Ihr so feines Essen habt. Auch Goldi war mit Eurem Geburtstagsbrief sehr glücklich und strahlte über ihr ganzes Gesicht, als sie ihn mir zum Lesen brachte. Sie hat Euch gleich auf demselben Briefbogen geantwortet, und in ein paar Wochen werdet ihr den Brief gewiß bekommen. Gert kommt fast jede Woche und besucht mich. Seine Klasse führt zu Chanukka etwas auf und er hat eine ziemlich große Rolle dabei zu spielen. Am 30. 12. ist seine Barmizwah in der Rykestr. Seine Pflegeeltern gehen am 15. fort von hier, und Gert kommt dann ins "Auerbach'sche". Er ist wirklich ein sehr netter und anhänglicher Junge, der mir sehr gut gefällt. Er läßt Euch beide herzlichst grüßen und Euch alles Gute wünschen. Wie ist das bei Euch mit Chanukka? Zünden die älteren Jungen nicht die Lichtchen an, und singt Ihr alle zusammen? Oder macht Ihr garnichts? – Mutti zündet jeden Abend Deinen kleinen Leuchter an, Peterle, und dann denkt sie zurück, wie Ihr, Peterle, jeden Abend ein Lichtchen mehr anzündete, bis der Leuchter voll war, und dann

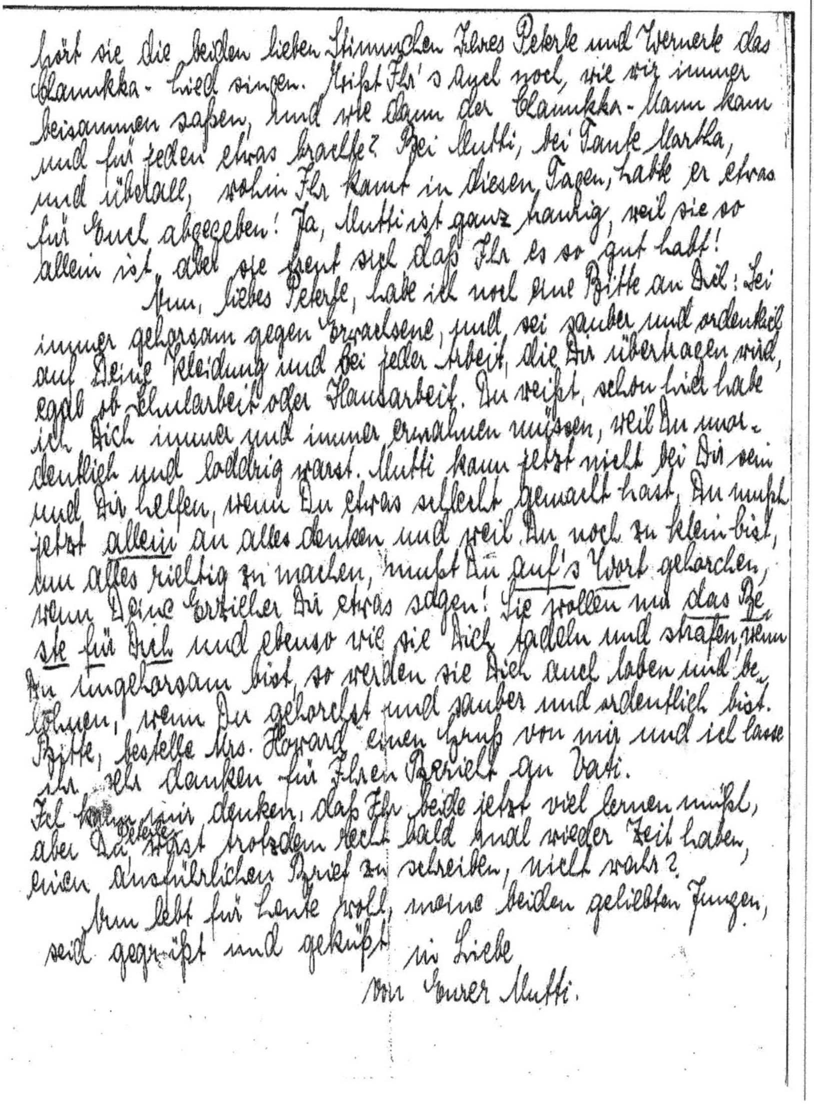
hört sie die beiden lieben Stimmchen Ihres Peterle und Wernerle das Clamukka-Lied singen. Wißt Ihr's auch noch, wie wir immer beisammen saßen, und wie dann der Clamukka-Mann kam und für jeden etwas brachte? Bei Mutti, bei Tante Martha, und überall, wohin Ihr kamt in diesen Tagen, hatte er etwas für Euch abgegeben! Ja, Mutti ist ganz traurig, weil sie so allein ist, aber sie freut sich daß Ihr es so gut habt!

Nun, liebes Peterle, habe ich noch eine Bitte an Dich: Sei immer gehorsam gegen Erwachsene, und sei sauber und ordentlich auf Deine Kleidung und bei jeder Arbeit, die Dir übertragen wird, egal ob Schularbeit oder Hausarbeit. Du weißt, schon früher habe ich Dich immer und immer ermahnen müssen, weil Du unordentlich und lodderig warst. Mutti kann jetzt nicht bei Dir sein und Dir helfen, wenn Du etwas schlecht gemacht hast, Du mußt jetzt allein an alles denken und weil Du noch zu klein bist, um alles richtig zu machen, mußt Du auf's Wort gehorchen, wenn Deine Erzieher Dir etwas sagen! Sie wollen nur das Beste für Dich und ebenso wie sie Dich tadeln und strafen wenn Du ungehorsam bist, so werden sie Dich auch loben und belohnen, wenn Du gehorchst und sauber und ordentlich bist.
Bitte, bestelle Mrs. Howard einen Gruß von mir und ich lasse ihr sehr danken für Ihren Bericht an Vati.
Ich kann mir denken, daß Ihr beide jetzt viel lernen müßt, aber Du Peterle wirst trotzdem recht bald mal wieder Zeit haben, einen ausführlichen Brief zu schreiben, nicht wahr?

Nun lebt für heute wohl, meine beiden geliebten Jungen, seid gegrüßt und geküßt in Liebe

von Eurer Mutti.

December 14, 1939

My dear beloved boys,

This morning I received your two letters (one for me and one for Vati) in your sweet little handwriting, my little Schnäuzelchen. This is my most beautiful Channukah present and it makes me very happy. I am happy also because of your nice and clear handwriting, dear Peterle. Mutti took care of the dictionary right away and sent it to you to get it soon and so that you can always learn a lot from it. What do you actually mean by "*Moden*" [fashion?] Are you taught manual skills and do you have to make the "bows, arches, baskets, etc. yourselves as, for instance, you have always done with your jigsaw, or how should I understand this? Please explain this to me in your next letter, won't you? I received the address for your little friend's letter, but you have apparently forgotten to enclose the letter ? Please say hello to your friend for me and tell him that I will gladly forward his letter. Alright, Peterle, next time pay attention and don't forget again, are you listening!? – You seem to gradually develop into a little artist. Is the house, that you drew in your father's letter, supposed to be the Schloss? That looks rather splendid and you also drew the arches, planes and ships very nicely. – Is Wernchen also learning to write in the children school? You probably helped him a little with his signature? Mutti is rereading all she has written to her boys and she notices that she never stops asking questions because she likes to know everything exactly. And now she is quickly asking yet something else that interests Mutti especially. Tell me, Peterle, how are you actually dressed? Are you both wearing your beautiful things – are you sometimes wearing your nice grey suits with the light blue blouses that I bought you or do all of you boys always wear the same things? Do you wear something fine on Sundays or holiday or are you always wearing the same clothes? What kind of caps and shoes do you wear? Please tell me sometimes so I can imagine what you look like now, you little Strolche. I suppose you have grown a lot! I am very happy that you celebrated Channukah together. The fact that you, dear Peterle, have the best grades is the greatest joy you could have given me. You truly appear to study diligently, now you must take great care for your next grades to be so good again and then you may ask me for a reward! It is wonderful that you are very active in sports, race and take beautiful walks in the woods. This makes you big, strong and always in good mood. I very much like your description of the old mill with the wild brook and I very much want to romp around there and play with you boys some time. Wouldn't this be wonderful, wouldn't it? – Since you both have left, Mutti does not walk at all anymore – it is no fun so alone. Here it is already terribly cold and it gets dark in the early afternoon. Then Mutti is glad when she can sit and work in a warm room. This Channukah was very lonesome for me because you were not with me. Every night Mutti lighted your little menorah, my dear Peterlein and when the candles where lighted, she thought of her two little boys. Today Mutti packed the menorah up and now it can rest for one whole year. – The whole page is packed with writing, it is late and Mutti is tired. So, be well today my two beloved boys, stay healthy and happy as up to now. I am embracing you [cut off text – basically mentioned all relatives and friends etc.]

14. XII. 39.

Meine beiden geliebten Jungen,

heute früh erhielt ich Eure beiden Briefe (1 an mich, 1 a
Vati) und Deine süße kleine Handarbeit, mein kleines Schnäuze
chen. Dies ist mein schönstes Chanukka-Geschenk, und ich
freue mich sehr damit, ebenso mit Deinem so fein sauber
geschriebenen Brief, liebes Peterle. Das Wörterbuch hat Mutti sofort besorgt und abgeschickt, sodaß Du es bald dort haben
wirst, und dann kannst Du immer fleißig daraus lernen.
Was meinst Du, liebes Peterle, eigentlich mit Euren „Moden"?
Habt Ihr Handfertigkeitsunterricht und müßt die "Pfeile, Bog
Körbchen usw. alle selbst machen, so z. B. wie Du immer mi
Deiner Laubsäge selbst gezimmert hast, oder wie ist das zu
verstehen? Erkläre mir das doch einmal in Deinem nächsten
Brief, ja? Die Adresse für den Brief Deines kleinen Freundes ha
ich bekommen, aber Du hast wohl vergessen, den Brief beizu
legen? Bestelle Deinem Freund einen schönen Gruß von mir
und sag ihm, ich werde seinen Brief gern weiterschicken.
Also, Peterle, beim nächsten Mal, aufpassen und nicht wied
vergessen, hörst Du!? – Du scheinst Dich so langsam zu ein
kleinen Maler zu entwickeln. Soll das Haus, das Du in den
Brief an Vati gemalt hast, das Schloß sein? Das sieht ja
ganz großartig aus, und die Bogen, Flugzeuge und Schif
hast Du auch sehr niedlich gemalt. – Kann Würmchen den
in der Kinderschule auch schreiben? Du hast ihm wohl
ein Bißchen geholfen bei seiner Unterschrift? Mutti liest e
einmal durch, was sie alles an ihre Jungen geschrieben
hat, und da merkt sie, daß sie nicht aufhört zu
fragen, weil sie alles so gern ganz genau wissen möch
Und nun fragt sie schnell noch etwas, und das inte
essiert Mutti ganz besonders: Sag mal, Peterle, wie ge

Berlin, January 14, 1940

My two darlings Peterlein und Werni!

I have received both letters of Christmas and New Year and everything that you wrote made me very happy. But you, dear Peterle, only write so little about Werni; as long as he cannot write to me himself and tell me everything, you, little Racker [rascal], should really tell more about him and not only about you. Mutti worries about the little Schnauzel [rascal] whether he is well, whether he likes his food and how he handles school. Therefore, dear big Peterle, write to me in detail; you do know your Mutti and realize yourself that a Mutti always worries about her children and can be happy only when she knows that her darlings are doing well! I can well understand, my dear Peterle, that writing is a lot of work for you, but you happily do it for your Mutti, right?! – It really is nice the way you celebrated Channukah and that, also at Christmas, you were being thought of with little presents. It is great also that you, Peterle, won some writing paper because now you can always write long letters. And what did you get, my beloved, little Wernchen? Why don't you tell Pepi all the things he should write to me. Mutti would like very much to exactly know everything and when you can, write a letter to me all by yourself, right? Then Mutti will be very proud when she receives the first letter written by you, her dear little Schnauzelchen. I look at your little handy work again and again and then I see my little Wernerle with his red cheeks diligently bent over his work, sitting in school. Is this so and is Mutti right? By the way, I recently received you little letter that you sent together with Egon Heisemann to his Mutti. I sent Gerhard's letter immediately to his aunt. – It is good that the dictionary I sent you, dear Peterle, made you happy; I am certain that you can use it well. It is meant for both of you and once Wernchen is ready, he can also use it, do you hear? Don't be mad and bicker! Your little Sylvester drawing is really neat. Did you really celebrate New Year? Is your toothbrush glass all frozen and how do you clean your teeth, Pepi? And also tell me of the tricks you have learned. Gerd B. has not been here at all anymore, very likely he moved in the meantime. – For a few weeks it has been terribly cold here and it snowed too, just like where you are. Mutti would have liked to build snowmen, just like you have done, but firstly: Mutti does not have a nice garden as you have and secondly: the snow would have been too wet and too cold! It was so cold that Mutti's nose almost froze shut when she walked in the street; can you picture this! Laughable, no? Now in winter we are all sitting in one heated room together. That is best so, and Mutti wishes it were already summer again already! Very likely you are not dressed so warm, because where you are it is probably not so terribly cold. I would like to know whether you wear the pretty gray suits with the silk blouses once in a while and also the other fine knitted things that we purchased together? How did you like the nice presents Vati gave you; the mechanical pencil, notebook and calendar. Well, I think you have been treated splendidly and now don't forget to thank Vati! – Vacations are over now and you must work very hard again. Is Werner also helping with housework or is he still too small, and what kind of job do you have for the next few week, dear Peterle? When you write again, Peterle, please send greetings for all; you do know to whom: Oma, Tante Pach, Klein, Tante Betty, Jacobsohns, Tante Kirchhoff und anyone else to want to. All of them are always inquiring about you both and are rather sad that you never send greetings to them. Well, Peterlein, please don't forget and write soon again. Soon Mutti will send you a pretty picture of herself so that you may not forget what your Mutti looks like.

I say "Good Night" to you for now, my two beloved boys; it is 10:30 in the evening and Mutti's eyes are falling shut and tomorrow morning comes quickly. Good night, stay well and in good spirit. I give you both thousand wishes and kisses with tender love

Your Mutti

495/

Bln., d. 14. I. 40.

Meine beiden Lieblinge Peterlein und Werni!

Eure beiden Briefe von Weihnachten und Sylvester habe ich erhalten und alles, was Ihr mir dazu schreibt, hat mich sehr erfreut. Du liebes Peterle, schreibst mir _so wenig von Werni_; solange er noch nicht selbst an mich schreiben und alles erzählen kann, mußt Du, kleiner Racker, schon auch von ihm etwas mehr berichten und nicht nur von Dir. Mutti macht sich Sorge um den kleinen Schnauzel, ob er auch gesund ist, ob ihm das Essen schmeckt und wie er mit der Schule fertig wird. Also, liebes „großes" Peterle, schreib mir mal alles genau; Du kennst doch Eure Mutti und weißt doch selbst, daß eine Mutti sich _immer_ um Ihre Kinder sorgt, und nur froh sein kann, wenn sie weiß, daß es Ihren Lieblingen gut geht! Ich kann ja verstehen, mein liebes Peterchen, daß das Schreiben Dir viel Arbeit macht, aber für Mutti tust Du es bestimmt gern?! – Es ist wirklich fein, wie Ihr Chanukka verlebt habt, und daß man auch zu Weihnachten mit kleinen Geschenken an Euch gedacht hat. Daß Du, Peterle, Schreibpapier gewonnen hast ist auch ganz großartig, da kannst Du ja mir immer lange Briefe schreiben! Und was bekamst Du, mein geliebtes kleines Wernchen? Sage Du doch mal dem Pepi was er alles über Dich an mich schreiben soll. Mutti möchte so gern alles ganz genau wissen, und wenn Du kannst, schreibst Du mal ganz allein einen Brief an mich, ja? Dann wird Mutti aber sehr stolz sein, wenn sie den ersten selbstgeschriebenen Brief von ihrem lieben kleinen Schnauzelchen bekommt. Deine kleine Handarbeit sehe ich mir immer wieder an und dann sehe ich mein kleines Wernerle mit roten Bäckchen fleißig über seine Arbeit gebeugt in der Schule sitzen. Ist es so, und hat Mutti Recht? Im übrigen habe ich neulich Euren kleinen Brief bekommen, den Ihr mit Egon Heinemann zusammen an seine Mutti geschickt habt. Den Brief von Gerhard habe ich sofort an seine Tante geschickt. – Es ist fein, daß ich Dir, liebes Peterle, mit dem Lexikon eine Freude gemacht habe, gewiß kannst Du es gut gebrauchen. Es ist für _Euch beide_ bestimmt, und wenn Wernchen erst soweit ist, dann soll er auch daraus lernen, hörst Du? und nicht etwa böse sein und zanken! Deine kleine

Sylvester-Zeichnung ist sehr niedlich. Habt Ihr denn auch Sylvester gefeiert? Ist Dein Zahnbecher schon ganz eingefroren, und woraus putzt Du Dir denn die Zähne, Pepi? Und dann erzähl mir mal, was Du für Kunststücke gelernt hast. Gert Pz. war nun garnicht mehr hier, sicher ist er inzwischen umgezogen. – Hier bei uns war es jetzt ein paar Wochen ganz schrecklich kalt und hat auch geschneit, genau wie bei Euch. Mutti hätte auch am liebsten Schneemänner gebaut, genau wie Ihr, aber 1. hat Mutti keinen so feinen Garten wie Ihr und 2. wäre ihr der Schnee zu naß und zu kalt gewesen! Es war so kalt, daß Mutti die Nase fast zufror, wenn sie auf die Straße ging, stellt Euch das mal vor! Ulkig, was? Jetzt im Winter sitzen wir alle in einer geheizten Stube zusammen, das ist so am besten, und Mutti denkt immer, wenn's nur schon wieder Sommer wäre! Gewiß geht Ihr nicht so warm angezogen, weil es wohl bei Euch nicht so schrecklich kalt ist. Ich wollte aber auch mal wissen, ob Ihr auch mal die schönen grauen Anzüge mit den seidenen Blusen tragt und all die anderen feinen Stricksachen, die ich doch mit Euch zusammen gekauft hatte. Wie haben Euch denn die feinen Geschenke gefallen, die Ihr vom Vati bekommen habt, der Drehbleistift, Notizbuch und Kalender. Ja, ich finde Ihr seid großartig beschenkt worden, und nun vergeßt aber nicht, Euch bei Vati zu bedanken! – Die Ferien sind ja nun vorüber, und da müßt Ihr wohl wieder sehr fleißig sein? Arbeitet Werner nun auch schon im Hausdienst mit, oder ist er noch zu klein, und welches Amt hast Du, Peterle, in der nächsten Woche? Wenn Du wieder schreibst, Peterle, dann schreibe auch mal Grüße für alle, Du weißt schon, Oma, Tante Pach, Klein, Tante Betty, Jacobsohns, Tante Kirchhoff und wen Du sonst willst. Sie alle fragen stets nach Euch beiden und sind ganz traurig, daß Ihr sie niemals grüßen laßt. Also Peterlein, bitte nicht vergessen und bald wieder schreiben! Mutti schickt Euch auch bald mal ein hübsches Bild von sich, damit Ihr nicht vergeßt, wie Eure Mutti aussieht!

Nun will ich Euch für heute „Gute Nacht" sagen, meine beiden geliebten Jungen, es ist $\frac{1}{2}$ 11 Uhr abends, Mutti fallen die Augen zu, und morgen ist wieder zeitig Tag. Lebt wohl, bleibt gesund und frohen Mutes und seid beide tausendmal gegrüßt und geküßt in inniger Liebe von Eurer Mutti.

Ihr eigentlich angezogen? Tragt Ihr beide Eure hübschen Sachen auch mal, die feinen grauen Anzüge mit den hellblauseidenen Blusen, die ich Euch gekauft hatte, oder geht Ihr Jungen dort alle egal in den gleichen Sachen? Zieht Ihr auch Sonntag und Feiertag etwas Feineres an, oder habt Ihr immer dieselbe Kleidung? Was tragt Ihr für Mützen und Schuhe? Schreib doch mal darüber, damit ich mir einmal vorstellen kann, wie Ihr beiden kleinen Strolche jetzt ausseht. Sicher seid Ihr auch sehr gewachsen!
Ich freue mich sehr, daß Ihr Chanukka zusammen gefeiert habt. Daß Du, liebes Peterle, die beste Zensur hast, ist die größte Freude, die Du mir bereiten konntest. Du scheinst ja wirklich sehr fleißig zu lernen, nun mußt Du Dir sehr große Mühe geben, damit die nächste Zensur auch wieder so gut wird, und dann darfst Du Dir auch etwas zur Belohnung von mir wünschen! Daß Ihr soviel Sport treibt, braust und schöne Waldspaziergänge ~~ist~~ macht, ist wunderbar. Davon wird man groß, kräftig und ist immer lustig. Deine Schilderung der alten Mühle mit dem wilden Bach gefällt mir sehr gut, und ich bekomme große Lust, mit Euch Jungs einmal zusammen dort herumzutollen und zu spielen. Das wäre fein, was? – Mutti geht, seitdem Ihr zwei fort seid, überhaupt nicht mehr spazieren, so allein macht das keinen Spaß. Bei uns hier ist es schon schrecklich kalt und zeitig am Nachmittag wird es finster. Da ist Mutti froh, wenn sie im warmen Zimmer sitzen und arbeiten kann. Chanukka war diesmal sehr einsam für mich, weil Ihr nicht dabei wart, und so zündete Mutti jeden Abend Deinen kleinen Leuchter an, mein liebes Peterlein, und dachte, wenn die hübschen Flammen an Ihre beiden kleinen Jungen. Heut hat Mutti den Leuchter wieder eingepackt und nun kann er wieder ein ganz

[illegible]

Berlin, February 11, 1940

My two beloved boys, Pepi and Werni!

Finally I have some news from you again. This made me very happy because your chatting, my dear "big Peterle" tells me that you, my two children, are healthy and in good mood. Mutti has already been very concerned, [I feared that] you may be sick because here it has been very cold. I am very happy that you are being hardened and wear knee socks. When one gets used to this, one does not feel the cold at all, as you, dear Peterlein, so correctly state. Seven degrees below zero really isn't so bad. On the coldest day here, we had 24 degrees below zero. That's quite a lot more and now is has become very cold again, after we had a few days of milder weather. – It must really be very cozy where you are, the way you describe it. Are you just sledding or do you also have the opportunity to skate? You do have your skates with you, Pepi, and if they are too small for you, they surely fit Werni. Do you remember that you always liked to play with Snips here? Yesterday I met Edith and Sommerfeld's little boy. They just came from skating and both cheeks were red like Borsdorfer apples. That's the time I am missing you two, I kept thinking that you two should come rolling around on your sled. - - - but you did not come and Mutti was only dreaming for a moment. Edith has grown and you two beloved boys, must have also! I am enclosing a letter from her to you; maybe you will write a short letter to her, when you can; she always inquires about both of you, but she especially concerned about you, dear little Wernerle! I am hearing nothing about Gert anymore, and Edith does not even see him in school. Maybe he does not attend anymore?! It's a pity, I always liked him very much. – You, Peterlein, must belong to the middle group and Werni to the group of the very little ones? I can imagine that you and Werni were dancing on the ceiling for joy, when Vati's money arrived. Well, I would like to be treated that well once. Do you have a real stamp collection album and do you understand everything correctly? Once I know, I too will give you a few stamps [Inserted below: 'because I will use these stamp on the letter to him'] and Vati will then give to you. Please tell me all you did for the exhibition! Whistles, little baskets, bows or something else? Do you also play with Wernchen sometimes or does he play only with the littlest ones? Let him add his greetings now and then. Now, dear Peterle, you wrote, when I once asked you for a picture of you, that you have been photographed, but the people kept the pictures themselves. Could you do Mutti a favor and ask the person who took the pictures that time, to give you a picture for your Mutti because she is yearning for you? Why don't you try it sometime, I truly believe that they will give you a picture for me. When I chat with you as I do now, I imagine that the three us of are sitting closely together talking to one another. Then I see you both in front of me with your shining eyes and hear your voices talking to me and I don't feel at all that we are so far apart from each other. Oh my beloved children, Mutti's thoughts are always with you and accompany you in all you do. How cozy were those Wednesday afternoons at Tante Martha's when we all sat together and played and Lorchen was angry because she did not receive enough attention! Do you also sometimes think of this? – Tante Minna Kranz, who always was so nice to you and whom you, dear Peterle, always told, when she came, what we served her the last time she was here for lunch. She now has left for South America to join her two boys, Onkel Ludwig and Lothar whom you also knew. Do you still remember how nicely Onkel Ludwig always played with you? Well, there are increasingly fewer of us.

Now my two beloved, Mutti again has told you quite a lot and is running out of news. We therefore must say goodbye again for today. Stay healthy, diligent and obedient and bring joy to your mentors. Write real soon a long, detailed letter - - - Greetings and kisses for you my dear Peterle and for you, Werni, my little sunshine, in tender love and devotion

Your Mutti

Everybody to whom you sent greetings, was most delighted and have read your letters, dear Peterle. You should continue thinking of them. They are sending their heartfelt greeting to you both and wish you both well!

[Kurrant writing]

Dear boys! I want to take the opportunity to send you greetings. I still come visiting every day and have also seen Tante Klein who, at the moment [illegible] (sciatica) and talks about you a lot. [illegible] Onkel B?, who now . . . [partially cut off]

Kind regards

Tante Pach and Klein

Berlin, d. 11. Febr. 1940.

Meine beiden geliebten Jungen, Pepi und Werni!

Endlich habe ich wieder einmal eine Nachricht von Euch erhalten, die mich sehr froh gemacht hat weil ich aus Deiner Plauderei mein liebes großes "Peterle" ersehe, daß Ihr, meine Zwei, gesund und guter Dinge seid. Mutti war schon in großer Sorge um Euch, daß Ihr nur nicht krank wäre weil es hier bei uns so sehr kalt war. Ich freue mich sehr, daß Ihr so abgehärtet werdet und Kniestrümpfe tragt, wenn man sich daran gewöhnt hat, fühlt man garnicht, daß es kalt ist wie Du, liebes Peterlein, sehr richtig sagst. 7 Grad unter 0 ist ja auch wirklich nicht so schlimm, unser kältester Tag hatte 24 Grad unter 0! Das ist schon eine Portion mehr, und es ist jetzt auch wieder sehr kalt geworden, nachdem es einige Tage etwas milder war. – Es muß bei Euch wirklich sehr gemütlich sein wie Du das alles so beschreibst. Schlittert Ihr nur, oder habt Ihr auch Möglichkeit zum Schlittschuhlaufen? Du hast ja Deine Schlittschuh dort Pepi, und wenn sie Dir zu klein sein sollten, so passen sie bestimmt dem Werni. Weißt Ihr noch, daß Ihr hier schon immer so gern mit Snips gespielt habt? Edith und den kleinen Jungen von Sommerfelds traf ich gestern, sie kamen vom Schlittenfahren und hatten beide Bäckchen so rot wie Borsdorfer Äpfelchen. Ihr zwei fehlt mir dabei, ich glaubte Ihr müßtet auch mit Euren Rodelschlitten angetollt kommen, – – aber Ihr kamt nicht und Mutti hatte nur für einen Augenblick mal geträumt. Edith ist groß geworden, und Ihr zwei geliebten Jungen, bestimmt ebenso! Ich lege einen Brief von ihr an Euch bei, vielleicht schreibt Ihr auch mal einen kleinen Brief an sie, sie fragt immer nach Euch beiden, und besonders sorgt sie sich um Dich geliebtes, kleines Wernerle! Vom Gert höre ich garnichts mehr, auch Edith sieht ihn nicht einmal in der Schule. Vielleicht geht er garnicht mehr dorthin?! Schade ich hatte ihn sehr gern. – Du Peterlein gehörst wohl zur Mittelgruppe und Werni zur Gruppe der ganz Kleinen? Ich kann mir denken, wie Du und Werni an die Decke gesprungen seid, als von Vati das Geld kam. Na, so fein möchte ich's ja auch mal haben! Hast Du denn ein ganz richtiges Briefmarken-album und verstehst Du denn auch alles ganz genau? Wenn ich das weiß, sollst Du von mir auch mal ein paar Marken bekommen, die Vati Dir dann geben wird, weil ich den Brief an ihn damit frankiere. Erzähl doch mal was Du alles für die Ausstellung gemacht hast: Pfeifen, Körbchen, Bogen, oder was sonst? Spielst Du mit [illegible] auch mal zusammen, oder ist er nur mit den Kleinsten zusammen? Laß ihm doch mal wieder Grüße ausschreiben. Nun, liebes Peterle, schreibst Du nur mal, als ich Dich um ein Bild von Euch bat. Ihr seid photographiert worden, aber diejenigen hatten sich die Bilder behalten. Kannst Du nicht mal Mutti den Gefallen tun und denjenigen, der Euch damals photographiert hat, bitten, Dir ein Bild für Beide (Mutti) zu geben, weil sie Sehnsucht nach Euch hat? Versuch es doch mal, ich glaube bestimmt, daß man Dir ein Bild geben wird. Wenn ich so mit Euch plaudere, kommt es mir so vor, als wenn wir Drei dicht beieinander säßen und uns unterhielten, da sehe ich Euch beide vor mir mit Euren glückstrahlenden Augen und höre Eure Stimmen zu mir sprechen, und es ist mir garnicht, als ob wir so weit voneinander getrennt sind. Ach, meine geliebten Kinder, Mutti ist mit ihren Gedanken immer bei Euch und begleitet Euch bei allem, was Ihr tut. Wie gemütlich waren doch immer die Mittwoch-Nachmittage bei Tante Martha, wenn wir alle zusammen saßen und spielten und Horsten übelnahm, weil sie nicht genug beachtet wurde! Denkt Ihr auch noch manchmal daran? - Tante Minna Kranz, die zu Euch auch immer so nett war, und der Du, liebes Peterle, immer, wenn sie kam, erzähltest, was sie das letzte Mal bei uns zum Mittag bekommen hatte, ist nun auch fort nach Südamerika zu ihren beiden Jungen, Onkel Ludwig und Lotte, die Ihr ja auch gekannt habt. Wißt Ihr noch, wie fein Onkel Ludwig immer mit Euch gespielt hat? Ja, es werden immer weniger.

Nun, meine geliebten Zwei, hat Mutti Euch wieder eine große Menge erzählt und weiß garnichts Neues mehr, und so müssen wir uns für heute wieder Lebewohl sagen. Bleibt gesund, fleißig und gehorsam und macht Euren Erziehern Freude. Schreibt recht bald wieder einen lieben, ausführlichen Brief --- ich grüße und küsse Dich, mein geliebtes Peterle, und Dich, meinen kleinen Sonnenschein, Wani, in inniger Liebe und Treue

Eure Mutti.

Alle, die Ihr habt grüßen lassen, haben sich sehr gefreut und Deine Briefe, l. Peterle, gelesen. Du sollst weiter an sie denken, und sie lassen Euch beide auch herzlich grüßen und Euch alles Gute wünschen!

Liebe Jungens! Ich möchte die Gelegenheit wahrnehmen, Euch auch mal Grüße zu senden. Ich komme noch alle Tage hin und war auch mal bei der Tante Klein, die augenblicklich leider krank ist (Gallenst.) und viel von Euch spricht. Den Onkel [illegible] [illegible] [illegible] ich heute auch. Herzl. Grüße Euer Onkel [illegible]

Schönen Gruß v. [illegible], Pachner und Klein

1931/57

Berlin, February 26, 1940

My two darlings!

It was truly a joy yesterday when I received a fat letter from Vati that contained 6 letters from you, beloved Peterle. And that again, after 14 days – you really worked hard and every letter was written so very clearly and with an extra story for everyone. I particularly liked Vati's birthday letter with the beautiful drawing. Is this all your own idea, Peterle, or do you have templates? I am delighted that you are the best in class and your explanation about the 0-20 point system was a lot of fun for me. I really think that you have already learned a lot there and I am very curious whether you will enroll in the actual school now at Easter. What are your thoughts on this and how is our little Schnauzel in school? Does he learn easily or does it give him much trouble? I believe that you never suffer from boredom because, as you always describe, the nice things you craft and the theater roles you play, must make the days fly by. Do you, dear Peterle, have a large role to play and are you wearing costumes? And Wernchen?? I can really picture him to be the boy who lies in bed and in his own Schnauzel language says: "Oh, I am still quite tired, etc.." Tante Pach and Klein, also Tante Martha are beaming with joy because of your letter. It really is very sweet of you, Peterlein, that this time you wrote to everyone, but now you must enclose a letter for Oma too. She is rather hurt because you never think to say hello. Well, Pepi, we understand each other, Right? Write a little letter and I will give it to her. – I would very much like to be with you and take part in all your joys and big and little concern! During the night I often dream that we are together and chat and play, but, when I awaken in the morning, I realize that all was only a dream. – It is good that now it has gotten warmer also where you are and hopefully it soon will be spring and you will certainly work in the garden a lot and do sports. It will really be very wonderful for the two of you, when you can romp around the entire day in the fresh air, without being under foot or make too much noise! And that also is what makes Mutti happy, because you could not do this here at all because Mutti would not have time to take walks with you. Mutti must work very hard, day in, day out and work in her profession to earn some money – but you do already know this. It is especially hard now in winter, since Mutti almost always had to go to the people, because it was too cold and no one wanted to come here. But, as you know, Mutti does it all and does not let herself get down so easily. At any rate, if the two of you were here, it would be double so hard and you two would have to help me quite a bit!! – Wernerle, how are you doing with your sucking? Do your fingers still taste so good at night, or have you given it up since your 6th birthday? It would be high time and I hope that you are doing this anymore! Please answer the question sometime. Mutti has sent a very tiny teddy bear with a milk bottle to Vati for her little Schnauz. You know my darling, it is as sweet as the tiny plush monkey that I gave you once and that you liked so much to take to bed with you? This teddy was attached to a chocolate bar and Mutti thought right away: Werni must get it! I think Vati will arrange it that you get it and you, dear Wernerle, will write me yourself whether you like him!? Today Mutti is enclosing the promised picture for you; It was ready earlier. Do you both live in the same room or not? If Werner sleeps in another room, I will send him another picture so that everyone has one. So, please let me know!

Now Mutti must sign off again, because she still has soooo much work - - - and the work does not get done by itself - - - and Vati too should still get a long letter - - - and it also does not write itself! – I very much hope that you two will write again very soon and will answer all my questions correctly! – In my thoughts I am sending you, my two beloved boys, thousand greetings and kisses in love and tenderness

Your Mutti

[Kurrant]

My dear boys – I was terribly happy about your letter and I thank you from my heart for it. That you like it [there] and that you are learning so many wonderful things is lovely. Continue to be hard-working, then you will become smart. This would be the greatest joy for your dear parents. Your dear Mutti visits us often and then we think of you a lot. So, stay real healthy and [illegible]. Heartfelt greetings from your old Tante Pach.

Dear Peterle and Wernerle!

That was a lot of fun to read your letter and all that you are learning. Too bad that you are no longer scampering around here at our house. Do you still remember how it was? Now, stay very healthy and keep working hard. Heartfelt greetings

Tante Klein

193/57 Berlin, den 26. Februar 1940.

Meine zwei Lieblinge!

Das war aber eine Freude, als ich vorgestern einen dicken Brief von Vati bekam, in dem 6 Briefe von Dir, geliebtes Peterle, lagen. Schon nach 14 Tagen - wieder -- da warst Du wirklich sehr fleißig und jeder Brief so fein sauber geschrieben und für jeden eine Extra-Geschichte darin. Ganz besonders hat mir ja Euer Geburtstagsbrief für Vati gefallen mit der hübschen Zeichnung. Denkst Du Dir das alles allein aus, Peterle, oder habt Ihr Vorlagen dafür? Ich freue mich sehr, daß Du der Beste in der Klasse bist, und Deine Beschreibung über die Punktberechnung von 0-20 hat mir viel Spaß gemacht. Ich glaube wirklich, Du hast dort schon viel gelernt und bin sehr gespannt, ob Du nun zu *Ostern* in die *richtige* Schule kommen wirst. Was denkst *Du* darüber, und wie geht's unserem kleinen Schmunzel in der Schule? Lernt er leicht oder macht es ihm viel Mühe? Ich glaube, Langeweile habt Ihr niemals, denn wie Du so alles beschreibst, was Ihr für schöne Sachen bastelt und Theater spielt, da müssen ja die Tage wie im Fluge vergehen! Hast Du, liebes Peterle, eine *große* Rolle zu spielen, und verkleidet Ihr Euch auch dazu? *Und* Wernchen?? Ich kann mir direkt vorstellen, daß er der Junge sein könnte, der im Bett liegt und mit Schmunzelsprache sagt: Ich bin *doch* aber müde usw." Tante Sach und Klein, ebenso Tante Martha, strahlten vor Freude über Euren Brief. Es ist wirklich sehr lieb von Dir, Peterlein, daß Du diesmal an alle geschrieben hast, nun mußt Du aber auch mal an Oma einen Brief beilegen! Sie ist schon ganz gekränkt, weil Du nie daran denkst, sie einmal grüßen zu lassen. Also, Pepi, wir haben

uns verstanden, nicht wahr? Schreibe einen kleinen Brief und ich werde
ihm ihn geben. Zu gern möchte ich bei Euch sein und an all Euren
Freuden und großen und kleinen Sorgen teilnehmen! Nachts träume
ich oft davon, daß wir zusammen sind uns unterhalten und
spielen, aber, wenn ich dann früh aufwache, merke ich, daß alles nur
ein Traum war. Es ist fein, daß es jetzt auch bei Euch wieder wärmer geworden ist, nun wird's ja hoffentlich bald Frühling sein, und
werdet Ihr gewiß viel Gartenarbeit machen und Sport treiben. Das
ist wirklich für Euch Beide ganz wunderbar, wenn Ihr so den ganzen Tag im Freien herumtollen könnt, ohne daß Ihr im Wege
seid oder zuviel Lärm macht! Und darum ist Mutti auch so
froh darüber, daß es Euch in dieser Hinsicht so gut geht, denn
hier wäre das ja garnicht möglich, da Mutti gar keine Zeit hätte,
mit Euch spazieren zu gehen. Mutti muß sehr fleißig sein – das
wißt Ihr ja auch – und tagaus, tagein, in ihrem Beruf arbeiten,
um etwas zu verdienen. Jetzt im Winter war das ganz besonders schwer, weil Mutti dann fast immer zu den Leuten hingehen
mußte, weil es zu kalt war und keiner herkommen wollte.
Aber, Ihr wißt ja, Mutti macht das schon alles und läßt sich
nicht so leicht runterkriegen. Jedenfalls wenn ich Euch Zwei bei
mir hätte, wäre alles doppelt schwer und Ihr müßtet mir schon
beide tüchtig helfen!! – Was machst Du eigentlich, Wernerle mit Deinem Nuckeln? Schmecken die Fingerchen nachts noch immer so
gut oder hast Du Dir das seit Deinem 6. Geburtstage abgewöhnt?
Zeit ist es längst dazu gewesen, und ich hoffe, daß Du das nicht
mehr tust?! Antworte mir doch einmal darauf. Mutti hat für
ihren kleinen „Schmanz" an Vati einen ganz kleinen Teddybären

2. Kinder

1331/57

mit Milchflasche geschickt. Weißt Du, Liebling, er ist so süß wie das ganz kleine Felläffchen, das ich Dir einmal schenkte, und das Du so gern ins Bett nahmst!? Dieses Teddychen hing an einer Tafel Schokolade, und Mutti dachte sofort: Das muß Werni bekommen! Vati wird es schon einrichten, daß Du es bekommst, und Du, liebes Wernerle, schreibst mir dann einmal selbst, ob Du Dich damit freust!? Heute legt Mutti auch das versprochene Bild für Euch bei, es war nicht früher fertig. Seid Ihr beide in demselben Zimmer oder nicht? Wenn Wernchen in einem anderen Zimmer schläft, dann schicke ich ihm noch ein anderes Bild, damit jeder eins hat. Also, schreibt mir darüber!

Nun muß Mutti wieder Schluß machen, denn sie hat noch sooooviel Arbeit --- und die macht sich nicht von selbst --- und der Vati soll auch noch einen langen Brief bekommen --- und der schreibt sich auch nicht von selbst! - Ich hoffe nun sehr, daß Ihr Beide recht bald wieder schreibt und mir dann auch alle Fragen richtig beantwortet! - Ich grüße Euch, meine beiden geliebten Jungen, tausendmal und küsse Euch in Gedanken mit aller Innigkeit und Liebe

Eure Mutti.

Meine lieben Jungens über Euren lieben Brief habe ich mich schrecklich gefreut und danke herzlich dafür daß es Euch so gut gefällt und Ihr so viel schöne Sachen lernt [illegible] fleißig [illegible] Freude [illegible] gesund [illegible] herzliche Grüße von Eurem alten [illegible]

Pach.

Liebes Peterle und Wernerle!
Das war aber eine Freude Euren lieben Brief zu lesen und was Ihr alles lernt. Schade Ihr seid nicht mehr bei uns [illegible] wisst Ihr noch wie das war? Nun bleibt recht gesund, seid weiter fleissig und herzliche grosse Tante [illegible]

-1-

2301/34

Berlin, March 10, 1940
Sunday morning
Sent on March 13th

My two beloved, little Strolche!

Now I finally must take time out for you and have a cozy chat with you! First I had to help Oma with her feet, since she practically could not walk anymore – now she can dance on them, the way you used to do early in bed, do you remember this? - I am now sitting at my desk in my treatment room with brilliant sunshine. You picture is in from of me and I am looking into your sweet good children eyes and talk with you. Yes, my dear Peterle, you are right, this winter the weather was really "weird", right now in particular, because here it is still snowing almost every day, in between time, the sun sometimes comes out. Then it is not so very cold anymore, but it does not seem as though Easter will be in 14 days from today. There is still a lot of snow in the streets, parts are old and dirty, some parts are new and beautifully white. Mutti is very happy that is already warmer where you are and that you can play in the snow without being cold – words fail me to tell you how much I enjoy the picture. Now I can finally see your friends and a piece of the garden. The sun must shine onto your faces because you all are making such grimaces? I suppose that the picture was taken shortly after your arrival. You, my dear Wernerle, do not look well and you are making a serious little face! Are you looking better now and are you two really healthy? I like both, your friend Gerhard and his governess, very much. What is the governess's name and is she still with you? She must be still very young herself and gets along with you well because she looks so joyful and nice. Thank you particularly, beloved Peterle, for the picture, because you had to spend one of your own francs. It is very sweet of you to give up stamps or chocolate to make me happy. Mutti knows real well that it may not have been so easy for her Peterle, all the more reason for me to be twice as happy with your picture; and also because you always write so diligently on Sundays and I am very happy of the way you always answer all my questions so nicely! If it were possible, Mutti would send you both something once in a while. Then you yourselves could fulfill your little wishes, like sweets, stamps or something else, but that is just impossible. Mutti can only send you a beautiful book and you, each one of you, my darlings, will receive a nice book for Purim 14 days from today (on March 24). For you, Wernerle, the "Regenwetterbuch" [rainy day book] that you may be able to read by yourself now, for you, Peterle, the "Feiertags-geschichten" [holiday stories]. I am certain you'll like these books with their beautiful illustrations. Peterle, you'll help Werni with his reading, won't you? And if there is something in your book that you don't understand, why don't you ask one of your older boys who has already learned more biblical stories than you. I think he will explain everything to you. I like the story with the "Adar-Scherri" most and you can write to me which story you liked best. Tomorrow Edith will bring me a picture of herself to fulfill you wish, and then I can mail the letter to you. Edith loves you both very much, she is pleased that you can be where you are..

I have also read your long letter to Vati, dear Peterle, and am very happy because of your nice and clear handwriting and your detailed descriptions. You, little Rackele, are now really busy every Sunday, when you write to diligently. You made a very sweet drawing for Oma. It seems to be spring greetings. You can be glad that you already have warm weather, here winter does not want to end and we are mighty cold.

2 children

10 o'clock !, Mutti must still write to Vati. I have yet another favor to ask you, dear Peterle. Vati was so nice and sent me your picture, so I may have it. Can you get another one for Vati soon? Please, if it costs money and you don't have any, ask them to give you one and

tell them, if Mutti could send you money, she would pay everything double and she will make everything good again later. Understood!

Good night, beloved children – again our chatting time has passed and we must now say goodbye because time races by and Mutti must still write to Vati because the letter must be mailed tomorrow early. Sleep well, dream sweet dreams and keep loving

Your Mutti

Thousand greetings from your Mutti, Tante Pach, Klein, Betty, Else, Martha, Oncle Georg, Klara

257/34

1.

Bln., d. 10. März 1940.
Sonntag vormittag.
abgesandt am 13. März.

Meine beiden geliebten kleinen Strolche!

Nun muß ich mir aber endlich eine Weile für Euch Zeit nehmen und mal wieder ein gemütliches Plauderstündchen mit Euch haben! Erst mußte ich Oma, die schon garnicht mehr laufen konnte, ihre Füße in Ordnung bringen – jetzt kann sie damit tanzen, wie Ihr Zwei es immer früh im Bett machtet, wißt Ihr's noch? – Ich sitze jetzt in meinem Behandlungszimmer bei strahlendem Sonnenschein am Schreibtisch. Euer Bild steht vor mir, ich blicke in Eure lieben guten Kinderaugen und spreche mit Euch. Ja, mein liebes Peterle, Du hast Recht, das Wetter war in diesem Winter wirklich „ulkig" und jetzt ganz besonders, denn hier schneit es noch immer fast jeden Tag, manchmal scheint dann auch die Sonne dazwischen, und es ist auch nicht mehr so sehr kalt, aber es sieht garnicht so aus, als ob heute in 14 Tagen Ostern wäre. Auf den Straßen liegt noch sehr viel Schnee umher, teils alter schmutziger, teils neu gefallener, der noch fein weiß aussieht. Mutti freut sich sehr, daß es bei Euch schon wärmer ist und Ihr so fein in dem Schnee herumspielt ohne dabei zu frieren. – Wie ich mich mit dem Bild freue, kann ich Euch garnicht sagen, sehe ich doch darauf endlich einmal Eure Kameraden und ein Stückchen des Gartens. Euch scheint wohl gerade die Sonne ins Gesicht, weil Ihr alle so die Gesichter verzieht? Die Aufnahme ist wohl kurze Zeit nach Eurer Ankunft gemacht worden? Du, mein geliebtes Wernerle, siehst so schlecht darauf aus und machst so ein ernstes Gesichtel! Siehst Du jetzt schon besser aus und seid Ihr auch bestimmt alle beide gesund? Dein Freund Gerhard und die

Erzieherin gefallen mir beide sehr gut. Wie heißt die Erzieherin, und ist sie noch bei Euch? Sie ist bestimmt selbst noch sehr jung und versteht sich gut mit Euch, denn sie sieht so lustig und nett aus. Ich danke Dir, geliebtes Peterle, ganz besonders für das Bild, weil Du dafür Deinen Franc hast hergeben müssen. Es ist sehr lieb von Dir, daß Du, um mir eine Freude zu bereiten, auf Briefmarken oder Schokolade verzichtet hast. Mutti weiß ganz genau, daß das ihrem Peterle vielleicht doch nicht so leicht gefallen ist, und darum freue ich mich doppelt mit Eurem Bild; ebenso darüber, daß Du jetzt immer am Sonntag so fleißig schreibst. Ich finde, wir unterhalten uns schon sehr ausführlich per Brief, und ich freue mich sehr darüber, wie fein Du mir alle meine Fragen beantwortest. Wenn es möglich wäre, würde Mutti Euch Beiden gern öfter etwas schicken, damit Ihr Euch selbst Eure kleinen Wünsche, wie Süßigkeiten, Briefmarken oder was sonst, erfüllen könntet, aber das geht eben nicht. Mutti kann Euch nur mal ein schönes Buch schicken, und so werdet Ihr, meine Lieblinge, heute in 14 Tagen (am 24. März) zu Purim jeder ein hübsches Buch von mir bekommen. Für Dich, Wernerle, „Das Regenwetterbuch" das Du gewiß nun auch schon lesen kannst, für Dich, Peterle, die „Feiertagsgeschichten". Bestimmt werden die Bücher Euch Freude machen mit den hübschen Bildern; Peterle, Du hilfst dem Werni beim Lesen, ja? Und, wenn Du in Deinem Büchlein etwas nicht verstehst, dann frage mal einen von Euren älteren Jungen, der schon mehr biblische Geschichte gelernt hat als Du, der wird Dir bestimmt alles erklären; mir hat die Geschichte mit dem Adar-scheni am besten gefallen, und Du wirst mir dann schreiben, welche Du am schönsten findest. – Morgen bringt Edith mir ein Bild von sich damit Du Deinen Wunsch erfüllt bekommst, und dann kann ich den Brief an Euch abschicken. Edith hat Euch beide sehr lieb, sie kommt

2 Kinder.

zufrieden, daß Ihr dort sein dürft.

Deinen langen Brief an Vati, liebes Peterle, habe ich auch gelesen und freue mich sehr über Deine hübsche saubere Handschrift und Deine ausführlichen Beschreibungen. So hast Du, kleines Rackele, nun jeden Sonntag Deine reichliche Beschäftigung, wenn Du immer so fleißig schreibst. Die Zeichnung für Oma hast Du sehr niedlich gemacht. Es soll wohl ein Frühlingsgruß sein. Ihr könnt froh sein, daß es bei Euch schon warm ist, hier will der Winter gar kein Ende nehmen, und wir frieren noch tüchtig.

10 Uhr! Mutti muß jetzt noch an Vati schreiben. Noch eine Bitte habe ich, liebes Peterlein. Vati war so lieb und hat Euer Bild an mich geschickt, damit ich es habe. Kannst Du bald für Vati ein anderes bekommen? Bitte doch, wenn es Geld kostet und Du keins hast, man möchte Dir eins schenken und sage, wenn Mutti Dir Geld schicken dürfte, würde sie alles doppelt bezahlen und sie wird später alles wieder gut machen! Verstanden?!

Gute Nacht, geliebte Kinder, wieder ist unser Plauderstündchen herumgegangen und wir müssen uns Lebwohl sagen, weil die Zeit immer weiter eilt und Mutti noch an Vati schreiben muß, denn morgen früh soll der Brief fort. Schlaft wohl, träumt süß, behaltet lieb

Eure Mutti.

Tausend Grüße von Mutti, Tante Pach, Klein, Betty, Else, Martha, Onkel Georg, Klara.

Berlin, March 27th 1940,

9 p.m.

My beloved good boys!

The clock in the dining room is just striking 9! You, my two darlings, are surely already blissfully and sweetly tucked into your little beds and are reliving in your dreams everything you did today – and your Mutti who has been working diligently from the early morning on all day finally finds a few minutes to chat again with you. Your picture, the latest one, is again in front of me, again I am looking into your good children's eyes – and now I am completely with you, in your midst, and we talk about everything, just like we did, do you remember it, my little ones, in our green room at your little table? How often the three of us sat there and we told each other what things had happened, I gave you sometimes my motherly advice, and you two, oh how often my beloved Peterle and you, my little one, you my sunshine, Wernerle, was it you who with a little caress or your well-intended childish advice gave me courage and hope again. – Easter and Passover are now already past, too. Surely you have gone on an Easter egg hunt in your yard? And have you received the books and pictures from Mutti and Edith already? Edith visited me again today and brought me her letter, looked at your picture and read your letters. She finds you, my dear Peterle, much changed. I agree, you both have gotten very big and your hair is resembles the mane of a lion! Don't they cut your hair regularly? You, dear Peterle, make such a serious face, I am not used to that from you at all. And Wernerle looks like a boy who's all grown up! I'm just so happy that he's stopped sucking on his thumb. It doesn't matter that you are not yet going to school, you're probably learning more in the home, and Werni also; but do pay attention and be diligent in your lessons and be neat and modest in all you have to do, so that your instructors like you and see that you are well raised boys. If I write this to you, my beloved children, believe me that your Mutti wants only the best for you, because if you are always neat, modest and diligent and very obedient, the grown-ups will be happy with you and you will reap the reward for it. – Your dream, my dear Peterle, is nothing new for me. Your Mutti dreams of you two every night. Yes, my beloved children, for now we shall dream of each other, talk with our pictures and in our letters tell each other all the things that we are unable to say to each other in person right now, and we want to pray every night to our dear God that the day we see each other again may come soon. Mutti has been doing this since you left and now let's do it the three of us and let's not be sad, my darlings, but we shall be content and grateful that you have the chance to grow up over there into free, healthy and productive human beings, even if you should think sometimes "oh, it was just so much better at home", today that would not be true anymore, a lot has changed since you went away, and not for the better at all, the apartment is smaller, the winter is so cold that we sat in the living room together with Klara – I thought of you often then – and at the school where nothing is really learned, the "Oldie" is still there, too. So be happy and content.

[...] very often and keeps reading your letters. She is now 10 years old and has gotten big. Your description, Peterle, of the train station is so clear that I feel I can see it all in front of me. It must be so nice where you are! You are really in the genuine countryside over there? When you do housework, do you learn to make your bed and to clean up your room? What else? I would like to know. It's very nice and good for you that you learn things like that early in life. In the meantime you must have gotten the picture of me that I sent to Vati. Now you know that your Mutti is with you all the time no matter what you are doing, whether you are sleeping at night in your little beds or whether you have to work diligently during the day. Mutti's thoughts are always with you, when you are happy she is happy with you, and when you have your little troubles she is troubled too and would like to help you.

So, my dear good children, my letter got longer than I thought and hopefully you, Peterle, do not have too much trouble reading it. I could easily chat a few more hours with you, but now Clara is calling mc for dinner and we have to end our chat. Farewell until next time, my two darlings, I embrace and kiss you with all my love and loyalty,

Your Mutti.

Do write again very soon!

Do you, Peterle, read the letters to Werni? Let him write something by himself some time.

Hbg. d. 27. März 1940.
abends 9 h.

Meine geliebten, guten Jungen!

Die Uhr im Eßzimmer schlägt gerade 9, Ihr meine beiden Lieblinge schlaft gewiß schon selig und süß in Euren Bettchen und erlebt im Traum noch einmal alles, was Ihr am Tage getan habt -- und Mutti, die heute auch von früh an fleißig gearbeitet hat, findet jetzt erst ein paar ruhige Minuten, um wieder einmal mit Euch zu plaudern. Wieder steht Euer Bild, jetzt auch das ganz neue vor mir, wieder sehe ich in Eure lieben guten Kinderaugen -- und nun bin ich ganz bei Euch in Eurer Mitte, und wir sprechen über alles, sowie wir es hier so oft taten, wißt Ihr's noch Kinderle, hinten in unserem grünen Zimmer, an Eurem kleinen Tischchen?! Wie oft saßen wir drei dort beisammen und erzählten uns, was wir erlebt hatten; ich gab Euch meinen mütterlichen Rat, und Ihr zwei, ach wie oft, geliebtes Peterle und Du, mein Kleinstes, Du mein Sonnenschein Wernerle, wart Ihr es, die Ihr mit Eurem lieben Streicheln oder einem gutgemeinten Kinderwort mir Mut und Hoffnung wiedergabt. - Ostern und Purim sind nun auch schon vorbei. Gewiß habt Ihr in Eurem Garten Ostereier gesucht!? Und habt Ihr schon die Bücher und die Bilder von Mutti und Edith bekommen? Edith war heute wieder bei mir, brachte mir ihren Brief, sah Euer Bild und las Eure Briefe. Sie findet Dich, mein liebes Peterle, sehr verändert aussehend. Ich finde auch, Ihr seid beide sehr groß geworden und außerdem habt Ihr ja eine Löwenmähne auf dem Kopf! Wird Euer Haar nicht öfter geschnitten? Du, liebes Peterlein, machst ein so ernstes Gesicht, ich bin das doch garnicht von Dir gewöhnt?! Und Wer sieht auch schon aus wie ein ganz erwachsener Junge! Ich bin ja so froh, daß er sich das Buckeln abgewöhnt hat. Es schadet nichts, daß Ihr noch nicht zur Schule geht, bestimmt lernt Ihr im Heim mehr und Werni auch; seid nur allebeide recht aufmerksam und fleißig in den Unterrichtsstunden und ordentlich und bescheiden bei allem, was Ihr zu tun habt, damit Eure Erzieher Euch gern haben und sehen, daß Ihr gut erzogene Jungen seid! Wenn ich Euch, meine geliebten Kinder, das schreibe, so glaubt mir, daß Eure Mutti es nur gut mit Euch meint, denn, wenn man immer ordentlich, bescheiden und fleißig ist und immer auf's Wort gehorcht, dann haben die Erwachsenen ihre Freude daran, und Ihr werdet auch Dank dafür haben! – Mit Deinem Traum, mein geliebtes Peterlein, hast Du mir nichts Neues erzählt. Mutti träumt jede Nacht von Euch beiden. Ja, geliebte Kinder, wir wollen vorläufig von einander träumen, uns mit unseren Bildern unterhalten und in unseren Briefen uns alles Liebe sagen, was wir im Augenblick nicht persönlich können; und wir wollen jeden Abend zum lieben Gott beten, daß der Tag unseres Wiedersehens bald kommen mög. Mutti tut das schon solange Ihr fort seid, und nun wollen wir's zusammen weiter tun und nicht traurig sein, Lieblinge, sondern wir wollen froh und glücklich sein, daß Ihr dort zu freien, gesunden und tüchtigen Menschen heranwachsen dürft; Wenn Ihr auch vielleicht manmal denkt, „ach, zu Hause war es besser", glaubt mir, heute wär es nicht mehr so, es ist vieles seit Eurem Fortgehen anders geworden -- nicht schöner jedenfalls, die Wohnung enger, der Winter so kalt, daß wir in einer Stube saßen mit Klara zusammen -- da dacht ich oft an Euch -- dann die Schule, wo doch kaum was gelernt wir und „die Olle" ist auch noch immer da. Seid glücklich und zu

25/01/34

3.

sehr oft und liest immer Eure Briefe, sie ist nun auch schon 10 Jahr alt und ist sehr groß geworden. – Deine Beschreibung, Peterle, von dem Bahnhof ist wirklich so deutlich, daß ich mir das alles richtig vorstellen kann. Es muß wirklich zu schön bei Euch sein! Ihr seid wol dort richtig auf dem Lande? Wenn Ihr Hausarbeit macht, lernt Ihr wohl Euer Bett zu machen und Euer Zimmer aufzuräumen? Oder was sonst? Das möchte ich gern mal wissen! Das ist sehr schön und gut für Euch, daß Ihr in so jungen Jahren das alles lernt. – Inzwischen habt Ihr bestimmt auch schon mein Bild bekommen, das ich an Vati geschickt habe. Nun wißt Ihr, daß Eure Mutti immer bei Euch ist bei allem was Ihr tut, ob Ihr nachts in Euren Bettchen liegt und schlaft, oder ob Ihr am Tage fleißig arbeiten müßt. Muttis Gedanken sind immer nur bei Euch, wenn Ihr Euch freut, freut sie sich mit Euch, und wenn Ihr Eure kleinen Sorgen habt, so sorgt sie sich mit Euch und möchte Euch helfen.

So, geliebte, gute Kinder, mein Brief ist länger geworden als ich geglaubt habe, und hoffentlich hast Du, Peterle, nicht zuviel Mühe, ihn zu lesen. Ich könnte noch viele Stunden mit Euch plaudern, aber eben ruft Clara mich zum Essen, und da müssen wir nun unser Plauderstündchen beschließen. Lebt wohl bis zum nächsten Mal, meine zwei Lieblinge, ich umarme und küsse Euch alle Beide in Innigkeit und Treue

Eure Mutti.

Schreibt recht bald wieder!

Liest Du, Peterle, dem Werni die Briefe immer vor? Laß ihn doch mal einen Gruß anschreiben!

27 Mar, 1940

Dear Peterle and Wernerle!

Tante Hilde and I were much delighted by your letter and thank you very kindly for it. You, dear Peterle, drew a very nice flower pot that surely was meant for Oma at [illegible]. How is your French going? Parlez vous française messieurs? And you, my Wernerlein what are you up to these days? I just hope that you my sweethearts are healthy. – We had a tough winter and were often sick with a cold. Now Oma is happy to tell you that the skin rash on her left hand has finally healed. I know that will make you happy, right? It's a pity that I cannot [illegible] a little for it. Well, maybe that too will happen soon. – You are filling your time so well that it will be impossible to get bored. Don't fight, and you, dear Peterle, please set a good example and be protective as an older brother. We are thinking about you a lot. – Tante Minna is in Brazil with Ludwig and Lothar. Onkel Karl is in Quito (Equador). Greetings also from Tante Betty and Jocobsohns. You, my dear little children, I kiss a 1000 times in my thoughts and Tante Hilde too is sending her regards.

Love,

Your Oma

Edith comes by often to ask about you.

27.3.40.

Liebes Peterle und Wernerle!
Tante Hilde und ich waren über Dein Brief-
chen sehr erfreut und wir danken Dir herz-
lich dafür. Du, l. Peter hast einen schönen
Blumentopf aufgemalt, der gewiß für Oma
zu Purim sein sollte. Wie steht es mit Eurem
Französisch? Parlez vous français messieurs?
Und Du, mein Wernerlein, was treibst Du
eigentlich? Hoffentlich seid Ihr meine
Süßen gesund. – Wir haben einen harten
Winter gehabt und waren viel erkältet.
Nun kann Euch Oma noch mitteilen, daß
die linke Hand von der Flechte geheilt ist.
Ich weiß, Ihr freut Euch darüber, nicht
wahr? Schade, daß ich nicht etwas dafür spen-
dieren kann. Na, vielleicht kommt das auch
noch. – Ihr habt Eure Zeit so schön eingeteilt,

daß Euch nicht langweilig werden kann.
Vertragt Euch nur und sei Du, l. Peterle,
dem Werner ein gutes Vorbild und die
Beschützer als älterer Bruder. Wir denken viel an Euch. — Tante Minna ist
in Brasilien bei Ludwig u. Lothar.
Onkel Kurt ist in Kito (Aequador).
Viele Grüße von Tante Betty u. Jacobsohns.
Euch, Ihr lieben Kinderchen küsse ich
in Gedanken 1000 mal und grüße auch
von Tante Hilde. In Liebe

Eure

Oma.

Edith kommt öfter nach Euch fragen.

Berlin, April 17th 1940

My beloved, good children

I was very happy about your two letters to Vati and me from March 31st, first of all because you, beloved Peterle, have learned to speak and write so well, and second, because our dear, little Wernerle added to it so nicely in his own handwriting. I am a tiny bit sad though that you do not write at all about whether you enjoyed the books and my picture. You will have received both in the meantime, because Vati did tell me so in his letter. Thus I hope that you will tell me about it in your next letter. Your description of your meals, dear Peterle, was a lot of fun. Are you always enjoying them? I think if you have to work so hard in the house, you must always be very hungry and surely you eat big portions?! That would make me very happy. And how about you, Wernerle? Are you also finishing what's on your plate every time? You have gotten very big, my beloved "little Wernerle" and so you should dig in, and finish everything on your plate every time so that you'll be strong and don't stay as thin as you look in the picture. – The Easter vacation is over now and you certainly will have to study again very diligently. Keep your clothes neat, always wash your hands before you eat, and don't get stains on your shirts and suits. Also be orderly in how you do your homework, without spots and stains. You know that here Mutti paid attention to all those things and cleaned it up when something was dirty, now you have to take care of your things and composition books yourselves. And you have to be very obedient, when you're being told something, and not stubborn. You always have to remember that you too will be grown-ups one day and will have say over children and one can only do that if one has been very obedient as a child oneself. Well, now I know that you will fulfill your Mutti's wish so that she may be proud of her two boys, right? – Edith is now visiting with me more frequently all the time, she can hardly wait from one of your letters to the next. At Easter she got into the next grade and is now very busy with school. Some days she has lessons from 8 am to 3 pm. You should have received her letter by now. – Tante Hilde still has the same position in the house of the temple on Lindenstrasse and is very happy about that. Tante Pach and Tante Klein, Tante Betty Jacobsohns und Tante Martha Kirchoff, all of them ask regularly about you and when we are together there's always talk about you. Since you, my beloved children, left it is always too quiet for me, I miss your singing and your sweet laughing children's voices so much. Yesterday, Mutti made creams and perfumes all day long and this afternoon Tante Betty will come for a big facial treatment. I am telling you, you rascals would have a field day with that. Mutti has gotten a face steam bath with a big blue glass cylinder – Tante Betty will put her head in it. If you could watch that you would be amazed and play barber like you once did before. Do you recall that? You still remember the big white treatment chair, no? It was perfect for climbing around on, as I'm just remembering now. The room looks like a doctor's office these days. And I think you'd enjoy your Mutti to complete the look in a white coat. Other than that nothing new has happened to Mutti. Every day is the same as the one before and it passes with sleeping, working, eating, reading the paper and dreaming of Peter and Werni. It's still as cold as if it was winter. Every morning when I get up I check the thermometer and it's always below zero although we're already in mid-April. It's probably a lot warmer where you are and I'm happy about that. Are you already spending much time in the yard?

Now I hope again to receive real soon a nice detailed letter from you where you will answer all questions I asked you. Be well my darlings. I embrace each of you and kiss you with all my love.

Your Mutti.

Stay healthy!

Kindest regards from Oma, Tante Hilde, Klara, Pachs, Tante Betty Jacobsohns, Edith.

Give my best regards to Mademoiselle Lauriac

[Illegible writing in left margin]

2501/59

Berlin, d. 10. April 1940.

Meine geliebten, guten Kinder

über Eure beiden Briefe vom 31. März an Vati und mich habe ich mich ja sehr gefreut, erstens, weil Du, geliebtes Peterle, schon so fein sprechen und schreiben gelernt hast, und zweitens, weil unser liebes, kleines Wernerle diesmal so hübsch angeschrieben hat. Ein ganz kleines Bißchen bin ich aber doch traurig, weil Ihr garnicht schreibt, ob Ihr Euch mit den Bildern und meinem Bilde gefreut habt. Bekommen habt Ihr doch Beides inzwischen, denn Vati hat mir das geschrieben! Ich hoffe nun also, daß Ihr mir in Eurem nächsten Brief etwas darüber erzählen werdet. Deine Beschreibung Eurer Mahlzeiten, liebes Peterle, macht mir viel Spaß. Schmeckt es Euch denn auch immer? Ich glaube, wenn Ihr so fleißig im Hause mitarbeiten müßt, habt Ihr bestimmt immer tüchtigen Hunger, und da eßt Ihr gewiß ordentlich große Portionen?! Ach, das würde mich wirklich sehr freuen! Und wie ist das mit Dir Wernerle? Ißt Du auch immer alles fein auf? Du bist sehr groß geworden, mein geliebtes „kleines Wernerle", und da mußt Du immer tüchtig essen, alles, was Du bekommst, damit Du kräftig wirst und nicht so dünn bleibst, wie Du auf dem Bilde aussiehst! - Nun sind die Osterferien wieder vorbei, und Ihr müßt nun gewiß wieder sehr fleißig lernen. Seid Beide recht sauber in Eurer Kleidung, wascht Euch immer die Finger, bevor Ihr etwas eßt, und macht Euch Eure Bluschen und Anzüge nicht fleckig. Auch Eure Schulaufgaben macht recht ordentlich und ohne Kleckse und Flecke. Ihr wißt doch, hier hat Mutti immer auf alles aufgepaßt und wieder sauber gemacht, wenn was schmutzig war, jetzt müßt Ihr selbst auf Eure Sachen und Schulhefte achten. Und Ihr müßt auf's Wort gehorchen, wenn Euch etwas gesagt wird, und nicht eigensinnig sein. Ihr müßt immer denken, daß Ihr auch mal groß sein werdet und über Kinder zu bestimmen haben werdet, und das kann man nur, wenn man selbst als Kind immer sehr gehorsam gewesen ist. So, nun weiß ich genau, daß Ihr Mutti diesen Wunsch erfüllen werdet, damit sie auf ihre beiden Jungen stolz sein kann. Nicht wahr? - Edith besucht mich jetzt immer häufiger, sie kann es schon immer garnicht von einem bis zum nächsten Brief von Euch erwarten. Sie ist zu Ostern versetzt worden und hat jetzt viel mit der Schule zu tun, manchen Tag hat sie von 8-3 Uhr Unterricht. Ihren Brief werdet Ihr ja inzwischen bekommen haben. - Tante Hilde hat noch immer dieselbe Stellung in der Lindenstraße im Haus des Tempels und ist sehr froh darüber. Tante Rachel und Tante Klein und Tante Betty, Jacobsohns und Tante Martha Kirchhoff alle, alle fragen regelmäßig nach Euch und wenn wir zusammen sind, wird immer von Euch erzählt. Seitdem Ihr, meine geliebten Kinder, fort seid ist es fast zu ruhig für mich geworden, Euer Gesang und Eure lieben lachenden Kinderstimmchen fehlen mir zu sehr. - Gestern hat Mutti den ganzen Tag Krems und Parfum gemacht und heute Nachmittag kommt Tante Betty zur großen Gesichtsbehandlung. Ja, ich sage Euch, das wäre ja jetzt so etwas für Euch Rangen, Mutti hat sich ein Gesichts-Dampfbad mit einer großen blauen Glasglocke zugelegt, da wird Tante

2) Betty ihren Kopf hineinstecken --- wenn Ihr da mal so zusehen
könntet, Ihr würdet ja staunen und dann Friseur spielen,
so wie Ihr's schon mal getan habt. Wißt Ihr noch? Den großen, weißen Behandlungsstuhl kanntet Ihr doch noch, nicht
wahr? Der war Euch ja zum Herumklettern gerade recht, entsinn
ich mich eben. Ja, das Zimmer sieht jetzt ganz aus wie
bei einem Arzt. Und ich glaube Eure Mutti dazu im
weißen Kittel würde Euch gefallen! - Sonst hat Mutti auch
nichts Neues erlebt. Ein Tag vergeht wie der andere mit
Arbeit, Essen, Zeitunglesen und Schlafen und von Peter und
Werni-Träumen. Kalt ist es noch wie im Winter. Jeden Morgen beim Aufstehen sehe ich auf's Thermometer und immer
ist es unter Null Grad, obgleich wir schon mitten im April
sind. Ihr habt es gewiß viel wärmer, und darüber bin
ich auch sehr froh. Seid Ihr schon viel im Garten?
Nun hoffe ich sehr, recht bald wieder einen lieben, ausführlichen Brief von Euch zu bekommen, in dem Ihr
mir alle Fragen beantwortet, die ich Euch gestellt habe.
Lebt wohl, meine beiden Lieblinge; jeden einzigen von Euch schließe ich im Geiste in meine
Arme und küsse Euch in inniger Liebe.
Eure Mutti.

Bleibt gesund!
Tausend Grüße von Oma, Tante Hilde, Klara, Paula, Tante Betty
Jacobsohns, Edith.
Bestellt Mademoiselle Lauriac einen herzlichen Gruß von mir!

Meinen lieben Jungens [illegible] einen Gruß für Euch aufzuschreiben kann ich [illegible] Muttis [illegible] nicht [illegible] lassen. Also bleibt recht gesund, schön artig und fleißig in der Schule [illegible] dann freut sich auch Euer [illegible]

Friday, May 17th 1940

Beloved Peterle, beloved Wernerle!

I hope very much that you are happy and healthy and that you are having nice weather so you will be able to play in the yard and engage in your sports. You probably have caught all the june bugs by now and soon there will be the little lady bugs that you always liked so much and you'll have fun with those. By now you will surely have received and thought about my two long letters from early May in which I was telling you so many things. Have you read the nice books that I sent to Purim for you? And what does Vati write, is he healthy and how is he doing? Please tell him hello from me when you write to him next, I would very much like to hear from him. – Today, I will write to Tante Martha and Marian in Hartford; Tante Martha will now write to you more often, and you, beloved Peterle, should always write back to her, this way I hear, my darlings, how you are doing, if you are in good health, and all the details. The address of Tante Martha is: Mrs Charles Stearn, 130 North Whitney Street, Hartford, Conn. Onkel Erich, Tante Lorle and Gerda, which you both know, live very close to Tante Martha, and Gerda will soon go to school. She has supposedly become a very big girl. So when you write to Tante Martha do not forget to send her your regards. – Other than that there is nothing new here. It is still not warm although per the calendar summer will soon start, and I am happy for you that in this regard you have it nicer and better. – Now, beloved boys, be well for today, write immediately to Tante Martha with as much detail as you have always done, we all cannot wait to get a letter from you two.

Be hugged and kissed with all my love,

Your Mutti.

[Sideline:]

Dear Peter and Werner: Marian and I send greetings to you. Keep well dear children!

Aunt Martha

- 2. -

Freitag, den 17. Mai 1940.

Geliebtes Peterle, geliebtes Wernerle!

Ich hoffe sehr, dass Ihr beide gesund und munter seid und schönes Wetter habt, sodass Ihr viel im Garten herumtoben und Sport treiben könnt. Gewiss ___t Ihr schon alle Maikäfer weggefangen und nun kommen bald die kleinen niedlichen Junikäferchen (Marienkäferchen), die Ihr immer so süss fandet, an die Reihe, mit denen Ihr dann auch Eure [illegible] werdet. Meine beiden langen Briefe von Anfang Mai, in denen ich Euch soviel erzählt habe, habt Ihr gewiss erhalten und Euch damit beschäftigt. Habt Ihr schon die hübschen Bücher gelesen, die ich Euch zu Purim geschickt habe? Und was schreibt Vati, ist er gesund, und was macht er? Bitte, grüsst ihn von mir, wenn Ihr wieder an ihn schreibt, und ich möchte sehr gern Nachricht von ihm haben.-Ich schreibe heute an Tante Martha und Marian in Hartford; Tante Martha wird jetzt öfter an Euch schreiben, und Du, geliebtes Peterle, schreibst dann auch immer an sie, ich erfahre dann wenigstens, wie es Euch, meine Lieblinge, geht, ob Ihr gesund seid, und alles Nähere. Die Adresse von Tante Martha ist: Mrs. Charles Stearn, North 130 Whitney-Street, Hartford/Conn. U.S.A. Onkel Erich, Tante Lorle und Gerda, die Ihr doch beide kennt, wohnen ganz in der Nähe von Tante Martha, und Gerda kommt jetzt bald in die hohe Schule. Sie soll ein sehr grosses Mädel geworden sein. Wenn Ihr also an Tante Martha schreibt, vergesst nicht, sie grussen zu lassen.- Sonst gibt es hier auch nichts Neues. Warm ist es noch immer nicht, trotzdem es nach dem Kalender bald Sommersanfang ist, und ich freue mich für Euch, dass Ihr es wenigstens schöner und besser in dieser Beziehung habt.-Nun, geliebte Jungen, lebt wohl für heute, schreibt umgehend an Tante Martha so ausführlich, wie Ihr es immer getan habt, wir alle warten sehnsüchtig auf einen Brief von Euch beiden.

Seid umarmt und geküsst in inniger Liebe von

Eurer Mutti.

Dear Peter & Werner: Marian & I send greetings to you. Keep well dear children! Aunt Martha.

20-1938

MEMORIES OF OUR ABORTED FLIGHT TO LIMOGES

AHEAD OF THE GERMAN ARMY BY BERNDT WARSCHAUER, STEPHAN LEWY, WERNER GOLDSMITH and ERIC GOLDFARB

When our mother wrote to us on May 17, 1940, she may not have realized that the German army had broken through the Maginot Line and was advancing rapidly on Paris. As a result, it was decided that our entire group of German Jewish children would set out for Limoges on June 13, 1940, with our educators, their suitcases and two large two-wheeled carts filled with food and luggage that the older boys were responsible for wrangling.

After a short trip in the bottom of a coal barge on the River Seine, we were divided into three groups and walked south until we arrived at a large farm near Fontainebleau sometime after dark. The owner allowed everyone to bed down in his barn on the straw, but as we started to do so, we found that the barn was already filled with a group of black French soldiers.

The following morning, the soldiers were gone, but we found that we were in the middle of a combat zone. Three French biwinged aircraft that had been parked across the street from the barn were shot down by German forces as they tried to take off. German motorcycles with sidecars soon arrived. One stopped and a soldier with a rifle pointed at us came into the barn asking where the French soldiers had gone. A cock crowed as he returned to his motorcycle without harming us; but a bomb landed in the courtyard in front of the barn during the third night of the battle of Fontainebleau, a battle no one has heard of.

On June 16, 1940, our entire group walked back all the way to the Chateau de Quincy, which was then occupied by French prisoners of war. Some time after the prisoners were moved to another location, the German army requisitioned a portion of the Chateau de Quincy as a place of rest for officers who had returned from the Polish front. Although we were frightened as the officers arrived at the Chateau in their army vehicles, it turned out that the officers were, by and large, kind to us, even though they knew that we were Jewish. They often gave us small gifts, for example, and helped us mail our letters back to Germany.

RECOLLECTION OF BERNDT WARSCHAUER (16 YEARS OLD)

(Translation by Norbert Bikales)

THE EXODUS

Quincy Chateau
13 June, 1940

6 a.m.
I was awakened by the noise of engines. The other boys also awoke. We jumped from our beds, ran to the windows, and saw French military trucks as well as their guns coming into our park. "Aha", I thought, "we are already in the combat zone."

7 a.m.
The soldiers were at their stations. One of them had already begun to play an accordion.

8 a.m.
After having coffee, we had to go back upstairs. We lay back down on our beds.

9 a.m.
The soldiers prepared our lunch in the kitchen. Others, lying here and there, just slept.

10 a.m.
Mr. de Monbrison came in brusquely. It had been decided that we would leave for Limoges. Afterwards he separated us, perhaps forever. We received our papers.

1 p.m.
Our last meal. We rolled our blankets and we prepared ourselves for our voyage.

Departure

4 p.m.
We left. The train had two cars, a big one for the people, and a smaller one for the bags and the five bicycles. The big boys were hitched to the cars. I am one of the larger ones, and we perspired heavily.

5 p.m.
We arrived at the Senart Forest. There were soldiers everywhere. The road was clogged with cars.

7 p.m.
We arrived at Corbeil. How we suffered on those train cars! Here's the Seine. All around us are refugees. All of the ships are already full. (A peniche is an engine-powered steel ship or vessel, larger than 15 meters, used for in-land water transportation. This type of ship is often modified in order to act as a docked water restaurant or hotel.)

8 p.m.
We finally found a boat. We began to board it.

9 p.m.
We laid ourselves down to sleep in a dirty hold, packed in like sardines in a box. The air was unbreathable, suffocating. I lay on my raincoat. Net to me, Gerard R. We stared into the dusty air. It was impossible to know if we were even moving. In any case, it was not a pleasant voyage.

10 p.m.
We had eaten nothing since lunch and were hungry. But those watching us are eating brazenly, and every half hour we could hear them crumpling their candy wrappers.

12 midnight
I could not sleep and thought about my house.

14 June 1940

4 a.m.
Right now I am on the bridge. The barge is held up in front of the floodgate.

6 a.m.
We are still in front of the floodgate.

8 a.m.
Finally we pass through.

10 a.m.
Breakfast: a half crust with pate.

Noon
Passing a large village. We search for water.

1 p.m.
We hear the firing of "D.C.A" (Department of Civil Aviation).

4 p.m.
Miss Richter, seated in a corner, has already been praying for a half an hour. Suddenly a woman cries out. Everyone must save themselves. What is it? We heard explosions and firings of the D.C.A. Everyone is ful of panic, and leaves the boat.

5 p.m.
We have left the boat and have piled all the baggage on a cart. The little ones have already left.

6 p.m.
We struggled up a hill. Behind us, the sky is blood red. The bombs! At this point we all have goose bumps. All along the little ones had been patrolling, charged with blowing up bridges. With all of this going on, Mr. Henri, our gardener, was drunk. Every five minutes, he stopped, cried, and said, "It's not my fault! This is war!" as if we didn't know!

7 p.m.
The sky is red. In front of me appears the image of ruined houses and people crying. Do you think that will ever leave your mind? [I'm not sure about this idiom - it could also mean "What thoughts are able to pass through your mind!"]

8:30 p.m.
The children are more than ten kilometers in front of us We are completely worn out. Henri cries in protest, "I cannot march anymore! One more step and I will rip off the wheel of the cart!" He's completely drunk. We decided to stop. But three boys had to carry the bread and the blankets to those who had gone ahead. I was volunteered for this chore. I had Wolfgang and Henri R. with me. Carrying bread and blankets, we moved on into the night.

8:45 p.m.
All around us the night was deep. Here and there were French paratroopers. From time to time there were gunshots. We followed their smoke in silence. I was never at ease. There was never a trace of the young children.

8:55 p.m.
Gerad came to meet us with his cart. He had left the children at a crossroad. What was going on?

9 p.m.
Stephan and Erick also arrived at our meeting point. The children had been directed toward Chailly la Biere. Those two go back to the cart, while we go on with Gerad to the road crossing to wait for the others.

9:15 p.m.
We are at the crossroad. Patrols every two minutes. We are interrogated. Gerard gives the information. "Where are you going?" "A Chailly." "Where are you from?" "From La Seine-et-Oise (very important), from Quincy sous Senart." "All alone?" "Non", and Gerad explains.

9:25 p.m.
Stephan and Erick as well as Mr. Gregoire are there. We can leave.

15 June 1940

12 midnight
We are still on our way. We often hear gunshots. Refugees are everywhere.

1:00 a.m.
Finally, we catch up to them! The boys are asleep in a barn. I throw myself down there as well, and force myself to get some sleep. But sleep doesn't want to come.

2:20 a.m.
Olga has a nervous breakdown. The soldiers make fun of her. (We are housed with 50 blacks, Indochines and other groups.) We are

expecting more bombarding, especially considering we are only 5 km from Fontainebleau.

4:00 a.m.
I go back towards the cart, but this time, on the streets!

5:00 a.m.
Profound silence is all around us. In the East, the sun is rising. The dew settles on the ground. One would not believe we are at war.

6:00 a.m.
We find ourselves back at the spot where we left our cart. But the cart and the boys are gone.

7:00 a.m.
We look for the cart.

7:30 a.m.
We found it . . . .

9:00 a.m.
Once again, we begin our travels.

9:30 a.m.
We are en route. Suddenly, we hear a terrible explosion beside the road, and immediately afterwards, a cloud of dust rises. Planes? Bombs? Worried, we look into the sky . . . . Nothing. Astonished, we look around us. A soldier from the D.C.A. (there are millions of them in the road) cried out to us, "That rolls in a ball!" Oh, yes, we are already in the middle of explosions.

10:00 a.m.
We hear continual explosions.

10:30 a.m.
We arrive and unpack our bags.

11:00 a.m.
We receive cocoa and crackers.

11:30 a.m.
Mr. Gregoire leaves by himself.

1:00 p.m.
Everyone gets three sardines in oil, but it is impossible to find bread anywhere. A German parachutist throws some bombs, but he is killed instantly.

2:00 p.m.
Paris will fall.

3:30 p.m.
We decide to get on our way.

4:00 p.m.
The cart is ready; we are getting close to the entrance of the barn, when a motorcyclist passes by us like a flash of lightening . . . . A moment later someone cries, "The Germans!" Everyone backs into the barn . . . I turn around and see a German soldier coming into the courtyard . . . He cries, "Where are the French soldiers?" Naturally he is carrying a rifle aimed towards us.

4:15 p.m.
We are crouched down on the ground. Sometimes we hear the sound of the machine guns. In the streets, the German troops head in the direction of Fontainebleau.

4:20 p.m.
Boom, boom . . . . the D.C.A. is in action. Above us appear French planes.

4:25 p.m.
The D.C.A. fires about 75 times and that is enough to bring the three planes down in flames.

7:00 p.m.
Time passes. We eat dinner: a piece of bread and a bit of chocolate. I lay my blanket on the ground and I fall asleep.

Boom, boom! I wake up. Boom . . . Boom! One would say - Bombs! I turn around and . . . there I am, in m home . . . But unfortunately, this is not a dream . . . . Outside, everything continues to explode. English bombs fall like rain on our town; one explodes 50 meters from us . . . . The angel of death passed closer than I believed . . . .

16 June 1940

8:00 a.m.
We leave and head back towards the Chateau.

10:00 a.m.
The path carries us . . . a crowd of people returning home accompany us.

12 noon
A short stop. It is unbearably hot.

2:00 p.m.
A German Colonel comes to join us . . . . He gives us handfuls of chocolate and candy.

4:00 p.m.
We are once again back at the Chateau. What took us three days to get there, only took us eight hours on the return! 45 kilometers - in eight hours (with two carts). Isn't that an amazing feat??

This is the end of our memorable escape, during which we learned well the meaning of the words: Life, War, and Hunger.

L'EXODE...

CHATEAU DE QUINCY

13 juin 1940.

6 heures. - Je suis réveillé par des bruits de moteurs. D'autres garçons se réveillent aussi. Nous sautons des lits, courons aux fenêtres et voyons des camions militaires français et même des canons entrer dans notre parc. Aha, pensé-je, nous voici déjà dans la zone de combat.

7 heures. - Les soldats se sont installés. L'un d'eux commence déjà à jouer de l'accordéon.

8 heures. - Après le café, il nous faut remonter. Nous nous allongeons sur les lits.

9 heures. - Les soldats préparent le repas de midi à la cuisine roulante. D'autres, couchés çà et là, dorment.

10 heures. - M. de Monbrison vient brusquement. Il fut décidé que nous partirions pour Limoges. Puis il se sépare de nous, peut être pour toujours. Nous recevons nos papiers.

1 heure. - Dernier repas. Nous roulons nos couvertures et nous nous préparons au voyage.

DEPART

4 heures. - Nous partons. Le train se compose de deux charrettes, une grande pour les vivres, une petite pour les bagages, et de cinq bicyclettes. Les grands garçons sont attelés aux charrettes. Je suis à la grande, et nous transpirons à grosses gouttes.

5 heures. - Nous arrivons à la forêt de Sénart. Partout des soldats. La route encombrée d'autos.

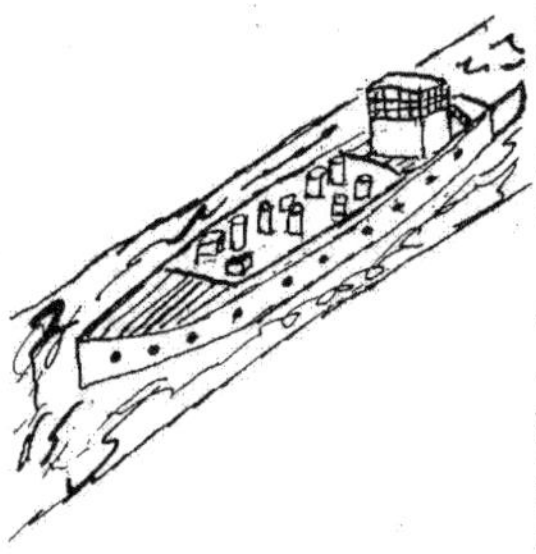

7 heures. - Nous arrivons à Corbeil. Que nous avons peiné avec ces charrettes! Voici la Seine. Partout autour de nous, des réfugiés. Toutes les péniches sont déjà occupées.

8 heures. - Nous avons enfin trouvé un bâteau. L'embarquement commence.

9 heures. - Nous sommes couchés dans une cale sale et serrés comme des sardines en boite. Un air irrespirable. Je suis couché sur mon manteau. A côté de moi, Gérard R. Nous fixons l'air poussiéreux. Impossible de constater si nous avançons. En tout cas, ce n'est pas un voyage d'agrément.

10 heures. - Nous n'avons rien mangé depuis midi et avons faim. Mais les surveillants mangent sans vergogne, et toutes les demi-heures on entend froisser le cornet aux bonbons.

Minuit. - Je ne peux pas dormir et pense à la maison.

14 juin 1940.

4 heures (du matin). - Tout à l'heure j'étais sur le pont. La péniche est immobilisée devant une écluse.

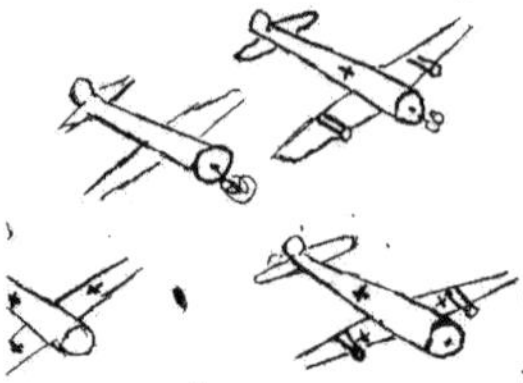

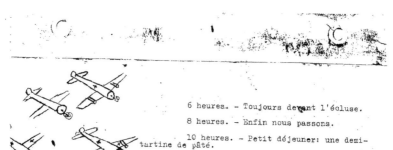

6 heures. - Toujours devant l'écluse.

8 heures. - Enfin nous passons.

10 heures. - Petit déjeuner: une demi-tartine de pâté.

Midi. - Passage d'un grand village. Nous cherchons de l'eau.

1 heure. - Nous entendons des tirs de D.C.A.

4 heures. - Mlle Richter, assise dans un coin, prie déjà depuis une demi-heure. Brusquement une femme crie. Tout le monde se sauve. Qu'y a-t-il? On a entendu des explosions et des tifs de D.C.A. Les gens, pris de panique, quittent le bâteau.

5 heures. - Nous avons quitté la péniche également, et empilons les bagages sur la charrette. Les petits sont déjà partis.

6 heures. Nous peinons sur une colline. Derrière nous, le ciel est rouge-sang. Les bombes! A ce mot on reçoit la chair de poule. Partout des petites patrouilles, chargées de faire sauter les ponts. Avec tout cela M.Henri, notre jardinier, est ivre. Toutes les cinq minutes,il s'arrête, pleure et dit : "C'est pas de ma faute, c'est la guerre !", comme si nous ne le savions pas...

7 heures. - Le ciel est rouge. Devant moi surgit l'image de maisons en ruines, de gens qui pleurent... Quelles pensées vous peuvent passer par la tête!

8 h.30. - Les petits sont à plus de deux kilomètres devant nous. Nous sommes complètement épuisés. Henri proteste en criant : "Je ne marche plus! Encore un pas, et j'arrache la roue de la charrette!" Complètement ivre! Nous décidons à nous arrêter. Mais 3 garçons doivent porter du pain et des couvertures à ceux qui sont en avant. Je suis volontaire de la corvée. J'ai Wolfgang et Heini R. avec moi. Chargés de couvertures et de pain, nous nous en-

4)

fonçons dans la nuit.

8 h.45. - Autour de nous - la nuit profonde. Par ci, par là - contrôles français de parachutistes. De temps en temps - des coups de feu.... Nous suivons notre chemin en silence. Je ne me sens pas à mon aise. Toujours pas de trace des petits.

8 h. 55. - Gerad vient à notre rencontre avec sa charrette. Il a laissé les petits à un croisement de routes. Que faire?

9 heures. - Stephan et Erick arrivent aussi à notre rencontre. Les petits se dirigent dans la direction de Chailly la Bière. Les deux s'en vont à la charrette, tandis que nous allons avec Gerad au croisement des routes pour attendre les autres.

9 h.15. - Nous sommes au croisement. Des patrouilles toutes les deux minutes. Nous sommes interpellés. Gerad donne des renseignements. "Où allez-vous?" "A Chailly". "D'où venez-vous?" "De la Seine-et-Oise" (très important), de Quincy sous Sénart." "Tout seuls ?" "Non," et Gerad explique.

9 h. 25. - Stephan et Erick, ainsi que M. Grégoire sont là. Nous pouvons partir.

15 juin.

Minuit. - Nous sommes toujours en route. On entend souvent des coups de feu. Des réfugiés partout.

1 heure. - Nous les rattrappons, enfin! Les garçons couchent dans une grange. Je m'y jette aussi et m'efforce de dormir. Mais le sommeil ne veut pas venir.

2 h.30. - Olga a une crise de nerfs. Les soldats rigolent d'elle. (Nous logeons avec 50 Nègres, Indochinois et autres coloniaux). On s'attend à un nouveau bombardement, d'autant plus que nous ne nous trouvons qu'à 5 Km. de Fontainebleau.

4 heures. - Je repars vers la charrette, mais cette fois-ci - sur des roues !

5 heures. - Profond silence autour de nous. A l'est se lève le soleil. La rosée se pose sur les prés... On ne croirait pas qu'il y a la guerre.

6 heures. - Nous nous trouvons à l'endroit, où nous avons laissé la charrette. Mais la charrette et les garçons sont partis.

7 heures. - Nous cherchons la charrette.

7 h.30. - Nous l'avons trouvée ...

9 heures. - De nouveau sur la route.

9 h.30. - Nous sommes sur la route. Tout à coup nous entendons une terrible explosion à côté de la route, et tout de suite après se lève un nuage de poussière. Avions? Bombes? Inquiets, nous cherchons dans le ciel... Rien. Etonnés, nous regardons autour de nous. Un soldat de la D.C.A. (il y en a des milliers sur la route!) nous crie: "Ça roule en boule!". Eh oui, nous en sommes déjà aux explosions.

10 heures. - Nous entendons des explosions continuelles.

10 h.30. - nous sommes arrivés et déballons nos bagages.

11 heures. - Nous recevons du cacao et une tartine.

11 h. 30. - M.Grégoire s'en va tout seul.

1 heure de l'après-midi. - Chacun reçoit 3 sardines à l'huile, mais pas de pain; im-

possible d'en trouver nullepart.- Un parachutiste allemand lance des bombes, mais il est tué tout de suite.

2 heures. - Paris serait tombé.

3 h.30. - Nous décidons de nous remettre en route.

4 heures. - La charrette est prête; nous nous approchons de l'entrée de la grange, lorsqu'un motocycliste passe devant nous comme éclair... Un moment après, quelqu'un crie : "Les Allemands!". Tout le monde recule dans la grange... Je me retourne et je vois un soldat allemand entrer dans la cour... Il crie :"Où sont les soldats français ?" Naturellement il porte un fusil braqué.

4 h.15. - Nous sommes couchés par terre. De temps en temps on entend le tac-tac de la mitrailleuse. Dans la rue passent les troupes allemandes dans la direction de Fontainebleau.

4.h.20. - Boum, boum... La D.C.A. est en action. Au-dessus de nous apparaissent des avions français.

4 h.25. - La D.C.A. tire environ 75 fois et cela suffit pour que les trois avions tombent en flammes ...

7 heures. - Le temps passe. On dine : uncake et un morceau de chocolat par personne. J'étends ma couverture par terre et je me couche. Bonne nuit !

Pfui... boum!... Je me réveille. Pfui... boum!... On dirait - des bombes ! Je me retourne et ... me voilà chez moi, à la maison ... mais ce n'est qu'un rêve, malheureusement... Dehors cela continue à craquer. Des bombes anglaises tombent en pluie sur notre village, une d'elles éclate à 50 mètres de nous.. L'ange de la mort est passé plus près que je ne l'ai cru...

16

LE RETOUR.

16 juin.

8 heures du matin. - Nous nous remettons en route, pour retourner au Château. 1

10 heures. - La route nous reprend... Une foule de ceux qui retournent chez eux nous accompagne...

Midi. - Une courte halte. Il fait terriblement chaud.

2 heures. - Une colonne allemande vient à notre rencontre... On nous jette des quantités de chocolat et de bonbons.

4 heures. - Nous sommes de nouveau au Château. Ce que nous a pris trois jours pour aller, nous l'avons fait en huit heures pour retourner !!! 48 Km. - en huit heures (avec deux charrettes), n'est-ce pas une action d'éclat ??

C'est ainsi que prit fin notre mémorable fuite, pendant laquelle nous avons appris ce que veulent dire les mots : la VIE, la GUERRE, la FAIM.

BERND WARSCHAUER (16 ans.)

Bernd Warschauer

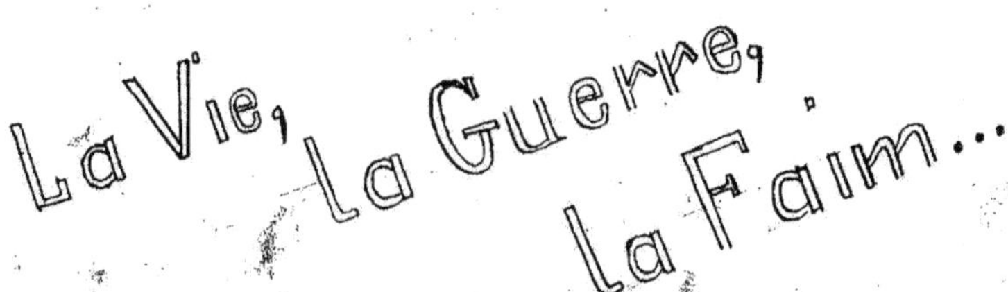

Bernd Warschauer, the author of this recollection, was shot and killed as he tried to escape from the train taking him to Auschwitz.

His picture can be found on page 55.

GENERAL INFORMATION PERTAINING TO THE CHATEAU DE QUINCY

by Stephan Lewy

1. Forty (40) children arrived from Berlin, Germany, on July 4, 1939. Our sponsors were Monsieur de Monbrison and a lady who was related to the House of Romanoff. (We were all boys.)

2. Some of the children came directly from their families and other from an orphanage in Berlin, known as "Auerbachishes Waisenhaus". Some of us had no parents, others just had one parent. I had a father only. Some of the names were Jerry Gerard (Gerhardt Rosenzweig), Wolfgang Blumenreisch, Walter Herzig, Günter Blatt, Berndt Warschauer and myself.

3. When we arrived on July 4, 1939, the Chateau was occupied by Spanish girls. We were transferred to the annex garçon, which was still in use when I visited Quincy in 1984, as an apartment house.

4. For three months we studied French and then we were sent to the school across the street. I remember with my 2 years of schooling I was transferred into first grade . . . a 13 year old boy going to school with six year old boys.

5. The only contact we had with the girls in the Chateau were basketball games, as you can see from one of the pictures.

6. Shortly after the beginning of the war, in September 1939, the girls moved out and all the boys moved into the Chateau. I started helping the gardener, who, as I recall, also came from Russia.

7. Peter describes our fleeing the German's very well. While we were on the barge however, the Germans came to "visit" us as we were huddling below deck. They observed, "they all look like a bunch of Jews." We expected machine gun fire, but nothing happened.

8. Upon our return, there were Germans housed in the castle and they knew that we were German Jewish refugees. All they did was put us to work. Madame Richter was basically in charge of us, but associated more with the Germans than us. There was also a Madame Howard (she had married an Englishman). Also I remember a Madame Lederer.

9. On October 4, 1940, the American Friends Service Committee or the Quakers took a group of us to live in three apartments in Pré St. Gervais near Paris. From there we were transported to unoccupied France to be taken care of by the OSE.

Stephan Lewy managed to come to the United States in 1942 because his parents lobbied Eleanor Roosevelt to obtain a visa for him. He served in the U.S. Army shortly after his arrival in this country and later became a certified public accountant.

His picture appears on pages 54 and 55.

The following are excerpts from an interview of Werner Goldsmith, who left Berlin with us, dated June 6, 1990, which is available at the U.S. Holocaust Museum as RG-50.030*0084. I have edited his response and corrected it where needed:

"Then we arrived at a place called Quincy Sous Senart, maybe 30 miles southeast of Paris, where Count Hubert de Monbrison owned a large chateau where he had served as host for a residential school that catered to White Russian teenage girls and later to refugees from Republican Spain. There were also a few Jewish girls from Germany. Shortly after we arrived on July 6, 1939, the school closed and we lived there alone under the tutelage of our counselors.

We were all Jewish children, but it wasn't a Jewish life. Our counselors and teachers were not Jewish. Mr. de Monbrison wasn't Jewish. We had no kosher cuisine. We had no Jewish rules and regulations. There was no Jewish instruction or anything. We led a totally non-Jewish assimilationist type of life. My guess is that most of the kids in the transport to this home came from assimilationist German-Jewish homes. There were no religious people that I can remember there among the kids. We all seemed to take to this secular type of life at Quincy rather easily. We seemed to fit in very, very nicely.

We learned French. I remember very well one of our teachers was a White Russian, Madame Richter, who really pounded French into us. I remember that to this day and we had other French teachers and émigré teachers and counselors . . . and none of them were Jewish and so, as I say, it was a secular atmosphere and we played and we had our instruction. We had our three meals a day. If there was anything lacking, it was parental love. That that was missing.

We fled south with thousands of other people . . . we were on the road . . . as the German armies approached Paris from the northeast, we were on our way to the southeast, by coal barge and then on foot traveling south, trying to go south. Everybody heading south to evade the approaching Teutonic horde. In other words, they had broken through the so-called impregnable Maginot Line. They had broken through and were rapidly approaching Paris, and that's when you had this helter skelter rush to the south. And we joined the rush. Our teachers and counselors told us we'll go south and hopefully we'll get there. Well, we didn't get there.

One night we spent on a coal barge going up the Seine, not down the Seine. And if you know the Seine, it meanders like that and going up is not only slow, it was painfully slow, extremely slow. We made very little progress and finally during one fine morning, the fine morning after the night on the barge . . . and the other people were on that barge sleeping, or trying to sleep . . . the fine morning afterwards, after having boarded it, the barge came upon hundreds of other barges all stuck in the sand. They were barring each other's way. There were barges and barges and barges, so we simply got out of our barge and continued the trip south on foot, carrying our belongings like thousand of other people. Traveling on foot the road south.

All day long. When we got off the barge in the morning and walked until it was evening time. We got to this farmhouse. We were on the road between the town of Corbeil on the north and the town of Melun in which direction we were moving or walking, on this third-rate country road, maybe second-rate country road . . . walking south and we came to this farmhouse and we decided, or our counselors decided . . . we didn't, kids didn't decide anything . . . teachers and counselors decided we were going to spend the night in the farmhouse and I remember vividly all night long there was pounding of cannon fire in the forest of Fountainblau, near the well-known forest of Fountainblau, cannons were firing and bang, bang, bang . . . all night long. It was very difficult to sleep. I got very little shut-eye. And so in the morning it finally got silent. Also I should mention some French troops, maybe a platoon of Frenchmen, joined us in that farmhouse and slept there or tried to sleep. Early in the morning they packed up and left to the south I guess. We stayed on for breakfast. As I said, in the morning it had gotten very quite, eerily still, and so as we finished breakfast some of us went out to the road, to the shoulder of the road and there were some, some farmers, French peasants standing there talking. The big crowd of people, the masses of people that had been the previous day walking, cluttering the road up, walking with their belongings down the road . . . all gone. The road was empty. Nothing moved on the road. Just a few farmers on the side of the road and a few children finishing breakfast early, moving to the shoulder of the road, and I heard one French farmer yelling into the tiny village down the road, north, what's going on now, what's happening? Words to that effect. And then the answer was shouted back, "les boches", a French pejorative expression meaning "those damned" Germans. And that's what it was. Well, you can see already the tension was rising among us. We didn't know what to expect. Anyway, the farmers stayed there on the shoulder of the road.

The kids stayed on the shoulder of the road. A few minutes later, noise. Motorized troops of the German Wehrmacht were coming down the road, zooming right by us. As they zoomed by us, our hearts once again grew lighter and we began to breathe again. We had no idea what would face us because there were rumors from eastern Europe, that the German Wehrmacht could be brutal as they were in the east, but in France, in the west of Europe, at this stage of the war, they weren't so brutal. They simply zoomed down the road and left us people standing there. They had no idea who was standing there . . . kids, some French adults, farmers . . . zoomed right along down the road and we were once again within the confines of the Third Reich. Our flight to the south had ended, so our counselors decided to move right back where we came from, back to our home at Quincy and so slowly we walked back on the road the way we came, only this time not by barge, simply on foot and we walked and the whole place . . . as I remember at that time was in a state of total discombobulation . . . you didn't know what was going on.

I mean everything was in a state of suspended animation. So we walked home. Nothing befell us. I mean we saw Germans along the road, supply, supply troops. Nobody bothered us. To them we were just some French kids walking along. Nothing. No problem. French civilians. Nobody bothered us. We just walked back to our home and that's the way our flight to the south ended, exactly nowhere. We were right back where we came from . . . at Quincy." Werner Goldschmidt's picture appears at page 52.

The following is a translation of a letter written by Eric Goldfarb to Madame Danielle Blin, the wife of the commanding officer at the Chateau de Quincy

Thornhill (Canada)
August 20 1996

Dear Madame Blin,

Peter Gossels told me that you have been interested in the history of the Chateau de Quincy and since I lived there at the same time as Peter, I am happy to send you some additional information that I recall about the years '39-'40.

As you already know, we were a group of forty boys who arrived at Quincy on July 4, 1939 fleeing from the Nazi persecutions in Germany. We were pupils of the Comité Israelite pour les enfants venant d'Allemagne et de l'Europe Central, whose office was at 38 Rue du Mont-Tabar, Paris. Our benefactor, Count Hubert de Monbrison, who owed the chateau, met us at the Gare de l'Est accompanied by members of the Committee and led us to Quincy.

We were put up in the Boys' Annex (the house that one can still find facing the community's school). The chateau was still a boarding school for young (teenage) girls. It is interesting to note that we were told that the girls at the school were refugees from Spain, but no one told us, I believe, anything about Russian girls. We knew nothing, or rather, I don't remember anything of Princess Theodore.

We passed the first months of our stay in France at the boys' Annex, learning French and becoming integrated into our new country. Mr. Jacobi, our director, Mr. Zimmerman, and Madame Freistadt-Lederer, our counselors, were also refugees from Germany.

It is, perhaps, difficult to relate now, after sixty years, everything that our new life represented. It was about finally living in a free country where we had nothing to fear, but for the sad fact that we all had left our parents behind, a place where we knew they were in danger. In any event, the summer of 1939, July and August, was a time of new discoveries: our July 14, a trip to Paris, baguettes, food that was so different from what we were used to, café au lait in bowls . . . .

We were divided into three groups, the little ones, the middle group and the older group to whom I was assigned. And the activities of the three groups differed, according to their respective heads.

From the beginning of September (1939) when the war began, our life changed a little, like that of everyone else. There were air raid warnings, passive defense (the windows painted blue and paper ribbons psted on the windows), the trench that we had dug ourselves in the garden, two meters deep in a zigzag form (in case of bombardment), which filled with water as soon as we finished it so we could not use it, even to play, the first aid courses, the construction of stretchers, evacuation exercises from the house in the middle of the night, the acrobatics of French aviation in the sky above Quincy . . . .

Then, at the beginning of October, I was placed in the middle course as I had become 13 years old, because our French was still rudimentary. But we were soon among the first and the pieces that were dictated to us were "prepareés" with the help of our memory, even though we did not understand well what the piece was all about. It was easy to avoid making mistakes. Our young teacher was single at the beginning of our classes, but quickly married and the "Mademoiselle" that we had become accustomed to quickly became a "Madame". Her young husband was drafted and we found her to be very sad.

Since they were originally from Germany, Messrs. Jacobi and Zimmerman were arrested and interned in a camp. And the young girls did not return to the chateau when autumn arrived. So we moved into the chateau and inherited a new director, a French woman, who must have been part of the staff of the boarding school and a counselor, Mlle. Richter, mentioned by Olga Efimovski in her book. Happily for us, we kept Mme. Freistadt-Lederer and the old laundry person from the Annex. Old Pierre was still part of the staff along with his dog, whom he called from the other end of the garden in Russian. There were also one or two White Russian teachers about whom I don't remember very much. One, I believe, had homosexual tendencies and did not remain at the chateau for long.

During the winter of 1939-1940, our life in the chateau became perhaps a "chateau life". Yes, life was not easy. Winter was rough, there was a lot of snow. There was still enough to eat. We worked every day. I remember well because the rice pudding (?) did not burn up and we constructed a big Norwegian pot ourselves, and when the milk turned, I let it curdle as one should and as a result I had made white cheese. Now that I think of it, where was our chef, because I see us often in the kitchen in the basement of the chateau. Then, I see us working in the garden helping the gardener pile up the grass cut from the great lawn which was transformed into a pile under the trees at the back of the garden. I see us explore all the corners of the garden, the tennis court, the old abandoned wells from which we drew water after the occupation, when we had lost our electricity and we could not draw water in the chateau. I see us climb the tallest pine tree on our grounds and planting a "flag" made from some white cloth obtained from the laundry, an act that did not endear us to the population of Quincy who said, "Look at those little strangers who are signaling to the Germans."

Then came May 1940. The end of the phony war, the invasion and the exodus. For us, we had to put a small valise together containing everything we owned; forty little valises were put onto a large two-wheel handcart as well as all the baggage of the directrice and Mlle. Richter and the valise of Alice Freistadt-Lederer. That was the carriage that we pulled and pushed across the Forest of Sénart with all of our might up to the edge of Corbeil. Having arrived at the Seine, exhausted, we put everything we owned at the bottom of a coal barge that was supposed to take us to Melun. The Seine was choked up with boats and barges and we were able to travel only a few kilometers. Bombardment during the night - a long stop. Early in the morning, we got off the barge, we resumed pulling and pushing our cart on the roads of France, heading South. When we could no longer go on because of fatigue, we arrived at a large farm at night where we would pass the night in the barn on the straw. There was also a regiment of Sudanese soldiers already in the barn.

But during the morning, as we were preparing to leave, we heard the sound of motorcycle motors, trucks, the Germans had trapped us again. As for them, the war was over. Therefore, we retraced our steps.

I don't know how long it took us to return to the chateau, how we ate. All I remember was the road, the dust, I hear one of the others boys who helped to pull the cart without stopping saying in his bad French, "I can not do any more." I hear the people in the villages we passed ask us what country do you come from? We evidently did not know that they meant to say, "what village?"

Upon returning to the chateau, our life returned to a semblance of normal with, nevertheless, certain difficulties. There was no longer any water, for example. I discovered that the big reservoir (of water) could be found under the roof of the left tower. It was empty and the pump was not working. That is when the wells raised our hopes, but the wheel was not working, as we had to pull the water up by means of a bucket and rope. And while some were pulling up water by the bucket from the well, others carried it on foot to the foot of the tower of the chateau, where we raised the water by rope up to and through a window when we threw the water into the immense reservoir inside. From today's vantage point, it was an absurd piece of work. In any event, I don't know how it all ended.

Then came the rationing of bread. It came to be that we became very jealous about our daily ration of 200-350 grams. One had to weigh each piece of bread. Imagine . . . .

Some time later, the Germans requisitioned the chateau. Our joint occupation of the chateau with the Germans was "cordial". The Germans then wanted to gain the goodwill of the people. In September 1940, the children of the chateau were dispersed (scattered) and for the most part we found each other once more at the Chateau de Chabannes, about which Peter must have told you.

I don't remember ever having anyone talk about the Russian boarding school or of "Princess Theodore". I can assure you that memory is selective. And if I don't remember, that doesn't mean that I never knew it.

On the other hand, I remember Count de Monbrison well. He was a very handsome man who came to find us at the railway station and drove his convertible in front of our bus accompanied by a lady. Upon our arrival at Quincy, he broke bread with us and made us welcome in friendship. After that, we saw him only on rare occasions. Events being what they are, I did not learn what happened to him. Frankly, I regret that.

As far as my personal life is concerned, I would simply like to add that I spent the war years in France, seeing combat with the French forces at Vercours and that I became a French citizen in 1948. And in a certain sense, Mr. de Monbrison is still there if he has not been forgotten.

Eric Goldfarb

The rest of Eric's letter needs no further translation. Eric Goldfarb, whose picture appears at page 54, managed to emigrate to Toronto, Canada, where he lived the rest of his life with his wife, Fée.

ERIC GOLDFARB
(905) 889 6288

1 507 - 7300 YONGE STREET
THORNHILL, ONTARIO, L4J 7Y5
CANADA

Thornhill, le 20 août 1996

Madame Danielle Blin
1, rue Léo-Lagrange
91480 QUINCY-SOUS-SÉNART
FRANCE

Madame,

C'est par Peter Gosssels que je suis au courant que vous vous intéressez à l'histoire du Château de Quincy, et comme j'y ai demeuré en même temps que Peter, j'ai le plaisir de vous envoyer quelques renseignements supplémentaires sur ce dont je me souviens des années 39 - 40.

Comme vous le savez déjà, nous étions un groupe d'une quarantaine de garçons qui sommes arrivés le 4 juillet 1939 à Quincy, fuyant les persécutions nazies en Allemagne. Nous étions pupilles du Comité Israélite pour les Enfants venant d'Allemagne et d'Europe Centrale, dont le siege social se trouvait alors au 38, rue du Mont-Tabor, Paris 1er. Notre bienfaiteur, le Comte H. de Monbrison propriétaire du château, nous accueillit avec les membres du Comité à la Gare de l'Est et nous mena à Quincy.

Nous étions logés à l'Annexe des Garcons (la villa qui se trouve encore maintenant en face de la place devant l'école communale), le château étant alors un internat pour jeunes filles. Il est intéressant de noter qu'on nous avait dit alors que les jeunes filles de l'internat étaient de jeunes refugiées espagnoles mais on n'a guère parlé, me semble-t-il, des jeunes filles russes. Nous ne savions rien - ou bien je ne m'en souviens pas du tout - de la Princesse Théodore.

Nous passâmes les premiers mois de notre séjours en France à l'annexe "Garçons", à apprendre le français et à nous intégrer dans notre nouveau pays. M. Jacobi, notre directeur, M. Zimmerman et Mme Freistadt-Lederer, nos éducateurs, étaient également des réfugiés d'Allemagne.

Il est peut-être difficile de relater maintenant, après une période de près de 60 années, tout ce que notre nouvelle vie représentait. Il y avait toute cette joie de vivre enfin dans un pays libre où nous n'avions rien à craindre, mêlée au triste fait que nous avions tous quitté des parents restés là-bas et que nous savions en plein danger. En tous les cas, l'été de 1939, juillet et août, ce fut la grande découverte: notre 1er Quatorze Juillet, l'excursion à Paris, les baguettes, la nourriture si différente de celle à laquelle nous étions habitués, le café au lait dans des "bols"...

Nous étions divisés en trois groupe: les petits, les moyens et les grands (dont j'étais). Et les activitée des trois groupes différaient selon les besoins respectifs.

Dès le début de septembre, avec le commencement de la guerre, notre vie, comme celle de tout le monde, changea un peu. Il y avait les alertes, la défense passive (les vitres peintes en bleu et des rubans de papier collés aux vitres), la tranchée, profonde de 2 mètres, en zig-zag, que nous avons creusée nous-mêmes dans le jardin (en cas de bombardement) et qui, dès que nous l'eûmes terminée, se remplissait d'eau sans que nous n'ayons jamais pu nous en servir - même pour jouer, les cours de premier secours, la construction de civières et les exercices d'évacuation de la maison en pleine nuit, les acrobaties de l'aviation française dans le ciel au-dessus de Quincy...

Puis, ce fut la rentrée du mois d'octobre. Bien que j'avais déjà 13 ans je fus placé au Cours moyen 1ère année (du fait que notre français était alors à peine rudimentaire). Mais bientôt nous étions parmi les premiers et même si nous ne comprenions pas très bien de quoi il s'agissait dans les dictées - elles étaitent "préparées", donc, avec un peu de bonne mémoire il fut facile d'avoir ZÉRO faute. Notre jeune institutrice était célibataire lors de la rentrée des classes mais se maria très vite et le "Mademoiselle" auquel nous venions à peine de nous habituer, devint vite un "Madame". Son jeune époux fut mobilisé - et nous la retrouvions bien triste.

Messrs Jacobi et Zimmerman étant originaires du pays belligérant furent arrêtés et internés dans un camp de prestataires. Et en automne, les jeunes filles n'étant pas retournées au château, nous y déménageâmes et par là héritâmes d'une nouvelle directrice, une Française qui devait faire partie de l'ancien personnel de l'internat, et d'une éducatrice, Mlle Richter, dont parle Mme Olga Efimovsky dans son livre. Mais heureusement pour nous, nous gardâmes Mme Freistadt-Lederer et notre ancienne lingère de l'annexe. Il y avait également, dans les dépendances, le vieux Pierre et son chien - qu'il appelait à tout bout de champ, en russe. Il y avait aussi un ou deux instituteurs - des Russes Blancs aussi, dont je ne me souviens plus beaucoup. L'un, me semble-t-il, avait des tendances homosexuelles et ne resta pas longtemps au château.

Pendant l'hiver 39-40 notre vie au château était peut-être "une vie de château". Oui, la vie n'était pas facile. L'hiver était rude, il y a vait beaucoup de neige. La nourriture était encore bien suffisante. Nous participâmes aux corvées quotidiennes. Je me souviens bien que, pour que le riz au lait ne brûle pas, nous construisions nous-même une grande marmite norvégienne; quand le lait tournait, je le faisait cailler comme il faut et ensuite, j'en faisais du fromage blanc pressé. A bien y penser, où était donc notre cuisinier, car je nous vois très souvent dans la cuisine au sous-sol du château? Puis, je nous vois travailler au jardin, aider le jardinier à entasser l'herbe coupée de la grande pelouse pour qu'elle se transforme en terreau au fond du jardin, sous les arbres. Je nous vois explorer tous les recoins du jardin - le court de tennis, le vieux puits abandonné d'où nous tirerons l'eau après l'occupation lorsque l'éléctricité sera en panne et que le ravitaillement en eau n'existe pas au château. Je nous vois grimper sur le plus haut sapin du parc et y planter un "drapeau" - un bout de chiffon blanc obtenu à la lingerie. Action qui ne nous a pas mis dans les coeurs de la population de Quincy: "Voyez, ces petits étrangers qui font des signaux aux Allemands!"

Puis vint mai 1940. Fin de la "drôle de guerre", l'invasion et l'exode. Pour nous, il fallait faire notre petite valise avec tout ce que nous possédions; une quarantaine de petites valises chargées sur une charrette à brancards et à deux roues, plus les multiples valises de la directrice et de Mlle Richter, la valise d'Alice Freistadt-Lederer. Charrette que nous tirâmes et poussâmes de toutes nos forces à travers la Forêt de Sénart jusqu'aux environs de Corbeil. Arrivés à la Seine, épuisés, nous chargeâmes tout ce que nous avions au fond d'une péniche qui devait nous emmener à Melun.... La Seine était gorgée de bateaux et de péniches et nous ne fîmes que quelques kilomètres. Bombardement au milieu de la nuit - arrêt prolongé. Au petit matin nous quittons la péniche, nous recommençons à traîner et à pousser notre charrette sur les routes de France en direction du sud. Fatigués, n'en pouvant plus, nous arrivons le soir à une grande ferme où nous allons passer la nuit dans la grange, sur la paille. Il y avait également un régiment de Soudanais.

Mais le matin, pendant que nous nous préparions à repartir, nous entendîmes des moteurs de motocyclettes, de camions. Les Allemands nous avaient rattrappés. Selon eux, la guerre "pour nous était finie". Nous rebroussâmes donc chemin.

Je ne saurais vous dire combien de temps il nous a fallu pour arriver au château, comment nous nous sommes nourris. Je vois seulement la route, la poussière; j'entends un de nos collègues, celui qui tirait la charrette, répéter sans arrêt, dans son mauvais français "je ne peux pas plus, je ne peux pas plus"; les gens dans les villages qui nous demandent "de quel pays venez vous?" - évidemment, nous, nous ne savions pas qu'ils voulaient dire "de quel village"?

De retour au château, notre vie reprit un semblant de normal, avec, pourtant, quelques difficultés. Par exemple, il n'y avait plus d'eau. J'ai découvert que le grand réservoir se trouvait sous le toit de la tour gauche. Il était vide et la pompe ne marchait pas. C'est là que le puits nous est revenu à l'esprit. La roue ne marchait plus, il fallut donc tirer l'eau à la corde; et pendant que les uns en tiraient seau après seau, d'autres portaient l'eau au pied de la tour du château d'où nous la montions à la corde et à bout de bras jusqu'à la lucarne et d'où nous le versions dans cet immense réservoir. Vu d'aujourd'hui, ce fut un travail, dirais-je, absurde; en tous les cas, je ne me souviens plus comment il se termina.

Puis ce fut le rationnement du pain. Il va de soi que nous étions très jaloux de nos 200 ou 350 grammes de ration quotidienne. Il fallait peser chaque bout de pain. Quand on y pense...

Peu de temps après les troupes d'occupation ont réquisitionné le château. Notre co-habitation avec les Allemands fut "cordiale", les Allemands voulant, en ce temps là, gagner la confiance du peuple. Au mois de septembre 1940 les enfants du château furent dispersés et pour la plupart, nous nous sommes retrouvés dès janvier 1941 au Château de Chabannes, dont Peter a dû vous parler.

Je ne me souviens pas d'avoir jamais entendu parler de l'épisode "Internat russe", ni de la Princesse Théodore". Mais je dois vous avouer que la mémoire est selective - et si je ne m'en souviens pas, cela ne veut pas dire, obligatoirement, que je ne l'aie pas su.

Je me souviens par contre très bien du Comte de Monbrison. C'était un très bel homme qui était venu nous chercher à la gare et qui roulait dans sa voiture décapotable devant notre car, accompagné d'une dame. Arrivé à Quincy, il brisa le pain avec nous en signe de bienvenue et d'amitié. Par la suite nous ne l'avons vu qu'à de rares occasions. Les événements étant ce qu'elles furent, je n'ai pas su ce qu'il était devenu. Franchement, je le regrette.

A titre personnel, je voudrais simplement ajouter que j'ai passé les années de guerre en France, que j'ai combattu dans les F.F.I. au Vercors et que je suis devenu Français en 1948. Et dans un certain sens Monsieur de Monbrison y était pour quelque chose, car s'il ne nous avait pas recueilli...

S'il vous fallait d'autres renseignements ou précisions, n'hésitez pas à me le faire savoir. Je me ferais un plaisir de vous les donner dans la mesure du possible.

Je vous prie d'agréer, Madame, l'expression de mes sentiments les meilleurs, et je vous serais obligé de bien vouloir transmettre à Monsieur votre mari mes salutations distinguées.

Eric Goldfarb

P.s. Lors de deux visites à Quincy, en 1969 et il y a quatre ans, ma femme et moi avions essayé de visiter le château - mais hélas, sans succès. Quoiqu'en 1992 nous avons pu faire un petit tour du parc accompagné d'une jeune recrue.

P.p.s. Peter m'a fait parvenir des extraits du livre de Mme Efimovsky. Je le trouve fort intéressant.

OUR MOTHER'S LETTERS CONTINUE

On October 3, 1940, however, the group of boys that had left Berlin on July 3, 1939, were taken from the Chateau de Quincy for the last time. Werner and I were sent to a Jewish orphanage at LaVarenne - St. Maur de Faussee, called the Orphelinat Bet Yessimin, about twenty miles southeast of Paris. There we were sent to the public school for the first time and I earned Billets d'Honneur each month for my school work. Some of the older boys were placed in apartments in Paris provided by the Quakers where they experienced some difficulty obtaining food.

While Werner and I were still in Paris, our mother wrote to the orphanage asking that we be returned to her. And in her letters and that of Lina dated December 1940 and January 8, 1941, they write as if she expected us to return to Berlin soon. Based on research by Simon Lütgemeyer, Egon Heysemann, whose image appears on page 54, did return to his parents in Berlin, was deported and murdered. Unbeknownst to Lotte, however, OSE put us on a train to Chabannes in the Unoccupied Zone of France early in January, 1941. An Emmy Award-winning film describing the children's lives at Chabannes was released by Lotte's granddaughter, Lisa Gossels, in 1999.

Sometime in March or early April, 1941, Lotte heard that we had been selected by a representative of the American Friends Service Committee to receive two of only two hundred visas to enter the United States, just as she was also applying for such a visa.

On May 29, 1941, Lotte wrote that she did not have the thousand dollars required to obtain a visa to come to the United States, but she continued to work on the project although she could not obtain the financial help she needed from her aunt, Martha Stern.

On September 1, 1941, Jews in Germany were compelled to wear a yellow star on their garments to make them stand out and invite taunts and threats from the rest of the population.

On September 9, 1941, Werner and I boarded the Serpa Pinto in Lisbon, Portugal on the way to our new homes in the United States. We landed in New York on September 24, 1941.

9 Oct. 1940

Dear children,

Write as soon as possible whether you are well and still at Quincy. We are well. We think of you all the time hoping to see you again soon.

Many greetings and kisses.

Your Mutti

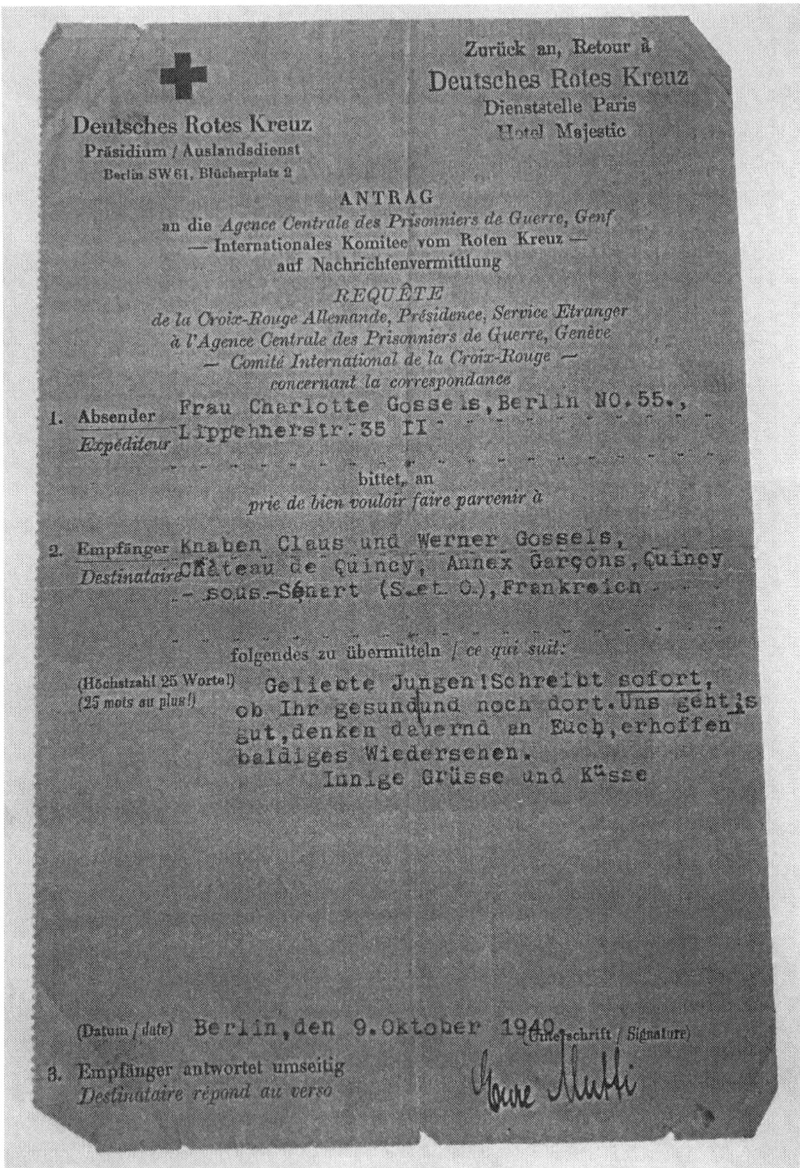

Deutsches Rotes Kreuz
Präsidium / Auslandsdienst
Berlin SW 61, Blücherplatz 2

Zurück an, Retour à
Deutsches Rotes Kreuz
Dienststelle Paris
Hotel Majestic

ANTRAG
an die *Agence Centrale des Prisonniers de Guerre, Genf*
— Internationales Komitee vom Roten Kreuz —
auf Nachrichtenvermittlung

REQUÊTE
de la Croix-Rouge Allemande, Présidence, Service Etranger
à l'Agence Centrale des Prisonniers de Guerre, Genève
— Comité International de la Croix-Rouge —
concernant la correspondance

1. Absender / *Expéditeur* Frau Charlotte Gossels, Berlin NO.55., Lippehnerstr. 35 II

bittet, an
prie de bien vouloir faire parvenir à

2. Empfänger / *Destinataire* Knaben Claus und Werner Gossels, Château de Quincy, Annex Garçons, Quincy - sous-Sénart (S. et O.), Frankreich

folgendes zu übermitteln / *ce qui suit:*

(Höchstzahl 25 Worte!)
(25 mots au plus!)

Geliebte Jungen! Schreibt sofort, ob Ihr gesund und noch dort. Uns geht's gut, denken dauernd an Euch, erhoffen baldiges Wiedersehen.
Innige Grüsse und Küsse

(Datum / *date*) Berlin, den 9. Oktober 1940. (Unterschrift / *Signature*) Deine Mutti

3. Empfänger antwortet umseitig
Destinataire répond au verso

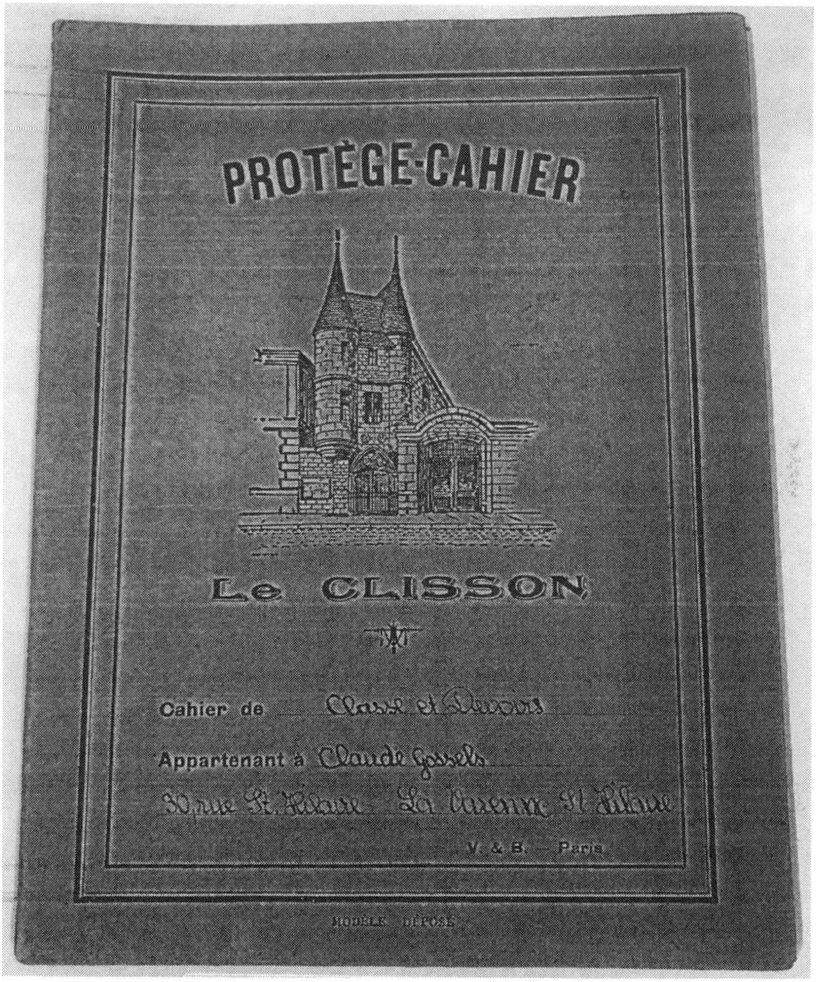

Extract from Peter's notebook, which contained his tests at the Ecole des Muriers.

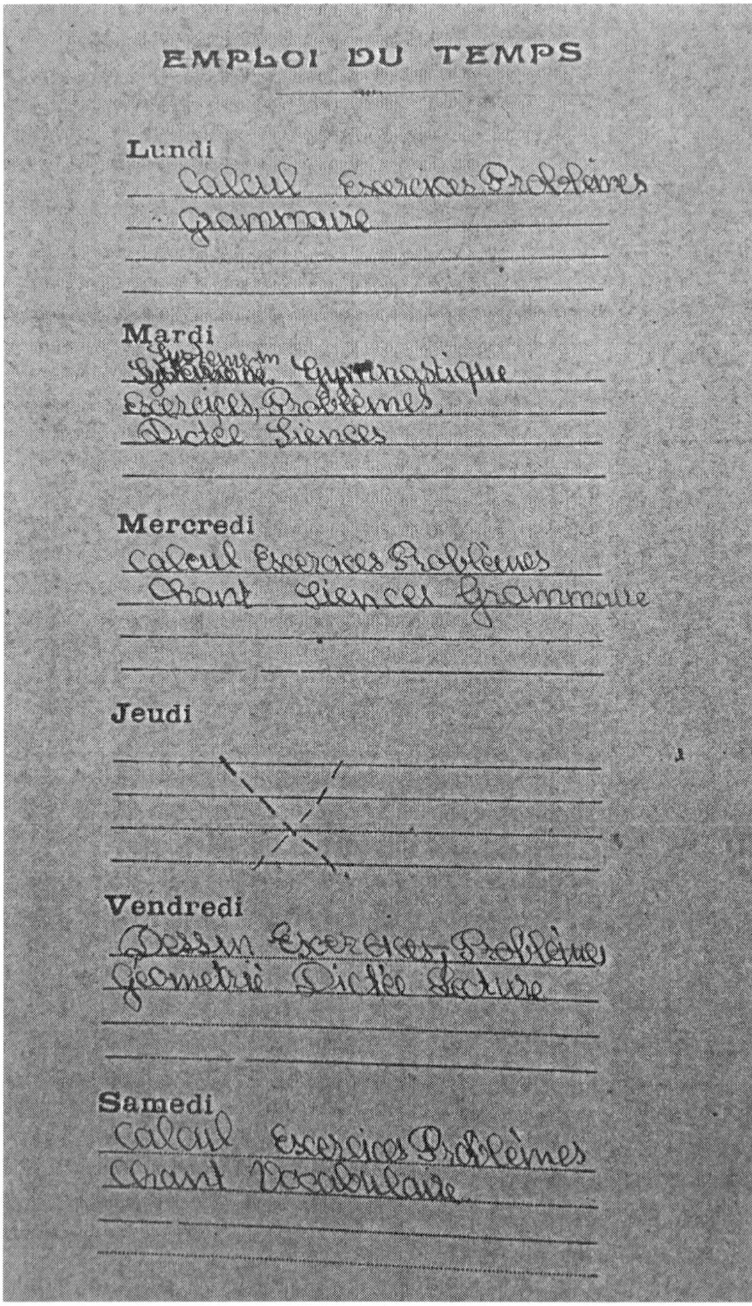

EMPLOI DU TEMPS

Lundi
Calcul Exercices Problèmes
Grammaire

Mardi
Système m [illegible]. Gymnastique
Exercices, Problèmes.
Dictée Siences

Mercredi
Calcul Exercices Problèmes
Chant Siences Grammaire

Jeudi

Vendredi
Dessin Exercices, Problèmes
Géometrie Dictée Lecture

Samedi
Calcul Exercices Problèmes
Chant Vocabulaire

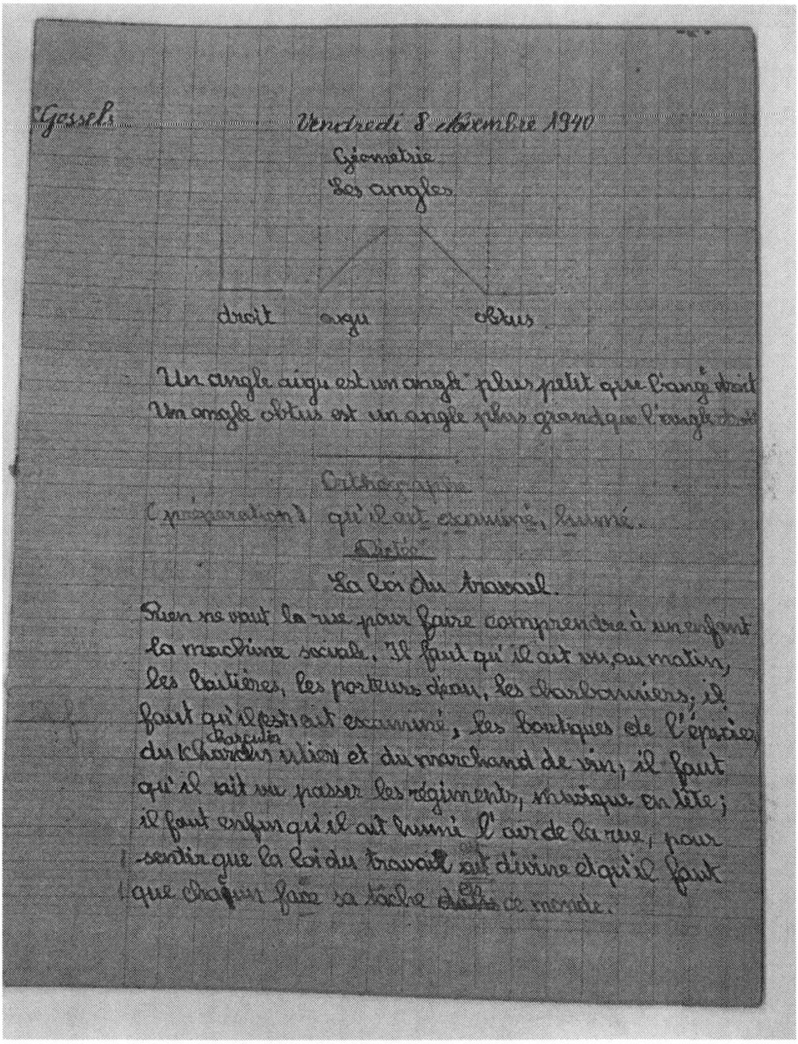

Gossels Vendredi 8 Novembre 1940

Géométrie

Les angles

droit aigu obtus

Un angle aigu est un angle plus petit que l'angle droit

Un angle obtus est un angle plus grand que l'angle droit

Orthographe

(préparation) qu'il ait examiné, humé.

Dictée

La loi du travail.

Rien ne vaut la rue pour faire comprendre à un enfant la machine sociale. Il faut qu'il ait vu, au matin, les laitières, les porteurs d'eau, les charbonniers; il faut qu'il ait examiné, les boutiques de l'épicier, du charcutier et du marchand de vin; il faut qu'il ait vu passer les régiments, musique en tête; il faut enfin qu'il ait humé l'air de la rue, pour sentir que la loi du travail est divine et qu'il faut que chacun fasse sa tâche en ce monde.

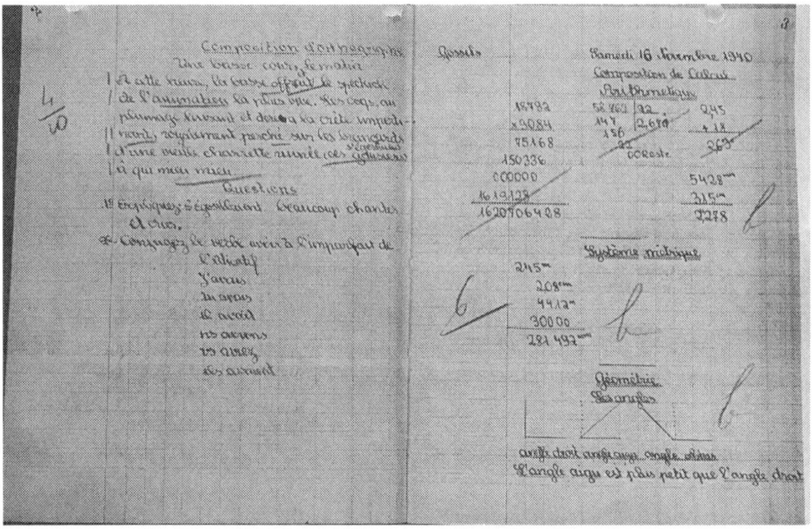
Composition d'orthographe
Une basse cour, le matin
À cette heure, la basse offrait le spectacle de l'animation la plus vive. Les coqs, au plumage luisant et dressant la crête impertinents, perché sur les brancards d'une vieille charrette ... à qui mieux mieux
Questions
1° Expliquez: s'égosillaient beaucoup chanter et crier.
2° Conjuguez le verbe avoir à l'imparfait de l'indicatif
J'avais
tu avais
il avait
nous avions
vous aviez
ils avaient
4/10
Samedi 16 Novembre 1940
Composition de Calcul
Arithmétique
Système métrique
Géométrie
Les angles
angle droit angle aigu angle obtus
L'angle aigu est plus petit que l'angle droit

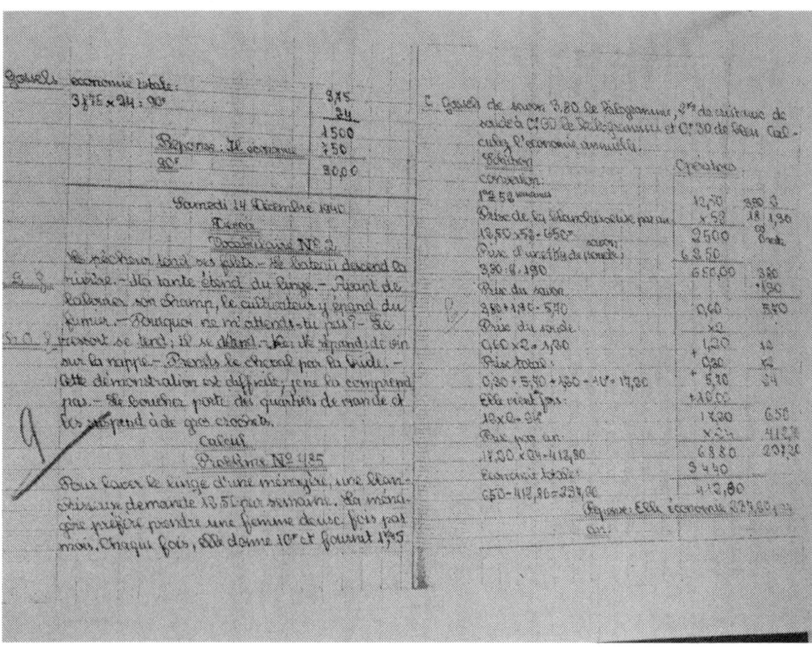
Samedi 14 Décembre 1940
Devoir
Vocabulaire N° 2
Le pêcheur tend ses filets. – Le bateau descend la rivière. – Ma tante étend du linge. – Avant de labourer son champ, le cultivateur y répand du fumier. – Pourquoi ne m'attends-tu pas? – Le ressort se tend; il se détend. – Il a répandu du vin sur la nappe. – Prends le cheval par la bride. – Cette démonstration est difficile; je ne la comprends pas. – Le boucher porte des quartiers de viande et les suspend à de gros crochets.
Calcul
Problème N° 425
Pour laver le linge d'une ménagère, une blanchisseuse demande 12,50 par semaine. La ménagère préfère prendre une femme deux fois par mois. Chaque fois, elle donne 10f et fournit 1,75
Calculez l'économie annuelle.
Solution
Opérations

VILLE DE SAINT-MAUR-DES-FOSSÉS

École des Mûriers

BILLET D'HONNEUR

Accordé à l'Élève Gossels Claude

pour son travail et sa conduite

Le 30 octobre 1940

Imp. [illegible]

Peter's certificate indicating that he was doing good work at the Ecole des Muriers, while he was living at a Jewish orphanage at La Varenne on the outskirts of Paris.

Berlin, Nov. 11th 1940

Beloved Peterle, beloved Wernerle!

A week and a half ago I sent you a letter and included a response form, stationary and an envelope. Since I have not yet heard back from you until now, I'm writing this card real quick. Do let me know immediately how you are doing by using the attached card, especially whether you are healthy and if you are now living there. Your Mutti is very worried about you and would like to have again a brief report from you. So please do write immediately, beloved boys. We are all in good health here and nothing has changed. For today, be well. I embrace and kiss you both.

All my true love - Your Mutti

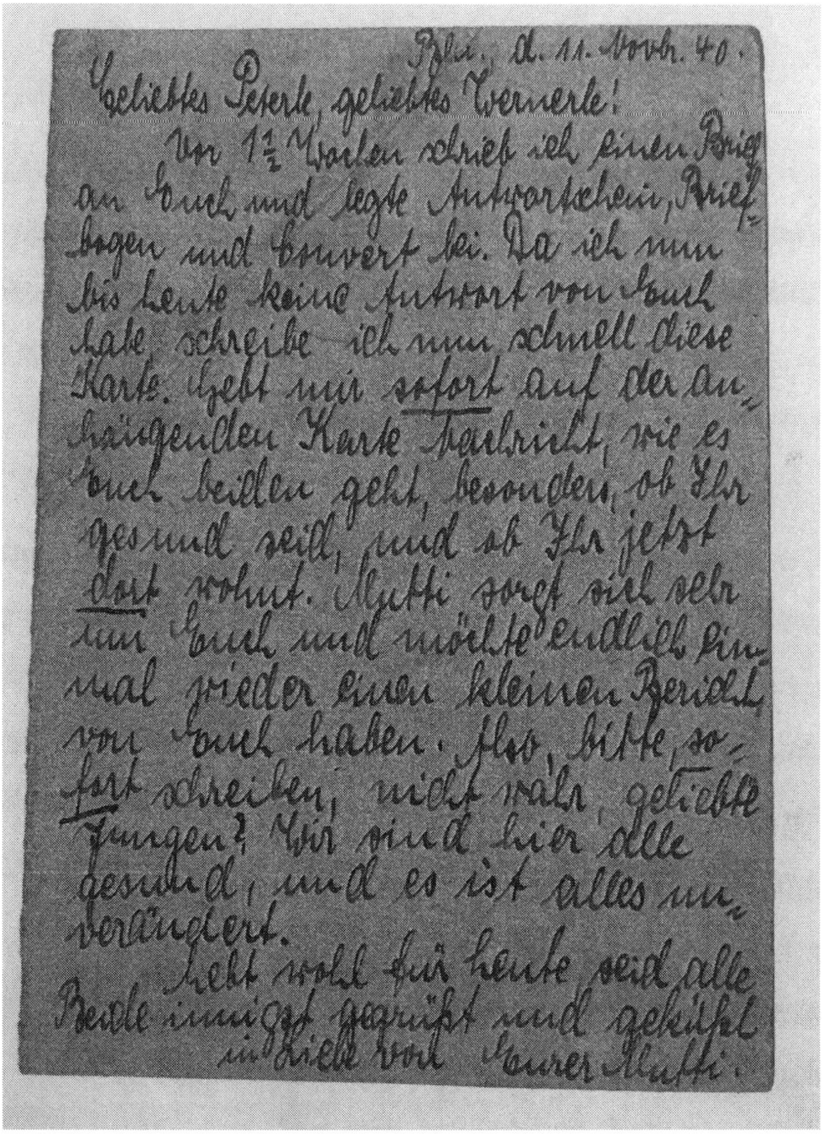

Bln., d. 11. Novb. 40.

Geliebtes Peterle, geliebtes Wernerle!

Vor 1½ Wochen schrieb ich einen Brief an Euch und legte Antwortschein, Briefbogen und Kuvert bei. Da ich nun bis heute keine Antwort von Euch habe, schreibe ich nun schnell diese Karte. Gebt mir <u>sofort</u> auf der anhängenden Karte Nachricht, wie es Euch beiden geht, besonders, ob Ihr gesund seid, und ob Ihr jetzt <u>dort</u> wohnt. Mutti sorgt sich sehr um Euch und möchte endlich einmal wieder einen kleinen Bericht von Euch haben. Also, bitte, so<u>fort</u> schreiben, nicht wahr, geliebte Jungen? Wir sind hier alle gesund, und es ist alles unverändert.

Lebt wohl für heute, seid alle Beide innigst gegrüßt und geküßt in Liebe von Eurer Mutti.

Charlotte Gossels

Berlin, N.0. 55, December 2nd 1940
Lippehnerstr. 35 II.

My beloved Peterle, my beloved Wernerle!

Finally I have found out where you my darlings have ended up. I have already written a few times to you, but to Rue Jean Jaurès in Paris because I was told that 22 children from Quincy had landed there and until this day I have not received an answer from you. Therefore I assume that you have never received the letter and the card from me.

Beloved boys, do write immediately now whether you are in good health and give details about everything you are doing there. As you know Mutti's thoughts are with you day and night and she has to know every little thing about how her two beloved boys are doing. How long have you been there now? Mutti missed you badly during this long time and was very worried about your well-being. Is it already as cold there as it is here? Now it is winter again and it's already been a year and a half since you have left. But now, my beloved boys, I want to tell you that we will see each other again soon. Have you heard yet that you are allowed to come back? I'm doing everything everything I possibly can so that you, my beloved children, can get back to me as soon as possible and I hope it won't be long now until we will see each other again. Then we will stay together and we will never ever part again. I have already received a fine sled, some balls and a hopping sack for you; these gifts are waiting for you so that you can play when you get here; Edith too is very much looking forward to you two.

We are all doing well and everything is as it was when you went away. You two must have grown into big boys now and I probably will not recognize you again.

Now, beloved children, I am enclosing stationary and an envelope as well as a reply form, so you only have to write, and I ask that you do it immediately after you read my letter. Mutti cannot wait to receive finally again a letter from you two that you wrote yourselves.

For today, be well, my beloved good children, I embrace and kiss you both with all my love

Your Mutti.

Oma, Tante Hilde, Tante Betty, Jacobsohns, Tante Martha, Tante Pach and Klein, Edith – everybody is sending a thousand regards and kisses to their two darlings Peterle and our Schnauzel.

Charlotte Gossels

Berlin N.O. 55, d. 2. Dezember 1940.
Lippehnerstr. 35. II

Mein geliebtes Peterle, mein geliebtes Wernerle!

Endlich habe ich nun erfahren, wo Ihr, meine Lieblinge hingekommen seid. Ein paar Mal habe ich schon an Euch geschrieben aber nach Rue Jean Jaurès in Paris, weil mir gesagt wurde, dort wären 22 Kinder aus Quincy hingekommen, und ich habe bis heute immer noch keine Antwort von Euch bekommen. Ich nehme also an, daß Ihr den Brief und die Karte von mir garnicht erhalten habt.

Geliebte Jungen, schreibt nun sofort, ob Ihr gesund seid, und recht ausführlich über alles, was Ihr dort macht. Ihr wißt doch, Mutti ist Tag und Nacht mit ihren Gedanken bei Euch und muß ganz genau alles über ihre beiden geliebten Jungen wissen. Seit wann seid Ihr dort? Mutti hat während der ganzen langen Zeit große Sehnsucht nach Euch gehabt und sich viel Sorge gemacht, ob Ihr auch gesund seid. Ist es bei Euch auch schon so kalt wie hier? Nun ist es schon wieder Winter und es sind bald 1½ Jahre, daß Ihr fortseid. Aber nun, geliebte Jungen, will ich Euch sagen, daß wir uns bald wiedersehen werden. Habt Ihr auch schon davon gehört, daß Ihr zurückkommen dürft? Ich tue alles alles, was ich nur kann, damit Ihr, geliebte Kinder, auf dem schnellsten Wege wieder zu mir kommen könnt, und ich hoffe, es wird nun nicht mehr lange dauern, bis wir uns alle wiedersehen. Dann bleiben wir zusammen und trennen uns nicht mehr. Ich habe schon einen feinen Rodelschlitten, Bälle und einen kleinen Hüft-Sack geschenkt bekommen; das wartet schon hier auf Euch, damit Ihr spielen könnt; Auch Edith freut sich schon so sehr auf Euch beide. Uns allen hier geht es gut, und es ist noch alles so, wie es war, als Ihr fortgefahren seid. Ihr Zwei seid ja bestimmt ganz große Jungen geworden, und ich werde Euch gewiß nicht wiedererkennen.

Nun, geliebte Kinder, lege ich Briefbogen und Briefumschlag gleich bei, ebenso einen Antwortschein, sodaß Ihr nur zu schreiben braucht, und ich bitte Euch, tut es gleich, wenn Ihr meinen Brief gelesen habt. Mutti kann es schon garnicht mehr erwarten, endlich einmal wieder einen selbst geschriebenen Brief von Euch beiden zu bekommen.

Lebt wohl für heute, meine geliebten, guten Kinder, ich umarme und küsse Euch alle Beide in innigster Liebe

Eure Mutti.

Oma, Tante Hilde, Clara, Tante Betty, Jacobsohns, Tante Martha, Tante Pach und Klein Judith, alle alle schicken tausend Grüße und Küsse an ihre zwei Lieblinge Peterle und unsern Schnauzel.

Berlin, 7 XII. 1940

My beloved good boys!

It is the happiest day for us all since your card arrived this morning. I stormed over to Oma who was still in bed and then to the Kleins and read them the entire thing. We are just so happy that you darlings are healthy and doing well. Of course, I am working, my beloved children, and I have to be very diligent, in my business and in my household. Clara is also still with us. I have not heard anything from Vati for a long time. I will now write regularly again and enclose reply forms. Now we will all see each other soon again. I have already written to your home that they should get the passes then it should go quick. We all are extremely excited to see you. Hopefully your letter will arrive soon. Be well, a thousand regards and kisses from all of us for you two.

All my love,
Your Mutti

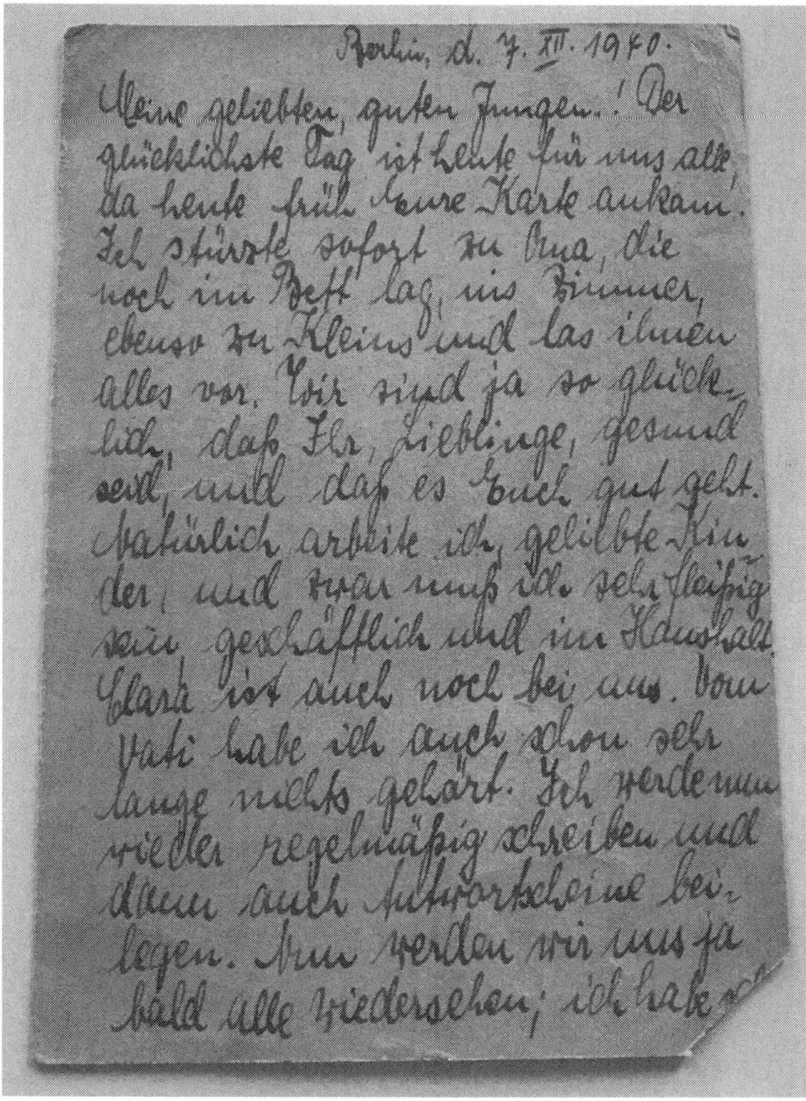

Berlin, d. 7. XII. 1940.

Meine geliebten, guten Jungen..! Der glücklichste Tag ist heute für uns alle, da heute früh Eure Karte ankam! Ich stürzte sofort zu Oma, die noch im Bett lag, ins Zimmer, ebenso zu Kleins und las ihnen alles vor. Wir sind ja so glücklich, daß Ihr, Lieblinge, gesund seid und daß es Euch gut geht. Natürlich arbeite ich, geliebte Kinder, und zwar muß ich sehr fleißig sein, geschäftlich und im Haushalt. Clara ist auch noch bei uns. Vom Vati habe ich auch schon sehr lange nichts gehört. Ich werde nun wieder regelmäßig schreiben und dann auch Antwortscheine beilegen. Nun werden wir uns ja bald alle wiedersehen; ich habe s

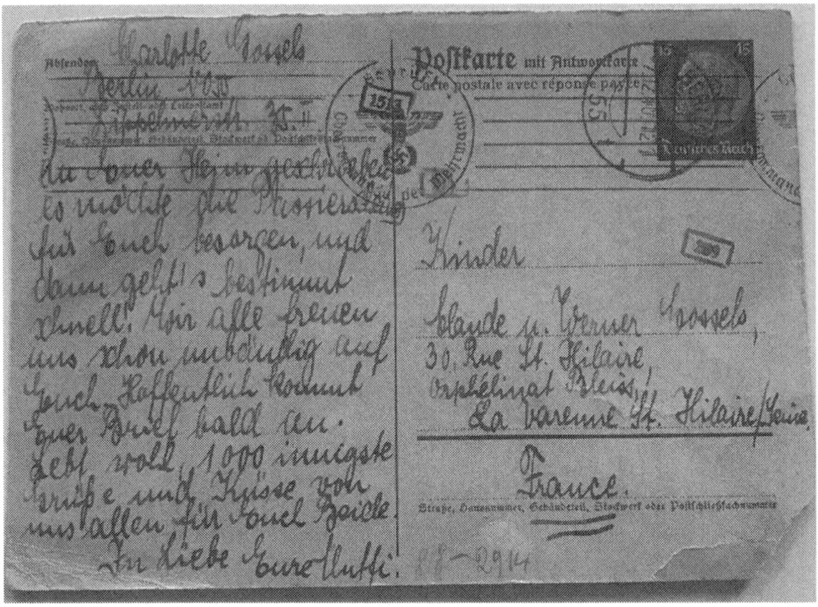

Absender: Charlotte Gossels
Berlin NO55
Lippehnerstr. 35 II

an Euer Heim geschrieben, es möchte die Papiere für Euch besorgen, und dann geht's bestimmt schnell! Wir alle freuen uns schon unbändig auf Euch. Hoffentlich kommt Euer Brief bald an. Lebt wohl, 1000 innigste Grüße und Küsse von uns allen für euch Beide.
In Liebe Eure Mutti.

Postkarte mit Antwortkarte
Carte postale avec réponse payée

Kinder
Claude u. Werner Gossels,
30, Rue St. Hilaire,
Orphélinat Weiss,
La Varenne St. Hilaire/Seine,
France.

Straße, Hausnummer, Gebäudeteil, Stockwerk oder Postschließfachnummer

Berlin, 9 December 1940,

My beloved Peterle and Wernerle!

This morning your long, detailed letter arrived, but unfortunately it's missing: the note from your instructor, the letter from Vati, and the old letter from you, beloved Peterle, after all, you wrote that you wanted to enclose all of that. The letter must have been too thick because it contained a notice from the control agency for foreign correspondence that the letter had been received damaged. It would really be a pity if these things had gotten lost! Maybe your instructor can add another note in your next letter? But my dear boys, I cannot tell you how much pleasure you gave with by your detailed description of your life over there and your pretty coloring of the stationary. I am especially glad to have received from you, my beloved Wernerchen, a letter written by your own hand! Given all your descriptions, beloved children, you are doing very well over there and you can imagine my joy reading your report about your good progress in school. You, dearest Wernerchen, write already very nicely, given that you are only in your first year of school over there, and you Peterle have very nice, clean handwriting, and Mutti thinks you are quite a big, big boy because you can already describe things with much detail and clarity. No, my darlings, I will certainly not be mad at you if you make a few mistakes here and there. Practice makes perfect and you are still young and will have plenty of time to learn everything thoroughly. Just keep writing like as you do and as often as you can, we thoroughly enjoy every line from you. Today Tante Betty and Jacobsohns are sending you a letter and Oma Pach and Tante Klein also want to write to you. Yesterday I visited Tante Martha and read her your card. Each and everybody is looking forward very much to their two darlings, Peterle and Werni. Tante Martha has kept a lot of your toys. You'll have a lot of fun with them!

We are all doing quite well so far. But her hand is still not completely healed. Our phone number is still the same ~~18~~-53.1871. But we will only have the telephone until December 31st. If you, beloved boys, were allowed to call, you would have to do it before then. Other than that there is nothing new here. I work diligently, Tante Hilde still has her job, and Oma is cooking a lot. So you see, everything is still as it was. Also with Clara nothing has changed. She has become a little smarter, but Oma is still often quite upset with her. Who's laughing there? I see you, my little rascals, grinning. Yes, we three have had to laugh about that situation often, didn't we? We will have a lot to talk about when you will be back here. Do tell me, beloved boys, what things that you have over there? You had so much underwear, socks, suits etc. Have you gotten new things over there, and will you bring back what you took when you left, or has much of it gotten lost?

I am really curious to see how you will get on in school again when you're back. Hopefully well. I am so pleased that you are doing so great over there. Do continue to be diligent and please your instructors and teachers. Give my kind regards to your instructors and the director and tell them I thank them a thousand times for all the good they are doing for my two darlings. The boys that are being sent to America are older than you, aren't they? I like the description of your house very much. It seems it is very well appointed and you must be quite comfortable there.

Now I have to end our chat because I have to get back to work and the bell just rang. 5 o'clock! The clients are gone and now I want to get the letter to the post office. Oma is also writing a few lines to you right now. Do write again soon. Stay healthy, cheerful and happy until we see each other again.

Kisses with all my love from your Mutti.

Don't forget to have your director attach a note and to give her my regards. I enclose stationary for your reply.

30–

Berlin, den 9. Dezember 1940.

Meine beiden geliebten Peterle und Wernerle!

Heute kam früh Euer langer, ausführlicher Brief
an, aber es fehlen leider: die Anschrift der Erzieherin, der Brief
vom Vati und der erste Brief von Dir, geliebtes Peterle. Du schreibst
doch, daß Du alles dies beilegen wolltest. Der Brief muß wohl
zu dick gewesen sein, denn es lag ein Zettel bei von der Prüf-
stelle für Auslandsbriefe, daß der Brief „beschädigt" eingegangen
sei. Es wäre ja nun wirklich sehr schade, wenn die Sachen verloren gegangen sind. Vielleicht schreibt Eure Erzieherin im nächsten Brief noch einmal an! Also, geliebte Jungen, ich kann Euch
garnicht sagen, was Ihr mir mit Eurer ausführlichen Schilderung
Eures dortigen Lebens und mit der hübschen bunten Bemalung
des Briefpapiers für eine große Freude bereitet habt. Ganz besonders froh bin ich aber einmal auch von Dir, mein geliebtes, gutes
Wernchen, einen richtigen selbst geschriebenen Brief bekommen zu
haben. Nach allen Euren Schilderungen, geliebte Kinder habt Ihr
es dort doch wirklich sehr gut, und Ihr könnt Euch ja vorstellen, mit welcher Freude ich Euren Bericht über Eure guten
Fortschritte in der Schule gelesen habe. Du liebstes Wernchen,
schreibst auch wirklich schon sehr fein, wenn man denkt, daß
Du doch erst das erste Jahr zur Schule gehst, und Du Peterle
hast ja schon eine feine saubere Handschrift, und Mutti glaubt
Du bist schon ein ganz, ganz großer Junge, weil Du schon alles
so ausführlich und deutlich erzählen kannst. Nein, meine
Lieblinge, ich bin bestimmt nicht böse, wenn Ihr auch mal
ein paar Fehler macht. Es ist noch nie ein Meister vom Him-
mel gefallen und Ihr seid ja noch jung und habt noch
genug Zeit alles gründlich zu lernen. Schreibt nur immer
weiter so und so oft Ihr könnt, wir freuen uns sehr über jede
Zeile von Euch. Heute schicken Tante Betty und Jacobsohns einen
Brief an Euch ab und Oma Pach und Tante Klein wollen Euch
auch schreiben. Gestern war ich bei Tante Martha und las ihr Eure
Karte vor. Alle, alle freuen sich schon sehr auf ihre beiden Lieblinge
Peterle und Werni. Tante Martha hat noch Eure ganzen Spielsachen
aufgehoben. Na, das wird ja eine Freude werden.

Uns allen hier geht es soweit gut. Omas Hand ist nun

auch besser, aber ganz gut noch immer nicht. Unsere Telephonnummer ist noch immer die alte ~~48~~ 53.1871, wir haben das Telephon nur noch bis 31. Dezember. Wenn Ihr, geliebte Jungen, also anrufen dürftet, so müßt Ihr es bis dahin tun! Sonst gibt es hier auch nichts Neues. Ich arbeite fleißig, Tante Hilde hat noch ihre Stellung, und Oma ist fleißig im Kochen. Also, Ihr seht, es ist noch alles wie es war. Auch mit Klara hat sich noch nichts geändert. Ein bißchen klüger ist sie nun doch schon geworden, aber Oma ärgert sich noch genug mit ihr herum. Wer lacht da? Ich sehe Euch, meine kleinen Strolche, grinsen! Ja, wir drei haben darüber manchmal lachen müssen, nicht wahr? Wir werden uns viel zu erzählen haben, wenn Ihr erst wieder hier sein werdet. Sagt mal, geliebte Jungen, wie steht es eigentlich mit Euren ganzen Sachen, die Ihr dort habt? Ihr hattet doch soviel Wäsche, Strümpfe, Anzüge usw. Habt Ihr schon Neues dort bekommen, und werdet Ihr das alles, was Ihr mitnahmt, wieder bringen, oder ist davon viel verloren gegangen?

Ich bin wirklich neugierig, wie Ihr dann hier in der Schule lernen werdet: hoffentlich gut! Ich freue mich so sehr, daß Ihr dort so gut mitkommt. Seid nur weiter recht fleißig und macht Euren Lehrern und Erziehern Freude. Grüßt Eure Erzieherinnen und Direktorin recht herzlich von mir und sagt ihnen, ich lasse Ihnen tausendmal danken für alles Gute, das sie an Euch, meine zwei Lieblinge, tun. Die Jungen, die nach Amerika sollen, sind wohl schon älter als Ihr? Die Beschreibung Eures Hauses gefällt mir sehr gut. So ist dort anscheinend alles sehr hübsch eingerichtet, und bestimmt fühlt Ihr Euch dort sehr wohl!

Nun muß ich unser Plauderstündchen wieder beenden, weil ich jetzt wieder arbeiten muß, es klingelt gerade!

5 Uhr! Die Kundschaft ist fort und nun will ich den Brief sofort zur Post bringen. Oma schreibt gerade auch noch ein paar Zeilen an Euch. Schreibt recht bald wieder, bleibt weiter gesund, munter und fröhlich, bis wir uns wiedersehen.

Seid alle beide innigst geküßt in Liebe

von Eurer Mutti.

Vergeßt nicht Eure Direktorin anschreiben zu lassen und meine Grüße zu bestellen!! Ich lege einen Briefbogen für Euch zum Antworten bei.

Berlin, December 19th 1940,

My beloved Peterle, my beloved Wernchen!

Yesterday Mr. Alexander came by and brought me good news from you two. Gert Alexander had written about you and told me that he had contacted you and had heard that you are both well and going to school. Is it true that you have news from Vati in Vichy? How long has that been? You had written that you had not heard from Vati in a long time? How can Gert A. then state something like that? – What else are you two up to? Do you still have a lot of work at school and do you still have to help a lot in the home like in Quincy? And what will you be doing for Hanukkah? Now the year is almost over and Mutti will get your little chandelier out and light it. – It has become quite cold and wintery here. Do you, beloved Wernerchen, have your second teeth yet, and do you have a lot of pain when they are coming out or is that going smoothly? – With us nothing new has happened since my last letter. Tante Betty had a small accident. When she stepped out of the subway, she fell on her face and got really banged up badly. She is still broken up about it and is getting slowly over her shock.

Now, beloved boys, do write again quickly. I'm badly awaiting a letter from you. For today, be well and many greetings and kisses to you with love from

Your Mutti.

A happy Hanukah celebration for you, beloved children, and all that are celebrating with you.

Berlin, den 19. Dezber. 1940.

Mein geliebtes Peterle, mein geliebtes Wernchen!

Gestern kam Herr Alexander und brachte mir gute Nachricht von Euch Beiden. Gert Alexander hatte über Euch geschrieben, daß er sich mit Euch in Verbindung gesetzt und gehört hat, daß Ihr Beide gesund seid und zur Schule geht. Ist es wahr, daß Ihr vom Vati aus Vichy Nachricht habt? Ist das schon lange her? Ihr habt mir geschrieben, Ihr hättet vom Vati schon lange nichts mehr gehört? Wie kommt denn Gert A. darauf, das zu behaupten? – Was macht Ihr Zwei denn sonst? Habt Ihr immer viel für die Schule zu arbeiten, und müßt Ihr auch im Heim tüchtig mithelfen, wie in Quincy? Und, was werdet Ihr zu Chanukkah machen? Nun ist das Jahr bald wieder herum und Mutti wird Euren kleinen Leuchter wieder raussuchen und ihn anzünden. – Es ist jetzt hier recht kalt und winterlich geworden. Hast Du, geliebtes Wernchen, eigentlich schon die zweiten Zähne, und hast Du viel damit auszuhalten, bis sie durchkommen, oder geht alles glatt? – Bei uns hat sich seit meinem letzten Brief auch nichts Neues ereignet. Tante Betty hatte vor ein paar Tagen einen kleinen Unfall. Als sie aus der Untergrundbahn stieg, fiel sie auf's Gesicht und hat sich alles tüchtig zerschlagen. Sie ist noch sehr kaputt davon und muß sich erst langsam wieder von dem Schreck erholen.

Nun, geliebte Jungen, schreibt recht schnell wieder, ich warte sehnsüchtig auf einen Brief von Euch. Lebt wohl für heute, seid Beide innigst gegrüßt und geküßt in Liebe von

Eurer Mutti.

Ein frohes, glückliches Chanukkah-Fest für Euch, geliebte Kinder, und alle, die es mit Euch feiern!

Chateau de Chabannes, France 1941

Berlin, January 8th 1941

My beloved good boys!

Your New Year's letter from 12/23 with the pretty drawing arrived this morning and you made me very happy with it. You, my dear, little Peterle, probably spent a lot of time and effort to create such a nice painting and I thank you very much for it. I am very happy, my beloved Wernchen, that you also wrote again. While you may not be able to write as long a letter as Peterle at this point, I am twice as pleased about every little word that you, my beloved little one, write to me and I think learning and especially writing does not come as easily to you, right? But you probably apply yourself very much so that your teachers may be happy with you. The little tooth which I would have loved to have had was not in your letter. Have you, dear Wernerle, gotten many new teeth yet, and do you get them easily or does it hurt? This time I am especially happy about your letter because you, dear Peterle, got to tell me in detail about everything. For sure, if they were not that nice to you in Quincy it was impossible for you to write openly and honestly how you were really doing; and I never thought of anything like that because you were always writing that you were doing well. Yes, yes, now I understand everything, beloved children! At the time Egon Heisemann wrote that the instructors were not nice to you and I was worried sick about you, my little ones, for weeks, until I heard from you again that you were doing well and so I figured that Egon who is much older than you might have been disobedient and had been punished for it. That was at the end of 1939. Now I am happy and relieved that you have survived all this and we'll have to spend many hours chatting about it, and hopefully with laughing faces.

[illegible notation]

What did you say to Madame Lederer when she simply took your suitcases away? There were no longer shirts and suits of yours in them, right? And did you have no way at all to report this incredible thing to the Baron de Monbrison? Maybe you were afraid to do so? In any case I am flabbergasted by the whole incident and speechless that something like that could happen. I am very happy, Peterle, that you acted so much like an adult by not giving her the money. – A moment ago Edith came by to ask if you had written. I showed her your letter and she is sending you the enclosed note. She cannot wait for your return! – Tomorrow or Sunday morning I will head over to Tante Martha and show her your letter. She is always very happy when I tell her about you. She is still the same and in her living room with Lorchen now everything still looks the same too. For some time now she has had a very nice radio device. – You should have received in the meantime my card from 12/24 and the letter sent after that, and I hope every day for an answer from Madame Bernheim, so that I will know whether she has done everything that's necessary from Paris or if the paperwork for your passes has to be filed from here through the Reichsvereinigung to Cologne. – Today your nice vacation days are over and you'll have to work hard again. Edith does not have to go back to school until the 6th. That you, dear Peterle, send your post along with someone else's if it happens to work out is very smart of you. In this way you're saving at least a half day. I really think you are a very grown up boy by now and consider things like an adult.

It is now 3 p.m., we just finished lunch break, and at 4:30 I have to be at the dentist's and at 5:30 I have my lesson.

So we'll have to bid each other good-bye for today until next time. Again many, many thanks for your lovely letter and the pretty drawing. My most cordial regards and kisses for you two.

With love,
Your Mutti.

I am enclosing stationary for your reply.

Berlin, den 8. Januar 1941. – 20.I

Meine geliebten, guten Jungen!

Euer Neujahrsbrief vom 23.12. mit der hübschen Zeichnung kam heute früh an, und Ihr habt mir eine sehr große Freude damit bereitet. Du, mein liebes, kleines Peterle, hast gewiß viel Zeit und Mühe dafür verwendet, um eine recht schöne Malerei zustande zu bringen, und ich danke Dir sehr dafür. Ich bin sehr froh, mein geliebtes Wernchen, daß Du auch wieder angeschrieben hast. Wenn Du auch noch keinen so langen Brief schreiben kannst wie Peterle, so freue ich mich doppelt mit jedem Wörtchen, daß Du, mein geliebtes Kleines, an mich schreibst, und ich glaube, so leicht fällt Dir wohl das Lernen, und besonders auch das Schreiben nicht! Nicht wahr? Aber Du gibst Dir bestimmt viel Mühe, daß Deine Lehrer mit Dir zufrieden sind! Das Zähnchen, mit dem ich mich sehr gefreut hätte, hat nicht in Eurem Brief gelegen. Hast Du, liebes Wernerle, schon viel neue Zähne bekommen, und bekommst Du sie leicht, oder hast Du Schmerzen dabei? Ich freue mich diesmal mit Eurem Brief ganz besonders, weil Du liebes Peterle, einmal alles ganz ausführlich hast erzählen können. Ja, wenn man in Quincy so wenig nett zu Euch war, da konntet Ihr ja nicht offen und ehrlich schreiben, wie es Euch wirklich ging; und ich hätte ja nie an so etwas gedacht, weil Ihr doch immer schriebt, es ginge Euch gut. Ja, ja, jetzt kann ich alles verstehen, geliebte Kinder! Damals schrieb Egon Heisemann, die Erzieher seien nicht nett zu Euch, und ich war wochenlang in größter Sorge um Euch, meine Kleinen, bis ich dann wieder von Euch hörte, es ginge Euch gut, und so glaubte ich, Egon, der doch viel älter ist als Ihr, war vielleicht ungehorsam und ist dafür bestraft worden. Diese Sache war Ende 1939. Ich bin nun glücklich und froh, daß Ihr das alles überstanden habt, und wir werden manche Stunde darüber zu plaudern haben, und hoffentlich mit lachendem Gesicht!

14 I '02 – 14 I 3

Was hast Du denn der Mme. Lettera gesagt, als sie Dir einfach die Koffer wegnahm? Waren da etwa auch noch Anzüge und Wäsche von Euch drin? Und hattest Du gar keine Möglichkeit, diese unerhörte Sache dem Baron de Monbrison zu melden? Du hattest vielleicht auch Angst das zu tun? Jedenfalls finde ich ja den ganzen Vorfall einfach doll und bin sprachlos, daß so etwas möglich war. Ich freue mich sehr, Peterle, daß Du so selbständig warst, ihr das Geld nicht zu geben! – Eben kam Edith fragen, ob Ihr geschrieben habt, ich zeigte ihr Euren Brief und sie schickt Euch beifolgendes Briefchen. Sie kann die Zeit Eurer Rückkehr schon garnicht mehr erwarten! – Morgen oder Sonntag vormittag werde ich zu Tante Martha gehen und ihr Euren Brief hintragen. Sie freut sich immer sehr, wenn ich ihr von Euch erzähle. Sie ist noch immer die Alte und auch in ihrer Stube mit Porzellan. sieht noch alles unverändert aus. Sie hat seit einiger Zeit einen schönen Radio-Apparat. – Meine Karte vom 24. 12. und die noch später abgesandte Post werdet Ihr inzwischen ja erhalten, und so hoffe ich von Tag zu Tag auf Antwort von Mme. Bernheim, damit ich endlich mal weiß ob sie von Paris aus das erforderliche erledigt hat, oder ob von hieraus über die Reichsvereinigung die Anträge für Eure Passierscheine von Paris nach Köln zu stellen sind. – Heute sind Eure schönen Ferientage nun auch wieder zu Ende, und da heißt es, wieder fleißig sein! Edith braucht erst wieder am 6. zur Schule. – Daß Du, liebes Peterle, wenn es gerade so paßt, Deine Post mit jemandem nach Paris mitschickst, ist sehr überlegt von Dir, dadurch sparst Du ja wirklich mindestens einen halben Tag. Ich glaube wirklich, Du bist jetzt schon ein ganz großer Junge und denkst wie ein Erwachsener über alles nach.

Es ist jetzt 3 Uhr, wir sind gerade nach Tisch, um ½ 5 muß ich beim Zahnarzt sein und um ½ 6 habe ich Stunde.

So wollen wir uns für heute wieder Lebewohl sagen bis zum nächsten Mal. Nochmals tausend Dank für Euren lieben Brief und die hübsche Zeichnung und innigste Grüße und Küsse für Euch beide in Liebe

Eure Mutti.

Ich lege einen Briefbogen für Euch zum Antworten bei!

My dear boys Peterle and Wernchen!

You have positively no idea how worried we have been about you because we did not receive any news at all from you and could not find out an address for you – We are happy that you are in good health and are doing well. You, dear Wernerchen, have a lot of trouble learning and writing, right? My hand is almost completely healed. That too shall pass. Do you know already when you'll be coming? Saying good-bye to the place will surely not be easy for you since you have also spent some good times there.

Here with us many things are quite different now. Many people are looking forward to you. Now and also from Tante Hilde kind greetings from your

Oma

080-3096

Meine lieben Jungen Peterle u. Wernchen!
Ihr wißt ja garnicht, was für Sorge wir uns
um Euch gemacht haben, weil wir gar keine
Nachrichten von Euch bekamen und keine Anschrift
von Euch erfahren konnten. – Wir freuen uns
daß Ihr gesund seid und es Euch gut geht.
Dir l. Wernerchen fällt das Lernen und Schreiben wohl sehr schwer? Meine Hand ist bis auf
wenig, besser. Auch das wird gut werden.
Wißt Ihr schon wann Ihr kommt? Der Ab-
schied von X. dort wird Euch gewiß nicht leicht
fallen, denn Ihr habt doch schöne Zeiten verlebt.

Bei uns sieht jetzt manches anders aus. Es freuen
sich schon viele auf Euch. Nun herzliche Grüße
von Tante Hilde u. Deiner
Oma

nhard Gruenfeld

~~McPherson Avenue~~

XXXXXXXXXXXXXXXX

11 Aberdeen Pl.

Febr. 18. 1941

Mrs. Kathreen Perlmutter
3636 Page Ave.
St. Louis Mo.

Dear Mrs. Perlmutter:

I like to ask your opinion about the letter I just received from Berlin, Germany and submit the translation of the same to you.

My dear Mrs. Gruenfeld:(follows exlanation where and how she got

I am trying to explain the whole situation to you in the shortest possible way. After seven years of married life I divorced my husband. Our two children, Claus, 10 years old and Werner, 7 year stayed with me in Germany until conditions forced me to send them to France. While I intended (migrate) to go to England and find a livelyhood as a domestic I never would have gotten my permit with my children. Therefore their emigration to France where they found a home in the Rothschild-Children's Home was the best solution for all of us, hard as it was for me to be separated from my children. - My trip to England never materialized, the war broke out and I am still in Germany. - The Rothschild Home was dissolved in 1940 and my boys sent to private homes and later orphan homes gave them a shelter. For some time the rumor went around that the children would be send back to their parents but the final outcome -- they shipped the children to unoccupied France.

The address: Claus and Werner Gossels,
Union Osé Chateau de Chabannes par St. Pierre
de Fursac (Creuse)

My latest informations speak of a children's transport to America through an American Committee via Marseille. -- I do not have any possibility of communication with my children or any official authority and therefore, I am asking you to help me to secure those much wanted informations for me.-- Could you find out if American Committees are working to bring those children over, if those stranded child-refugees frm France will find a place and family in America when they come and if anything is known about time and transportation of the little ones.- Hoping that you'll try everything possible to secure these informations for me I remain, in deep gratitude

Charlotte Gossels
Lippehner Str. 35,II., Berlin N.55

Mrs. G. E. Gruenfeld

SRLE - Case #A-18,512

oke to you
or that there
You will note
is.

28 February 1941

Dear ones,

Write as soon as possible whether you are in good health, what you are doing, whether you are staying [in France] or whether you are going to America and where you may be going. Oma is sick. All heartfelt greetings.

Your Mutti

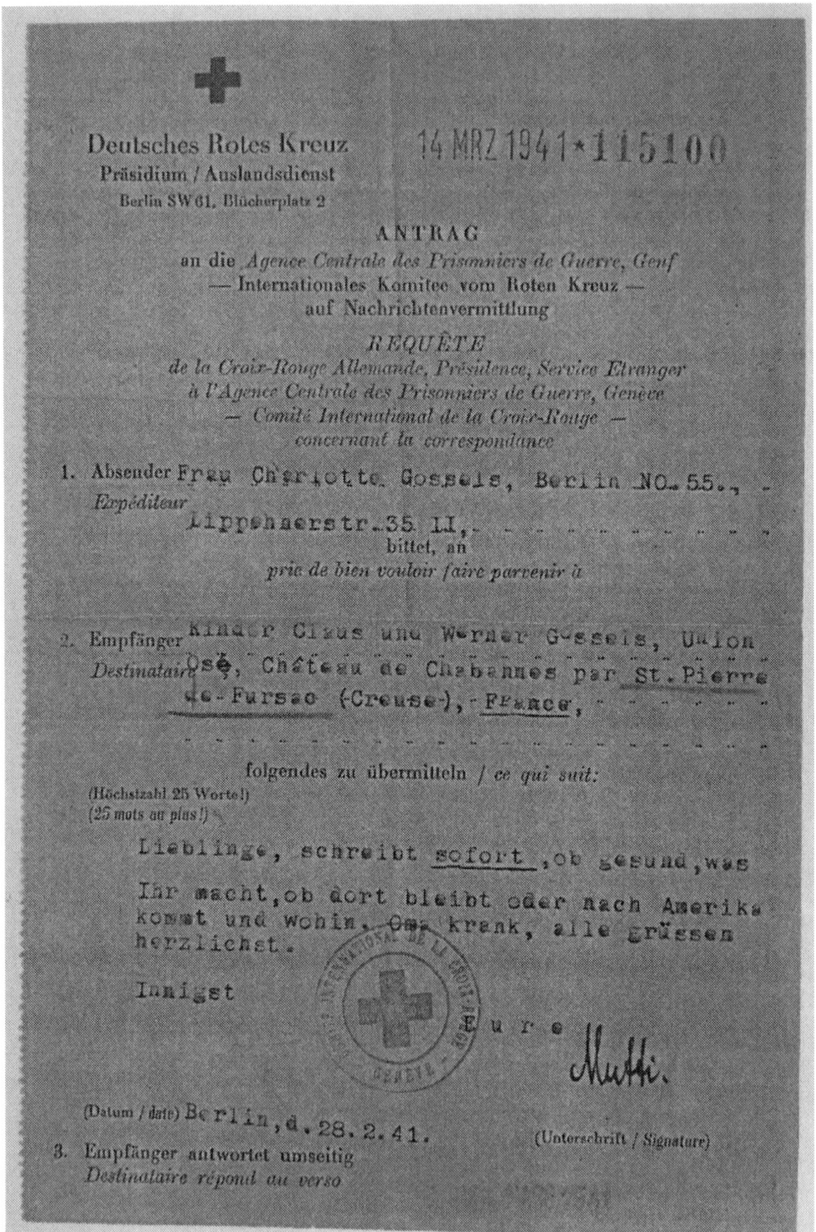

Deutsches Rotes Kreuz
Präsidium / Auslandsdienst
Berlin SW 61, Blücherplatz 2

14 MRZ 1941 * 115100

ANTRAG
an die *Agence Centrale des Prisonniers de Guerre, Genf*
— Internationales Komitee vom Roten Kreuz —
auf Nachrichtenvermittlung

REQUÊTE
de la Croix-Rouge Allemande, Présidence, Service Etranger
à l'Agence Centrale des Prisonniers de Guerre, Genève
— Comité International de la Croix-Rouge —
concernant la correspondance

1. Absender / *Expéditeur* Frau Charlotte Gossels, Berlin NO. 55., Lippehnerstr. 35 II,
bittet, an
prie de bien vouloir faire parvenir à

2. Empfänger / *Destinataire* Kinder Claus und Werner Gossels, Union Osé, Château de Chabannes par St. Pierre de-Fursac (Creuse), France,

folgendes zu übermitteln / *ce qui suit:*
(Höchstzahl 25 Worte!)
(25 mots au plus!)

Lieblinge, schreibt sofort, ob gesund, was Ihr macht, ob dort bleibt oder nach Amerika kommt und wohin. Oma krank, alle grüssen herzlichst.

Innigst

Eure Mutti.

(Datum / *date*) Berlin, d. 28. 2. 41.

(Unterschrift / *Signature*)

3. Empfänger antwortet umseitig
Destinataire répond au verso

Berlin, N.0.55. 4th April 1941
Lippehnerstr. 35 II.

Dear Doctor Lippmann!

Your detailed letter made me extremely happy and I thank you again for it. I can imagine what a happy Sunday it must have been with wonderful presents, the movies, a hotel, etc. One would have liked to eavesdrop as the two boys were sleeping alone in a hotel – just like grown-ups!

And then the wonderful treats, toffee, candy, honey cake, - well, just to think of it makes one's mouth water; one can only hope and wish that the two rascals know how to deal with all that and didn't end up with an upset stomach given all these treats. I am very happy and it is really a great comfort to me that my Claus'chen has finally realized that as an older brother he has to take care of his little brother and needs to protect him. I wrote it to him in almost every letter and since he has now gotten older and more mature he must have come to understand his mother's worries. I would be very grateful, dear Doctor, if you would let me know when the migration to the United States (I heard it will happen from Marseilles!) would take place. To know this is of the utmost significance to me because my own preferred emigration to the United States depends on it; my paperwork for it is already in place. – The children were and are still for all of us here the center of our lives. Everybody asks about them and takes an interest in their development. Edith, the little friend of the two boys, which has become a big, pretty girl, visits me often as she is still attached to the boys and sends them her kindest regards. – My dear mother has been very sick for 6 weeks now with a thrombosis in her left leg and our days and especially nights have been filled with worry, while the entire burden of household, nursing, and professional work has been resting on my shoulders and is still resting on them. Sometimes there are not enough hours in the day to get all the tasks done – and the nights are often very bad. A few days ago things improved a little, but it is a long-lasting disease that requires much rest and the greatest patience.

I gave my Tante Martha and Onkel Erich in Hartford (USA) a report about the children and will keep them informed. As a precaution, I am giving you once again the addresses, maybe the boys will write to them by themselves (per air mail!)

1) Mrs Charles Stearn, 130 North Whitney Street, Hartford, Conn. (USA)

2) Mr. Erich Lewis, 260 Sisson Avenue, Hartford, Conn. (USA)

My Onkel Erich is doing quite well over there; most of all they are happy that all three of them are together and were not torn apart. Gerda, now already 15 years of age, is fluent, got a scholarship and gives reason to the highest hopes. My uncle can unfortunately not study anymore as there are just not enough dollars and Tante Lorle is the breadwinner in the family earning all the money by making candy. The worst is now behind them and they have come to terms with all the rest.

Other than that, we are in good health and Tante Betty too now has recovered; everybody is sending their best regards.

For today I will now conclude my report to you in the hope that these lines reach you in best health. I thank you again from the bottom of my heart and hope to hear from you again soon.

Yours truly,
Charlotte Gossels

[illegible]

Berlin N.O. 55, den 4. April 1941.
Lippehnerstr. 35. II

Sehr geehrter Herr Doktor Lippmann!

Über Ihren so ausführlichen Bericht habe ich mich wirklich riesig gefreut und danke Ihnen vielmals dafür. Ich kann mir vorstellen, was das für ein beglückter Sonntag war mit so wunderbaren Geschenken, Kino, Hotel etc. Da hätte man mal Mäuschen sein mögen, als die beiden Jungen so allein im Hotel geschlafen haben --- richtig wie die Großen! -- und dann die herrlichen Bäckereien, Krokant, Bonbons, Honigkuchen, - na, ich danke, da läuft einem das Wasser im Munde zusammen; da kann man auch nur hoffen und wünschen, daß die beiden kleinen Strolche gut damit umzugehen verstehen und sich nicht mit all den guten Sachen den Magen verdorben haben. Ich bin sehr froh darüber, und es ist wirklich eine große Beruhigung für mich, daß mein Hans'chen nun endlich eingesehen hat, daß er für sein kleines Brüderchen immer als älterer Bruder sorgen und ihn beschützen muß. Ich schrieb es ihm fast in jedem Brief und, nachdem er nun älter und auch reifer geworden ist, hat er wohl auch gelernt, Muttis Sorgen zu verstehen! Ich wäre Ihnen, sehr geehrter Herr Doktor, von Herzen dankbar, wenn Sie mich wissen lassen würden, wann die Weiterwanderung nach U.S.A. (ich hörte von Marseille aus!) erfolgen soll. Dies zu wissen, ist für mich von allergrößter Bedeutung, da hiervon meine eigene <u>bevorzugte</u> Auswanderung nach den Vereinigten Staaten abhängt; meine Papiere hierfür sind bereits beisammen. -- Die Kinder waren und sind bis heute noch hier bei uns allen der Mittelpunkt. Jeder fragt nach ihnen und nimmt Anteil an ihrer Entwickelung. Edith, die kleine Freundin beider Jungen, die ein großes, hübsches Mädel geworden ist, kommt in alter Anhänglichkeit viel zu mir und läßt herzlichst grüßen. -- Meine liebe Mutter ist seit 6 Wochen an einer Thrombose im linken Bein schwer erkrankt, und wir haben

sorgenvolle Tage und besonders Nächte hinter uns, ~~da~~ während derer die ganze
Last von Haushalt, Krankenpflege und beruflicher Tätigkeit auf meinen
Schultern lastete und immer noch lastet. Manchmal reichen die
Tagesstunden nicht aus, um alle Arbeit zu bewältigen --- und d
Nächte sind häufig sehr schlecht. Seit einigen Tagen ist eine klei
Besserung eingetreten, aber es ist eine langwierige Krankheit
die viel Ruhe und größte Geduld erfordert. – An meine Tante
Martha und meinen Onkel Erich in Hartford (U.S.A.) habe ich al
über die Kinder berichtet und halte sie weiter auf dem Laufenden.
Vorsorglich teile ich Ihnen nochmals beide Adressen mit; vielleicht,
daß die Jungen einmal selbst dorthin (per Luftpost!) schreiben.

1) Mrs. Charles Stearn, 1309 North Whitney-Street, Hartford/Conn. (U.S.A.
2) Mr. Erich Lewis, 260, Lisson-Ave., Hartford/Conn. (U.S.A.)

Meinem Onkel Erich geht's drüben ganz gut; vor allem sind sie
froh, daß sie 3 zusammen sind und nicht auseinander gerissen.
Gerda, nun schon 15 Jahre, spricht fließend, hat ein Stipendium
bekommen und gibt Anlaß zu den besten Hoffnungen. Onkel kann
leider nicht mehr studieren, da die Dollars fehlen und Tante
Loile ernährt die Familie mit Konfektfabrikation. Sie
haben nun schon das Schwerste hinter sich und haben sich
auch mit allem anderen abgefunden.

Sonst geht's uns allen gesundheitlich gut; Tante
Betty ist auch wieder auf dem Posten und alle, alle senden
herzliche Grüße.

Ich will nun für heute meinen Bericht schließen in der
Hoffnung, daß diese Zeilen Sie bei bester Gesundheit antreffen,
und mit nochmaligem herzlichen Dank und dem Wunsche,
recht bald wieder von Ihnen zu hören.

Ihre ergebene

Charlotte Gossels.

17 April 1941

My dear youngsters,

I am happy that you are well and that you have seen Vati. My American papers have arrived. Write a soon as possible when you are traveling.

Greetings and kisses from everyone.

Mutti

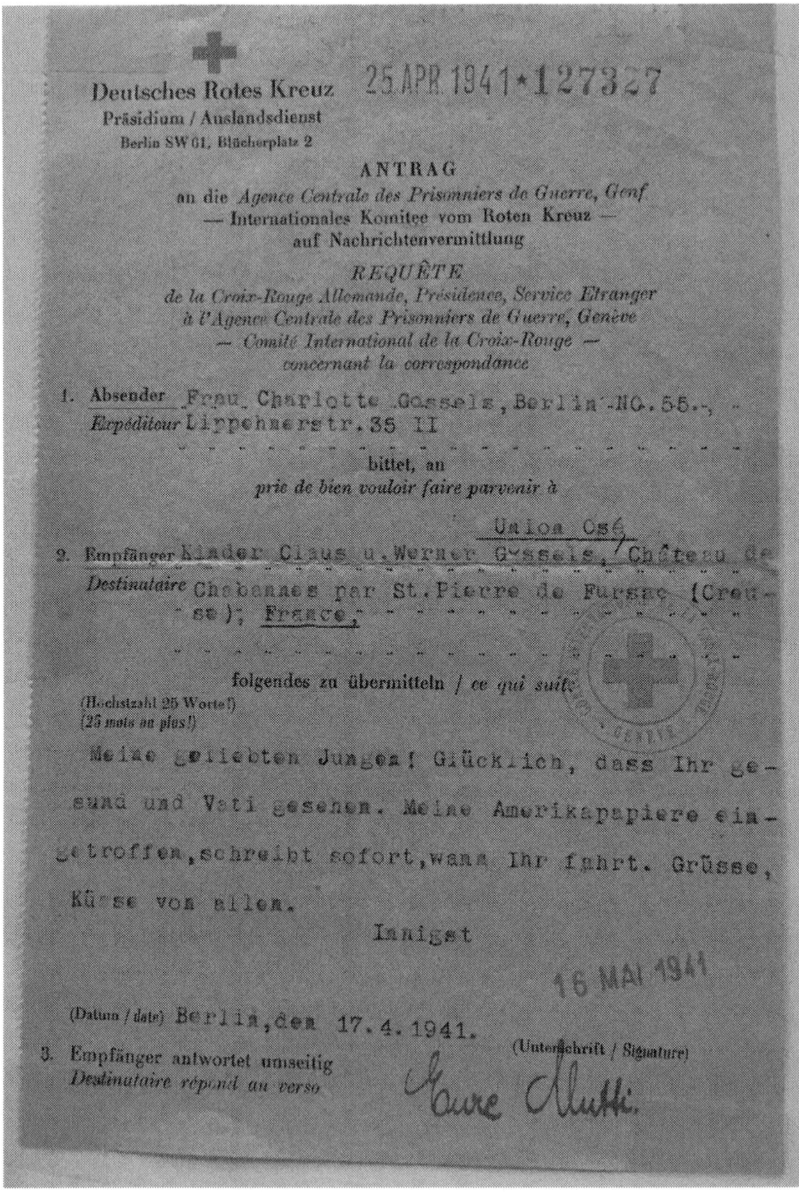

Deutsches Rotes Kreuz
Präsidium / Auslandsdienst
Berlin SW 61, Blücherplatz 2

25 APR 1941 * 127327

ANTRAG
an die *Agence Centrale des Prisonniers de Guerre, Genf*
— Internationales Komitee vom Roten Kreuz —
auf Nachrichtenvermittlung

REQUÊTE
de la Croix-Rouge Allemande, Présidence, Service Etranger
à l'Agence Centrale des Prisonniers de Guerre, Genève
— Comité International de la Croix-Rouge —
concernant la correspondance

1. Absender / *Expéditeur* Frau Charlotte Gossels, Berlin-NO. 55., Lippehnerstr. 35 II

bittet, an
prie de bien vouloir faire parvenir à

2. Empfänger / *Destinataire* Kinder Claus u. Werner Gossels, Union Osé, Château de Chabannes par St. Pierre de Fursac (Creuse); France;

folgendes zu übermitteln / *ce qui suit:*
(Höchstzahl 25 Worte!)
(25 mots au plus!)

Meine geliebten Jungen! Glücklich, dass Ihr gesund und Vati gesehen. Meine Amerikapapiere eingetroffen, schreibt sofort, wann Ihr fahrt. Grüsse, Küsse von allen.

Innigst

16 MAI 1941

(Datum / date) Berlin, den 17. 4. 1941.

(Unterschrift / Signature) Eure Mutti.

3. Empfänger antwortet umseitig
Destinataire répond au verso

Werner and Peter at Chabannes

Werner and Peter at Chabannes

Werner and Peter at Chabannes

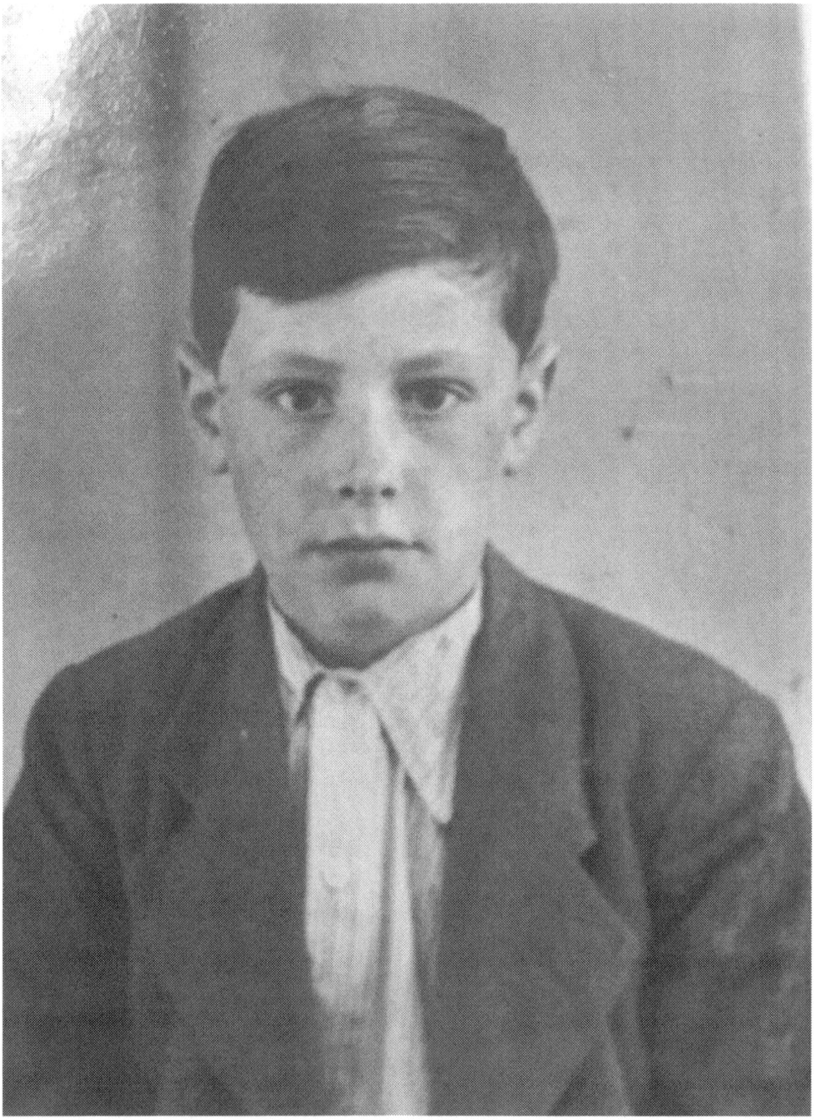

Peter at Chabannes

Chabannes, 24 April 1941

Dear Vati and Maman,

We are in good health. We are graduating at Grand-bourg on June 14, 1941. The weather was good on April 17. Werner, a friend and I made a tent. It was so hot that we took off our shoes and socks. We ate in the garden all day. Now we have cut down a tree because we have run out of coal. It was very hot. April 18: It was not very pleasant today. It is raining and stupid (?). A boy and I are in the barn toasting our bread. Right now, it is evening when the sun begins to shine. I am very thirsty and Werner and I bought ourselves a bottle of lemonade. April 19: It was not very pleasant this morning, but the sun began to shine at nine past 10 a.m. I am staying in the barn and toasting my bread. April 20: This morning the two school teachers returned. We greeted them with flowers. They were very happy to receive them. During the evening, Monsieur Chevrier gave us a festive card (?) and told us that our teacher will have a birthday tomorrow. The older group played a soccer match against Fursac, but lost 1-0. April 21: I went across the meadows to pick some flowers. It was cold and humid. After we had our coffee, we brought the flowers to our teacher who was very happy to receive them. Our vacations are over. There are very few lessons to learn. It was almost pleasant this evening. April 28(?): It was very hot. After noon, Cosman came from Toulouse. I exchanged some duplicates [stamps] for some beautiful stamps from a collection of 10,000 stamps. Today is the first time we will be studying in the evening? April 23: This morning, my friend, Gerard du Rothschild, arrived and we . . . and it is said that they are going to leave the following day, but during the afternoon they say that my friend will stay here and I was very happy.

You write that we are not on the OSE list. But we are not part of OSE, we are with the Quakers. We are only under the care of OSE until we leave here. We gave the cakes to the teachers. Many kisses. Claus

P.S. Thank you for the good things.
(Werner's signature appears on the side of the first page.)

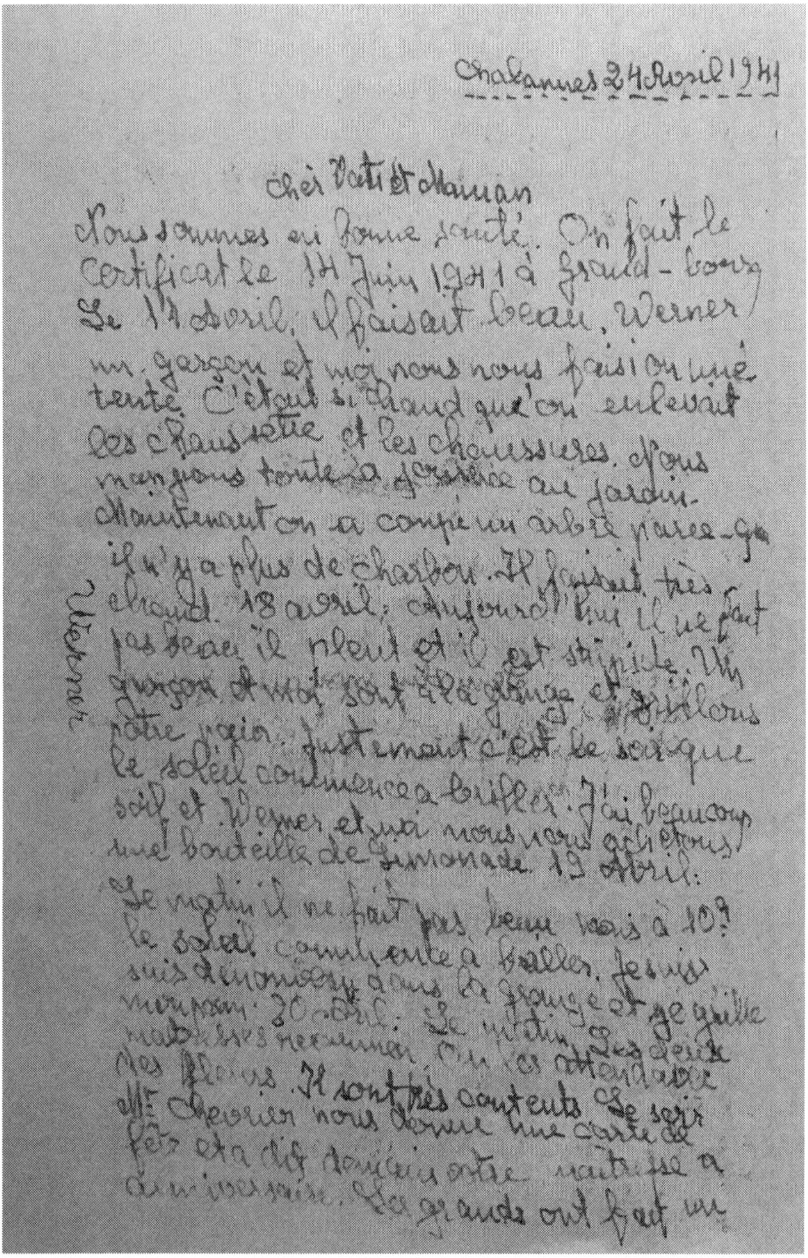

Chalannes 24 Avril 1941

Chèr Vati et Maman

Nous sommes en bonne santé. On fait le
Certificat le 14 Juin 1941 à Grand-bourg
Le 17 Avril, il faisait beau, Werner
un garçon et moi nous nous faisions une
tente. C'était si chaud qu'on enlevait
les chaussette et les chaussures. Nous
mangions toute la journée au jardin.
Maintenant on a coupé un arbre parce-que
il n'y a plus de charbon. Il faisait très
chaud. 18 avril; Aujourd'hui il ne fait
pas beau il pleut et il est stupide. Un
garçon et moi sont à la grange et [illegible]
notre [illegible]. Justement c'est le soir que
le soleil commence a briller. J'ai beaucoup
soif et Werner et moi nous nous achetons
une bouteille de limonade. 19 Avril:
Le matin il ne fait pas beau vers à 10?
le soleil commence à briller. Je suis
[illegible] dans la grange et je quitte
mon [illegible]. 20 Avril. Le matin [illegible]
[illegible] On les attend avec
des fleurs. Il sont très contents. Ce soir
Mr Chevrier nous donne une carte de
fête et a dit [illegible] notre maitresse a
anniversaire. Les grands ont fait un

Werner

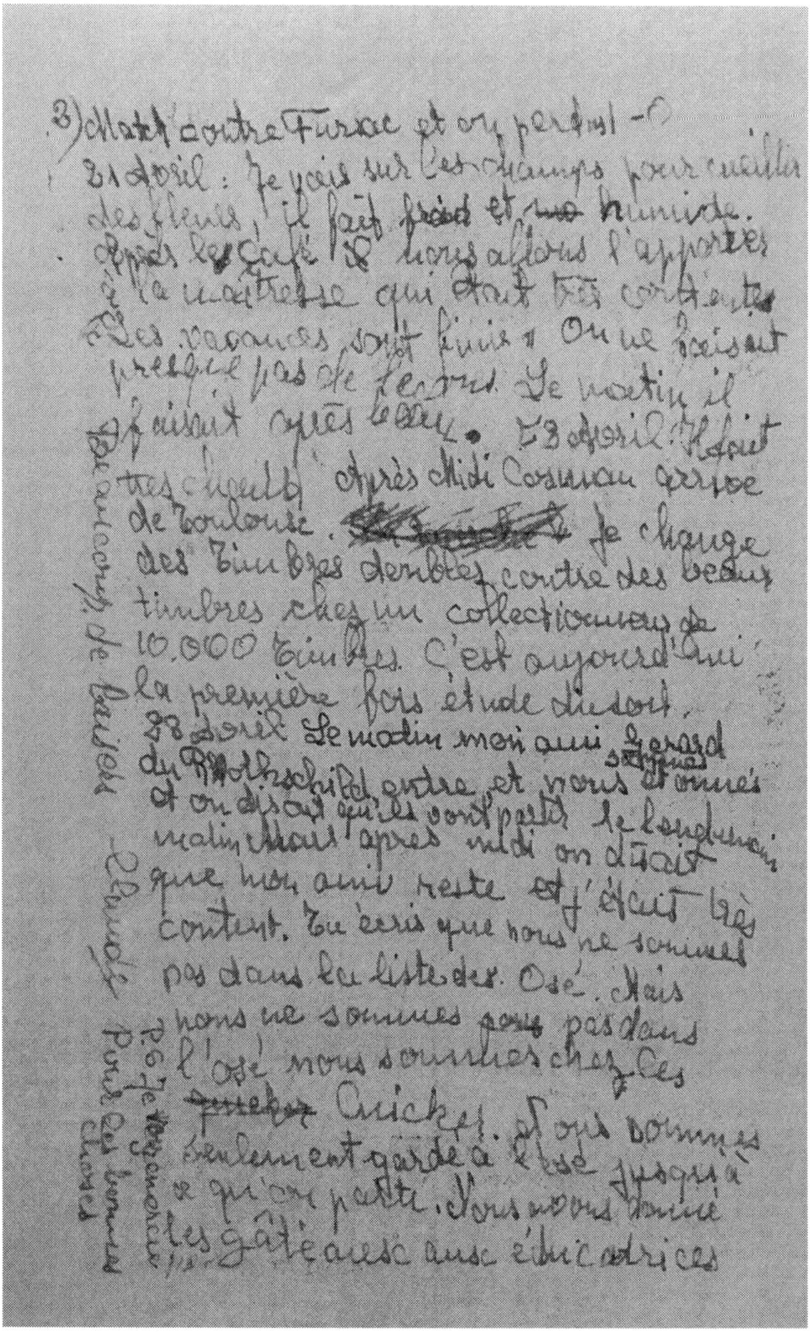
3) Match contre Furac et on perdu 1-0
21 Avril : Je vais sur les champs pour cueillir
des fleurs, il fait ~~froid~~ et ~~mo~~ humide.
Après le café nous allons l'apporter
à la maîtresse qui était très contente.
Les vacances sont finis. On ne faisait
presque pas de leçons. Le matin il
faisait après beau. 23 Avril : Il fait
très chaud. Après Midi Cosman arrive
de Toulouse. [illegible] Je change
des timbres doubles contre des beaux
timbres chez un collectionneur de
10.000 timbres. C'est aujourd'hui
la première fois étude du soir.
28 Avril Le matin mon ami Gerard
du Rothschild entre et nous étonnés (surpris)
et on disait qu'ils vont partir le lendemain
matin. Mais après midi on disait
que mon ami reste et était très
content. Tu écris que nous ne sommes
pas dans la liste des Osé. Mais
nous ne sommes ~~pour~~ pas dans
l'Osé nous sommes chez les
~~[illegible]~~ Quakers. Nous sommes
seulement gardé à l'Osé jusqu'à
ce qu'on partir. Nous avons donné
les gâteaux aux éducatrices

Beaucoup de baisers — Claude
P.S. Je te remercie
Pour les bonnes
choses

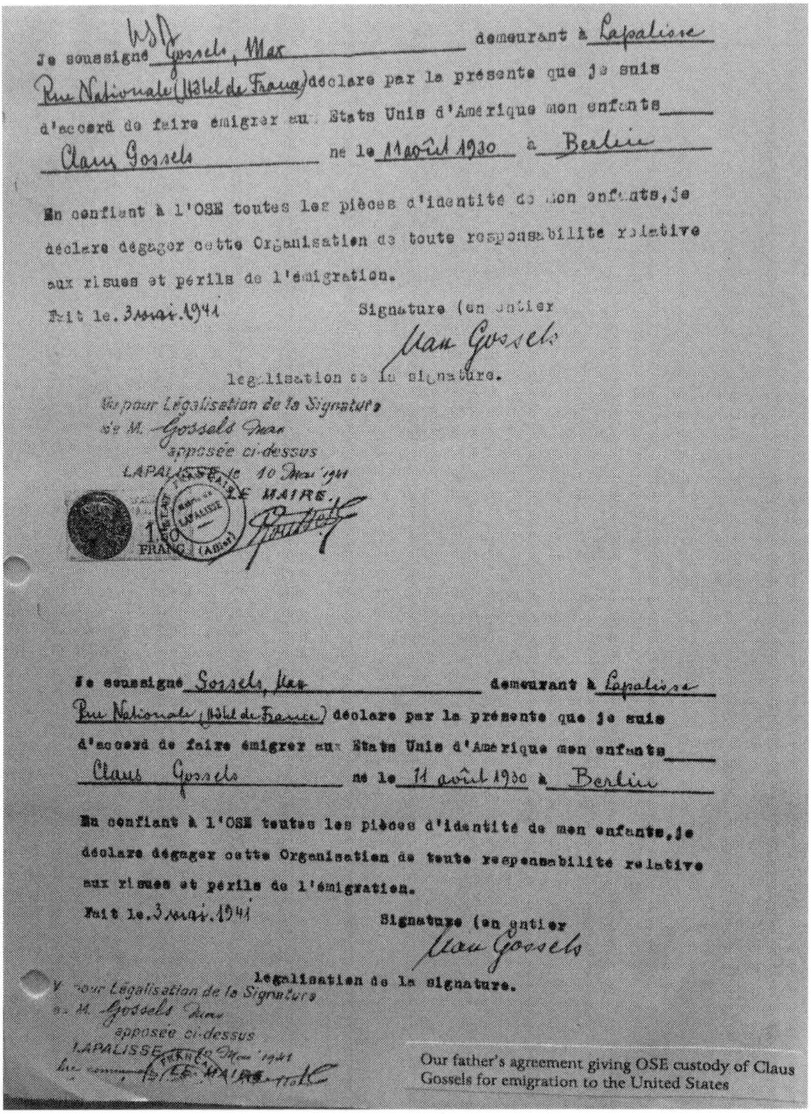

Je soussigné Gossels, Max demeurant à Lapalisse Rue Nationale (Hôtel de France) déclare par la présente que je suis d'accord de faire émigrer aux Etats Unis d'Amérique mon enfants Claus Gossels né le 11 août 1930 à Berlin

En confiant à l'OSE toutes les pièces d'identité de mon enfants, je déclare dégager cette Organisation de toute responsabilite relative aux risues et périls de l'émigration.

Fait le 3 mai 1941

Signature (en entier

Max Gossels

legalisation de la signature.

Vu pour Légalisation de la Signature de M. Gossels Max apposée ci-dessus

LAPALISSE le 10 Mai 1941

LE MAIRE.

1.50 FRANC

Je soussigné Gossels, Max demeurant à Lapalisse Rue Nationale (Hôtel de France) déclare par la présente que je suis d'accord de faire émigrer aux Etats Unis d'Amérique mon enfants Claus Gossels né le 11 août 1930 à Berlin

En confiant à l'OSE toutes les pièces d'identité de mon enfants, je déclare dégager cette Organisation de toute responsabilite relative aux risues et périls de l'émigration.

Fait le 3 mai 1941

Signature (en entier

Max Gossels

legalisation de la signature.

Vu pour Légalisation de la Signature de M. Gossels Max apposée ci-dessus

LAPALISSE le 10 Mai 1941

Le Maire

Our father's agreement giving OSE custody of Claus Gossels for emigration to the United States

[illegible numbers]
Charlotte Gossels

Berlin 8.055, May 22nd 1941
Lippehnerstrasse 35 II.
To May 29th

Dear Doctor Lippmann!

You cannot imagine how happy you made me with the letter and the picture of my two beloved boys. I was coming home late at night from work, found the letter on my night table and two pairs of eyes that for me had only been living in my memory, beloved and sunny, were looking at me. My sincerest thanks go to you and your friend Claus [illegible]! – I am happy that the children are in good health and look so well nourished; they must have lucked out after all over there, especially with being in the countryside where they can get all exercise they want and horse about to their heart's content. The notice about the emigration of the children creates ambivalent feelings for me, because, believe me, it is bitterly hard for a mother, especially for one like me, who is all by herself, to be always selfless towards her children, who after all are all she has got left. When shall we ever see each other again? The conditions that the United States are requiring for immigration are still too difficult and almost impossible to meet for a regular mortal. The affidavit that my aunt recently gave me based on my children's trip to the United States, is not even sufficient for me, although I obtained at the same time an additional affidavit from a friend of my aunt's. All not enough! Additional guarantees, possibly a deposit of 1000 dollars, are required, and nobody can give that much! I wrote again to Hartford, but my aunt is just not a rich woman, a widow herself with two children that she still has to partially support – and one really should not blackmail her. Now I have one more hope that once the children are over there this can create a situation in which clemency will be shown as an exception.

I did give Gerhart's aunt a full report. Her current address is: Berlin S.W. [illegible]ackerstrasse 3.

My oldest one seems to be becoming slowly a man His drawings are fun to look at and I am very happy about the progress both children are making in school. I can imagine how unhappy my little Peter is that he is not yet allowed to take the exam. Over there in America, their studies will start from scratch again and there will be a lot of new impressions. – Judging by the picture both children have grown up very much and have become much more mature. My little sunshine, Werni, looks so terribly like an adult in his suit and tie, and I think my beloved Peterle is at his now almost 11 years still as soft and sensitive as a little girl?! When I look at the picture I want to hold them both against my chest and never let them go again. My thoughts will accompany my beloved children and will follow them in their voyage across the ocean. May God be with them and in his fatherly goodness spare them any hardships so that they may arrive in good health in the new country that shall become their home. That is my dearest wish!

I myself keep working with all my might and an iron resolve on my own emigration to the Unites States. Maybe my aunt can still do something, she really would like to help me and my children. It all just takes so long.

I am enclosing a small picture of myself. I have to close now and thank you again from the bottom of my heart and with my best regards

Yours truly
Charlotte Gossels

P.S.: Maybe Peterle and Werni can see their Vati once more before their trip so that at least a loving hand will caress them once more and a loving mouth will kiss them.

Please be so kind as to inform me as soon as you hear of the children's address so that I can forward it to my relatives in the United States.

With kind regards,
Ludwig L

Charlotte Bonsch.

Berlin S.O. 36. den 22. Mai 1941.
Lippehnerstr. 35.II.
an 29.5.

Sehr geehrter Herr Doktor Lippmann!

Sie können sich nicht vorstellen, was Sie mir mit dem Brief und dem Bild meiner beiden geliebten Jungen für eine Freude bereitet haben. Ich kam spät nachts von der Arbeit nach Hause, fand den Brief auf meinem Nachttisch, und zwei für mich nur noch in der Erinnerung lebende, geliebte, sonnige Augenpaare strahlten mich an. Haben Sie und Ihr Freund Claus Mago herzlichen, innigen Dank! – Ich bin froh, daß die Kinder gesund sind und so gut genährt aussehen; sie haben es dort doch anscheinend gut getroffen, ganz besonders auch, weil sie auf dem Lande sind und sich tüchtig auarbeiten und austoben können. Die Aussicht von der Weiterwanderung erfüllt mich mit zweierlei Gefühlen, denn, glauben Sie mir, es ist bitter schwer für eine Mutter, besonders für eine solche wie ich, die so allein dasteht, immer nur selbstlos ihren Kindern gegenüber zu sein, die ja schließlich ihr Einziges sind was ihr geblieben ist. Wann wird man sich wohl wiedersehen?! Die Bedingungen, die U.S.A. für die Einwanderung stellt, sind immer noch zu schwierige und für einen gewöhnlichen Sterblichen so gut wie unerfüllbar. Das Affidavit, das meine eigene Tante mir kürzlich auf Grund der U.S.A.-Reise meiner Kinder stellte, reicht nicht einmal für mich aus, obgleich ich gleichzeitig ein Zusatz-Aff. von einem Freunde meiner Tante erhielt. Alles zu wenig! Es werden noch größere Bürgschaften, evtl. Depot von 1000 Dollars, verlangt, und das gibt kein Mensch! Ich habe wieder nach Hau

fort geschrieben, aber meine Tante ist eben keine reiche Frau, selbst
Witwe mit zwei Kindern, die sie z.T. noch unterhalten muss---
und so kann man ja doch auch keine Erpressungen machen. Nun
habe ich noch die eine Hoffnung, daß man, wenn vielleicht erst die
Kinder drüben sind, diese etwas schaffen können, und man dann
mehr Milde in diesem Ausnahmefalle walten lassen wird.

An Gerhart's Tante habe ich Bericht erstattet. Ihre jetzige
Adresse ist: Berlin S.W., Yorkmackerstr. 3.

Mein Ältester scheint sich so langsam zu einem kleinen Mann
herauszubilden. Seine Zeichnung macht mir Spaß. außerdem freue
ich mich sehr über die guten Fortschritte, die beide Kinder in der
Schule machen. Ich kann mir denken, wie unglücklich mein kleiner
Peter ist, weil er das Examen noch nicht machen darf. Na, in Amerika, geht das Lernen dann wieder von vorn los und da gibt
dann wieder viele neue Eindrücke. - Nach dem Bilde sind
beide Kinder sehr groß und verständig geworden. Mein kleiner
Sonnenschein, Werni, sieht so schrecklich erwachsen aus in dem
Anzug mit dem Schlips, und ich glaube, mein geliebtes Peterle,
ist heute mit seinen nun bald 11 Lebensjahren, immer noch so
weich und empfindsam wie ein kleines Mädchen?! Wenn ich
das Bild so vor mir habe, möchte ich sie Beide an mein
Herz drücken und nie mehr hergeben. Meine Gedanken
begleiten meine geliebten Kinder und werden ihnen folgen
bei ihrer Reise über den Ocean. Möge Gott mit ihnen sein
und sie in seiner väterlichen Güte vor allem Schweren
bewahren, daß sie gesund in dem neuen Lande ankommen
mögen, das ihnen Heimat werden soll. Dies ist mein innigster Herzenswunsch!

Ich selbst arbeite mit aller Macht und eiserner Energie
weiter an meiner eigenen Auswanderung nach U.S.A. -- vielleicht

kann meine Tante doch noch etwas tun, denn sie will ja mir mit meinen Kindern helfen. Es dauert nur alles so lange.

Ich füge ein kleines Bild von mir bei. Ich will nun für heute wieder schließen mit nochmaligem herzlichsten Dank und den besten Grüßen

Ihre ergebene

Charlotte Gossels.

P.S.: Vielleicht könnten Peterle und Werni vor ihrer Reise wenigstens noch einmal ihren Vati sehen, damit eine liebende Hand sie wenigstens noch einmal streichelt und ein geliebter Mund sie küßt.
Bitte, seien Sie doch so gut, mir, sobald Sie eine Adresse der Kinder erfahren, ~~um~~ diese umgehend mitzuteilen damit ich an meine Verwandten nach U.S.A. berichten kann!

Bz. 29.5.
mit Luftp. Brief
Ludwig

23 May 1941 * 138637

German Red Cross
Presidency/Foreign Affairs
Berlin SW 61, Blücherplatz 2

APPLICATION
to the *Agence Centrale des Prisonniers de Guerre, Geneva*
– International Committee of the Red Cross –

For the transmission of messages

REQUÊTE
de la Croix-Rouge Allemande, Présidence, Service Étranger
à *l'Agence Centrale des Prisonniers de Guerre, Genève*

– Comité International de la Croix-Rouge –
concernant la correspondence

1. Sender
   Expéditeur

   Mrs. Charlotte Gossels, Berlin NO. 55
   Lippehnerstrasse 35 II.

Asks to transmit to
Prie de bien vouloir faire parvenir à

2. Receiver
   Destinataire

   Children Claus and Werner GOSSELS, Union Ose
   Château de Chabannes par St. Pierre de Fussac (Creuse), France

the following
ce qui suit

(Maximum of 25 words!)
(25 mots au plus!)

Darlings! Happy to receive your message from March. All are well, hope you too. You off to America in July? Write immediately address, also to Aunt Martha, Hartford!
Love

5 June 1941

(Date/Date) Berlin, 14 May 1941

3. Receiver replies on reverse
Destinataire répond *au verso*

(Signature/Signature)
Your Mutti

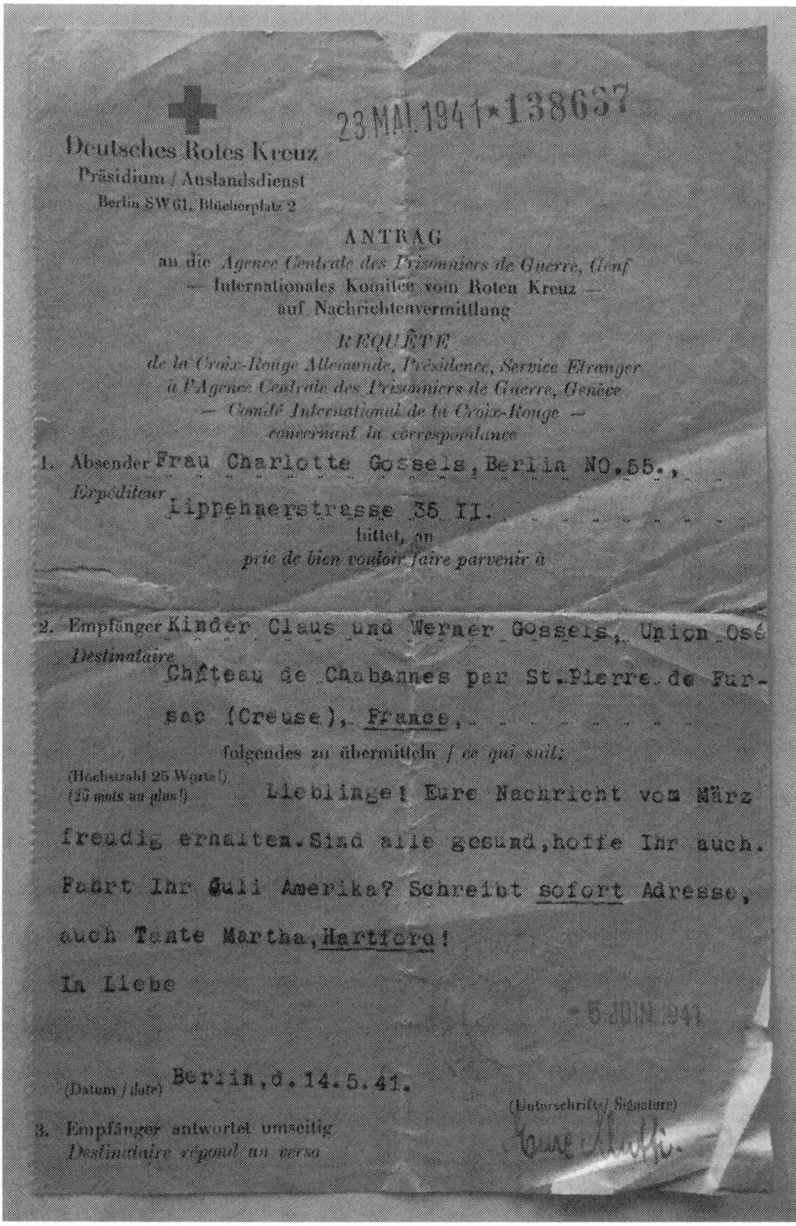

Deutsches Rotes Kreuz
Präsidium / Auslandsdienst
Berlin SW 61, Blücherplatz 2

23 MAI 1941 * 138637

ANTRAG
an die *Agence Centrale des Prisonniers de Guerre, Genf*
— Internationales Komitee vom Roten Kreuz —
auf Nachrichtenvermittlung

REQUÊTE
de la Croix-Rouge Allemande, Présidence, Service Etranger
à l'Agence Centrale des Prisonniers de Guerre, Genève
— Comité International de la Croix-Rouge —
concernant la correspondance

1. Absender *Expéditeur* Frau Charlotte Gossels, Berlin NO.55., Lippehnerstrasse 35 II.
bittet, an
prie de bien vouloir faire parvenir à

2. Empfänger *Destinataire* Kinder Claus und Werner Gossels, Union Osé Château de Chabannes par St.Pierre de Fursac (Creuse), France,
folgendes zu übermitteln / *ce qui suit:*
(Höchstzahl 25 Worte!)
(25 mots au plus!)

Lieblinge! Eure Nachricht vom März freudig erhalten. Sind alle gesund, hoffe Ihr auch. Fahrt Ihr Juli Amerika? Schreibt sofort Adresse, auch Tante Martha, Hartford!
In Liebe

- 5 JUIN 1941

(Datum / *date*) Berlin, d. 14.5.41.

(Unterschrift / *Signature*)

3. Empfänger antwortet umseitig
Destinataire répond au verso

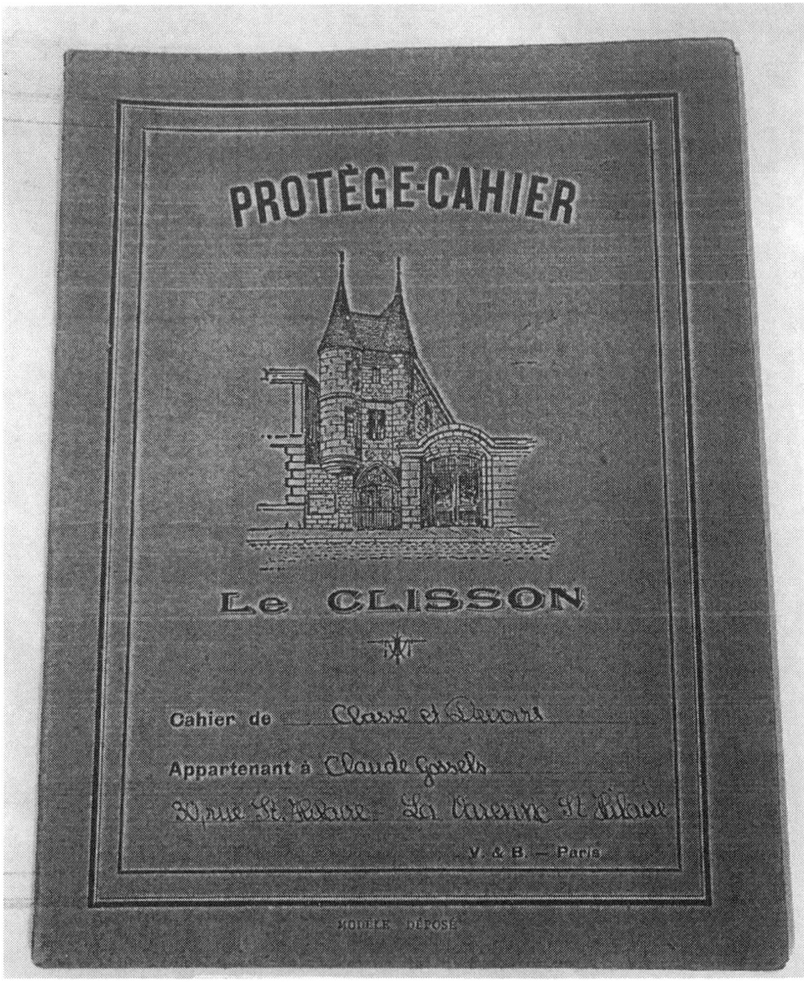

Extract from Peter's notebook, which contained his tests at the Ecole de Chabannes", not the Ecole des Murlers.

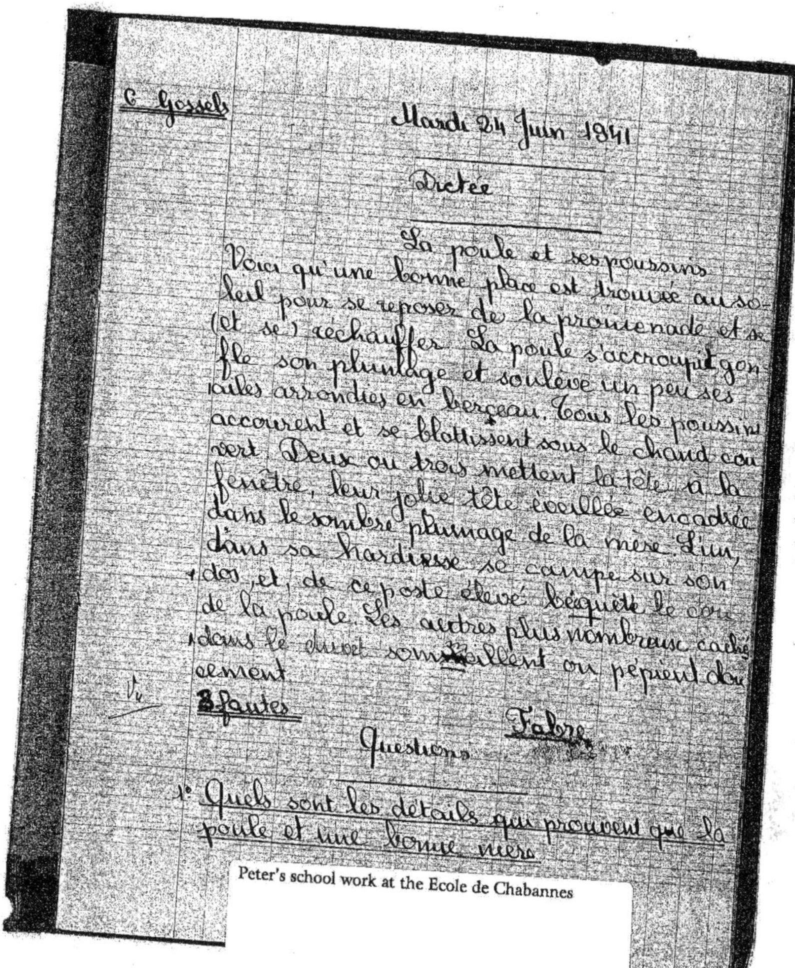
C. Gossels

Mardi 24 Juin 1941

Dictée

La poule et ses poussins

Voici qu'une bonne place est trouvée au soleil pour se reposer de la promenade et se
(et se) réchauffer. La poule s'accroupit gon-
fle son plumage et soulève un peu ses
ailes arrondies en berceau. Tous les poussins
accourent et se blottissent sous le chaud couvert. Deux ou trois mettent la tête à la
fenêtre, leur jolie tête éveillée encadrée
dans le sombre plumage de la mère. L'un,
dans sa hardiesse se campe sur son
dos, et, de ce poste élevé béquète le cou
de la poule. Les autres plus nombreux cachés
dans le duvet sommeillent ou pépient dou-
cement.

Vu

3 fautes

Fabre

Questions

1° Quels sont les détails qui prouvent que la
poule est une bonne mère

Peter's school work at the Ecole de Chabannes

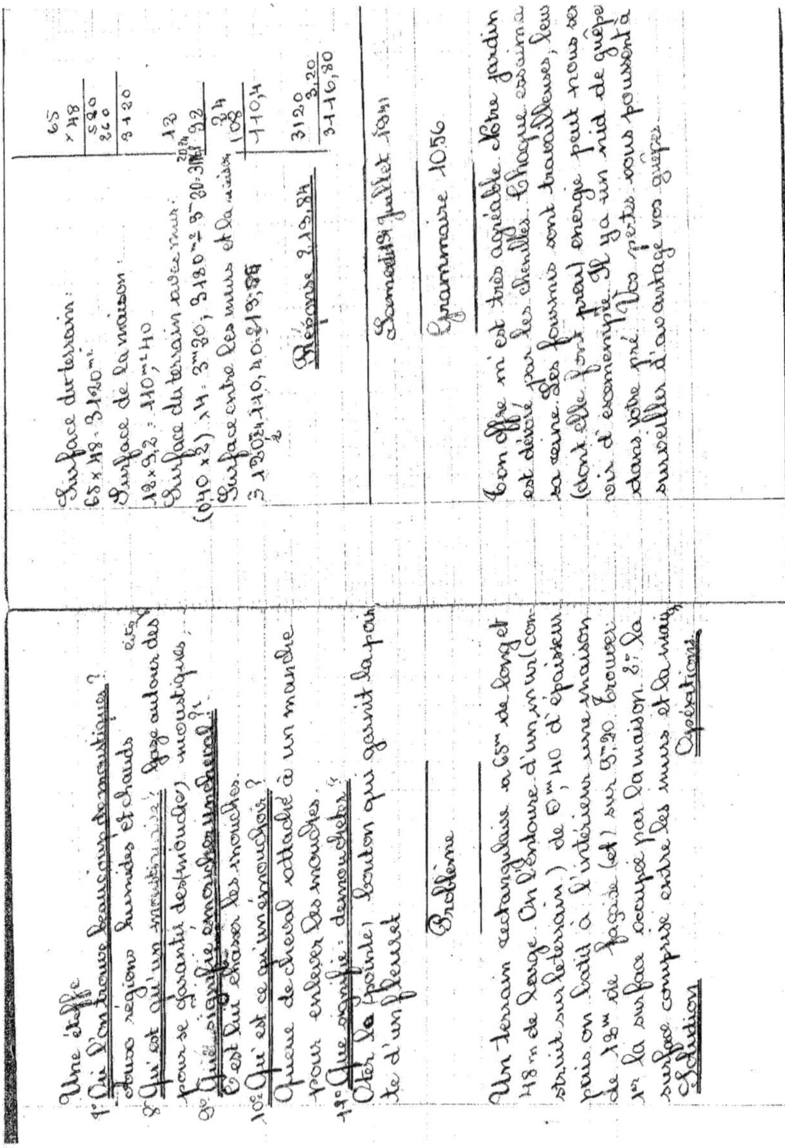

Une étoffe
7° Où l'on trouve beaucoup de moustiques ?
Aux régions humides et chauds etc.
8° Qu'est qu'un moustiquaire ? Gaze autour des
pour se garantir des (mouches) moustiques ;
9° Que signifie émoucher un cheval ?
C'est lui chasser les mouches.
10° Qu'est ce qu'un émouchoir ?
Queue de cheval attaché à un manche
pour enlever les mouches.
11° Que signifie : demoucheter ?
Ôter la (pointe) bouton qui garnit la pointe d'un fleuret

Problème

Un terrain rectangulaire a 65m de long et 48m de large. On l'entoure d'un mur (construit sur le terrain) de 0m,40 d'épaisseur puis on batit à l'intérieur une maison de 12m de façade (et) sur 9m,20. Trouver 1° la surface occupée par la maison. 2° la surface comprise entre les murs et la maison
Solution Opérations.

Surface du terrain :
65 × 48 = 3120m²
Surface de la maison :
12 × 9,2 = 110m²40
Surface du terrain avec mur :
(0,40 × 2) × 4 = 3m20 ; 3120m² − 3m20 = 3116
Surface entre les murs et la maison
3 120 − 110,40 = 213,84

Réponse 2.13,84

65 × 48 = 520, 260 = 3120
12 × 92 = 24, 108 = 110,4
3120 − 3,20 = 3116,80

Samedi 19 Juillet 1941

Grammaire 1056

Ton offre m'est très agréable. Notre jardin est dévoré par les chenilles. Chaque essaim a sa reine. Les fourmis sont travailleuses, leur (dont elle font preu) énergie peut nous servir d'exemple. Il y a un nid de guêpe dans votre pré. Vos pertes vous poussent à surveiller d'avantage vos guêpes.

Quel est son itinéraire

1° Les cultures industrielles en France sont le charbon au Nord et à l'Est et autour du massif central. Le fer près des bassins houillers. La laine en Berry à Mulhouse Lille, Troyes, Reims. La Betterave en Picardie

2° Je prends la Seine jusqu'à Paris. Je remonte la Marne et je prends le canal de la Marne au Rhin

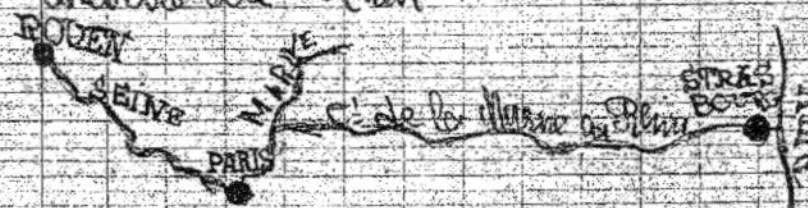

0

2 1/2

Note : 4/2

Composition de Sciences

1° Que savez-vous de l'évaporation ?
L'évaporation est quand un liquide se met à la forme gazeuse sans bouillir.
Comment active-t-on le séchage du linge mouillé ?
On active le séchage du linge en le pendant sur une place bien éclairée par le soleil ou dans un courant d'air

17

Pourquoi ne faut-il pas se placer dans courant d'air après une longue marche ?
Il ne faut pas se placer dans un courant d'air après une longue marche parce qu'on a chaud en se mettant dans un courant d'air on applique froid et on est malade

3

2° De quoi sont formés l'os ? Que devient un os placé dans le feu ? - dans un acide ?
L'os est formé de la moelle et de l'osséine.
Un os placé dans le feu commence à fumer et (l'osséine sort,) il ne reste que la partie dure.

1

Note 4

Enfant ayant appris le français pendant 2 ans. Excellents résultats — Enfant intelligent

L'Institutrice
Faillassoux

Chabannes Creuse — le 2 Août 1941.

During Franklin Delano Roosevelt's campaign for President in 1931, he sent his wife, Eleanor Roosevelt, to the Appalachian hills of West Virginia to report on the condition of the mining families living there. While gathering information about the people in that region, Eleanor met Clarence Pickett, who was the President of the American Friends Service Committee (the Quakers) and they remained friends.

In 1940, Clarence Pickett founded the United States Committee for the Care of European Children (USCOM) primarily to evacuate English children from British cities that were ravaged by German bombers. When Congress failed to enact the Wagner-Rogers bill that would have ordered the State Department to issue as many as 10,000 visas to European refugee children, Eleanor Roosevelt joined Clarence Pickett to persuade the State Department to issue some visas to children under the care of his USCOM. They succeeded in getting only 200 visas in 1941.

Sometime in March or April, 1941, a representative of the Quakers selected Werner and me as candidates to receive two of the two hundred visas that they hoped to obtain from the American Consulate in Marseille. No one knows why we were selected.

We were sent to Marseille, obtained our visas there, traveled to Lisbon on a train through Spain and sailed to America on the Serpa Pinto on September 9, 1941, under the auspices of the U.S. Committee for the Care of European Children created by the Quakers with financing from the Hebrew Immigrant Aid Society (HIAS) and the American Jewish Joint Distribution Committee.

After we arrived in New York on September 24, 1941, Werner and I, now under the jurisdiction of the U.S. Committee for the Care of European Children, were placed with separate Jewish families in South Brookline, Massachusetts: Werner with Louis and Mary

Gordon and I with Lawrence and Rose Singal, who had volunteered to take them in and care for them as part of their family. Werner and I lived only about a mile apart in South Brookline and saw each other at school, at the Temple and otherwise. We were both being followed by social workers of the Jewish Child Welfare Association in Boston until we reached our majority.

OUR MOTHER'S LAST LETTER TO US

November 10, 1941

My dear boys, Peter & Werner,

I waited each day with longing for your news until, at last, two days ago a detailed letter came to me from Aunt Lucy from New York in which she wrote that you had arrived there, but that you have not been placed in a permanent home yet so that she has not been able to visit you, something she would gladly have done.

I also understand that you, my dear Peter, had an accident during your trip and that you must stay in a hospital in New York. You may be sure, my dear little wanderer, that you must bear many more pains, and you, my dear Werner, have in the meanwhile decided to care for your brother in longing manner.

I hope that you, dear Peter, will have been released from the hospital in the meanwhile and that you will soon be with your foster parents so that you two will no longer be separated from each other.

It would make me very happy if you would write me a completely detailed account of your lovely trip, your arrival in New York and especially about Peter's accident. Was it the leg or the arm or what else? And are you still in pain or has everything healed? I must know everything exactly, otherwise I will be very worried.

I assume that you will have spoken with Aunt Lucy already when you will have received this letter. You must tell her everything, what makes you happy and what depresses you. You know that when you were still little she already loved you very much all the time and therefore you can have confidence in her and tell her everything.

In the event that I have heard correctly that you will remain in the neighborhood of New York, perhaps Aunt Fanny and Uncle Leo might visit you. Have you heard anything from Aunt Martha and Uncle Erich?

For a number of months already, we have received no mail from you.

How is it there as far as your schooling is concerned? Now you must adjust once more. But when one is still so young as you two, it goes quickly and hardly matters and it is also much easier to learn English than French.

Did you already know that Egon Heismann is here again and lives one floor above us with the Abrahams. He asks about you all the time. During the six months that he has been here, he has become a big boy and already earns money. He can't say enough about Werner, especially.

I also get together often with Erwin Cossman's father, but, as I heard, Erwin didn't travel together with you.

Were there many children in the group that you traveled with, or just the two of you?

I was delighted with your pictures on my birthday and if you should have such pictures again, send them to me without my having to ask for them.

Now another year has almost finished and the three of us want the firm will and the confidence that we will see each other again soon.

Work hard in school and make your foster parents happy. As I heard, you will be placed with a family and not into a home, but I don't know anything exact about it, and I am waiting for your exact answer concerning this. In either case, whatever it may be, whether a home or a family, always be obedient and work hard! And always care for each other because you both always belong together.

Concerning us, there isn't much else to tell. Oma is better again so that she can cook and keep busy in the house again. Aunt Hilde and I are busy working and don't have much time for other things.

All is still the same with Aunt Betty and the Jacobsohn's and also with Aunt Kirchhoff, all of whom send you their best wishes.

Now, dear boys, live well for today, write immediately how you are doing. Send your letter to Aunt Lucy so that it may be sent to me by airmail, otherwise it will take too long to reach me.

I embrace and kiss you both with Love.

Your
Mutti

From Oma, hearty greetings and kisses.

Dear Peter, a good and rapid recovery and don't be unhappy, everything will be alright soon.

Charlotte Gossels Berlin NO.55., den 10. November 1941.
Lippehnerstrasse 35.II.

Meine geliebten Jungen, Peterle und Werni!

Sehnsüchtig wartete ich jeden Tag auf Nachricht von Euch, bis endlich vor ein paar Tagen von Tante Lucy aus New York ein ausführlicher Brief an mich kam, indem sie mir schreibt, dass Ihr dort angekommen, XXXX aber noch nicht endgültig untergebracht seid, sodass sie Euch noch nicht besuchen konnte, was sie so gern getan hätte. Ich erfuhr auch, dass Du, mein geliebtes Peterle, unterwegs einen Unfall gehabt hast und im Krankenhause in New York liegen musstest. Gewiss hast Du, mein lieber kleiner Strolch, viel böse Schmerzen aushalten müssen, und Du, mein geliebtes Wernerchen, hast Dich inzwischen bestimmt um Deinen Bruder gesorgt und Sehnsucht gehabt. Ich hoffe, dass Du, geliebtes Peterle, indessen, aus dem Krankenhause entlassen und schon bei Deinen Pflegeeltern bist, sodass Ihr beide nun nicht mehr von einander getrennt seid. Ihr würdet mir eine sehr grosse Freude machen, wenn Ihr mir nun einmal ganz ausführlich über Eure schöne Reise, die Ankunft in New York und ganz besonders über Peterchens Unfall schreiben würdet. War es das Bein oder der Arm, oder was sonst?? Und hast Du noch Schmerzen, oder ist alles gut geheilt? Ich muss alles genau wissen, sonst mache ich mir zu grosse Sorgen. Ich nehme an, dass Ihr, wenn Ihr diesen Brief erhaltet, Tante Lucy schon gesprochen haben werdet. Ihr sollt ihr alles erzählen, was Euch Freude macht, und was Euch bedrückt. Ihr wisst doch, dass sie Euch, als Ihr noch kleiner wart, schon immer sehr lieb hatte, und so dürft Ihr Vertrauen zu ihr haben und ihr alles erzählen. Da ich erfahren habe, dass Ihr in der Nähe von New York bleiben werdet, könnt Ihr vielleicht auch mal Tante Fanny und Onkel Leo besuchen. Hört Ihr mal etwas von Tante Martha und Onkel Erich? Wir haben schon seit Monaten keinen Brief mehr von ihnen. Wie ist es dort mit der Schule? Nun müsst Ihr wieder umlernen, aber, wenn man noch so jung ist, wie Ihr es beide seid, geht das schnell und macht einem fast garnichts aus, und es ist auch viel leichter Englisch zu lernen als Französisch. Dass Egon Heisemann wieder hier ist und eine Treppe über uns, bei Abrahams wohnt, wisst Ihr das eigentlich schon? Er fragt jedesmal nach Euch. Er ist in dem halben Jahr, das er nun hier ist, ein grosser Junge geworden und verdient schon Geld. Er kann, besonders von Dir, Wernerchen garnicht genug erzählen. Mit Erwin Cosmann's Vater komme ich auch öfter zusammen, aber, wie ich hörte, ist Erwin nicht mit Euch zusammen gefahren. Wart Ihr beim Transport viele Kinder, oder nur Ihr beide? Mit Euren Bildern zu meinem Geburtstage habe ich mich sehr gefreut, und, wenn Ihr wieder mal welche habt, schickt sie mir, ohne, dass ich erst danach frage. Nun ist schon bald wieder ein Jahr herum, und wir Drei wollen den festen Willen und die Zuversicht haben, dass wir uns bald wiedersehen werden. Gebt Euch viel Mühe in der Schule und macht Euren Pflegeeltern Freude. Wie ich hörte, sollt Ihr in eine Familie kommen und nicht in ein Heim; aber etwas Genaues weiss ich nicht darüber, und erwarte daher Euren genauen Bescheid. Jedenfalls, wie es auch sei, ob Heim oder Familie, immer gehorchen und fleissig sein! Und immer Einer für den Anderen sorgen, denn Ihr Beide gehört für immer zusammen.... Von uns ist nichts Besonderes zu erzählen. Oma geht's wieder besser, sodass sie wieder kochen und sich im Haushalt beschäftigen kann. Tante Hilde und ich arbeiten fleissig und haben nicht viel Zeit für andere Dinge. Bei Tante Betty und Jacobsohn's und auch bei Tante Kirchhoff, die Euch alle sehr grüssen lassen, ist noch alles beim Alten.

Nun, geliebte Jungen, lebt wohl für heute, schreibt umgehend, wie es Euch geht. Schickt Euren Brief an Tante Lucy, damit er "per Luftpost" an mich abgeht, da es sonst zu lange dauert bis ich ihn bekomme. Seid Beide umarmt und geküsst in Liebe von

Eurer Mutti

Sometime in 2005, Peter decided to translate his mother's last letter and to share it with everyone in the family. It was a deeply moving experience for us all.

I was in a memoir writing class at the time and felt compelled to write a letter of my own to this extraordinary woman.

Nancy Lee Gossels

2005

Dear Lotte,

I have wanted to write to you for such a long time. You are the mother-in-law I never met, the grandmother my children never knew. We have so few tangible objects to remember you by – some photographs, an Hagadah and the remarkable letters that you wrote to your two young sons, Peter, my husband of nearly 47 years, and his younger brother, Werner. They were not yet nine and not yet six when they saw you for the last time as you put them on a train in Berlin bound for the safety of France on July 4th, 1939. An early photograph shows you as a beautiful, young girl, looking pensive and confident. A later photograph shows you as an intelligent, exuberant and happy young woman. You were tall and slender with an elegant, almond-shaped face and the Lewy nose which your son, Peter, and our daughter, Lisa, have inherited from you. The very last photograph, though, shows you looking older and sadder. There is pain in your eyes. You had reason to be sad.

Life in Berlin in those years was horrific. But you were a courageous woman. When you saw your boys encircled by a group of Hitler youth, you ran outside to take them by the hand and lead them safely home. You had the courage to divorce the man who was your husband when your children were only 6 and 3; it was not the conventional thing to do in those days when marriages turned sour, but you were not one to be intimidated by anyone. When you understood the danger looming ahead for your sons, you managed through persistence and tenacity to get them the visas needed for them to leave Germany. I can not imagine what it must have felt like for you to part with your beloved boys. I often wonder whether I could have done as you did. I pray that you had some comfort knowing that you were responsible for their escape to a safe haven.

You were also granted a visa, but you could not leave your dear mother behind, who was ailing. By the time you next applied, it was too late. Your mother was sent to Therezinstadt where she died. And we never knew for certain what happened to you. Peter tried so hard to find you; he always hoped that somehow, somewhere you had survived the horror. And so he never said Kaddish for you, the memorial prayer for the dead. That is, until 1991 when the records of Auschwitz were made available to the public. Your name was listed among those who were murdered there. We made the journey to Auschwitz with our three children, Lisa (who is named for you), Amy and Daniel, to honor you, to be witnesses to that place of death, that sterile museum of now silent terror. When Peter led a service in the Memorial room, there were no dry eyes. You died on March 2 in 1943. You were 39 years old. Peter now says Kaddish for you.

I have read and reread your last letter many time – it was written on November 10, 1941. I can not read it without weeping.

The love you had for your sons and the pain you felt at your separation are so apparent. Do you remember your words? Peter translated them from the German. Here are some excerpts: "My dear boys, Peter & Werner,

I waited each day with longing for your news until, at last, two days ago a detailed letter came to me from Aunt Lucy from New York in which she wrote that you had arrived there, but that you have not been placed in a permanent home yet . . . I also understand that you, my dear Peter, had an accident during your trip and that you must stay in a hospital in New York. You may be sure, my dear little wanderer, that you must bear many (sore) pains . . . It would make me very happy if you would write me a completely detailed account of your lovely trip, your arrival in New York and especially about Peter's accident. Was it the leg or the arm or what else? And are you still in pain or has everything healed? I must know everything exactly, otherwise I will be very worried. I assume that you will have spoken with Aunt Lucy already when you will have received this letter. You must tell her everything, what makes you happy and what depresses you. You know that when you were still little she already loved you very much all the time and therefore you can have confidence in her and tell her everything. . . . For a number of months already, we have received no mail from you. How is it there as far as your schooling is concerned? Now you must adjust once more. But when one is still so young as you two, it goes quickly and hardly matters and it is also much easier to learn English than French. . . . Were there many children in the group that you traveled with, or just the two of you? I was delighted with your pictures on my birthday and if you should have such pictures again, send them to me without my having to ask for them. Now another year has almost finished and the three of us want the firm will and the confidence that we will see each other again soon. Work hard in school and make your foster parents happy. . . . And always care for each other because you both always belong together. . . . Now, dear boys, live well for today, write immediately how you are doing. . . . I embrace and kiss you both with Love, Your Mutti"

I want you to know, dear Lotte, that your boys do care for each other. They have grown into men you would be proud of. You would smile to know that they both live in the same town and see each other very often, sharing Shabbat dinners, holidays and festivals together and mutual interests in town affairs. They have inherited your spirit and your courage. They are both activists. They are outspoken for what they believe in, they have held public office in their communities. They have a strong sense of justice; they are philanthropic and they are caring. For over 30 years Peter was a major light in a synagogue where he was driven by his strong desire to revitalize Judaism by working to bring joy to service and to reinvigorate its liturgy – all this so as not to allow Hitler a posthumous victory. Our two families have dedicated a room in your memory at Wayland's Public Library and created funds to promote human dignity in your name. You have 8 grandchildren and 11 great-grandchildren.

Though Werner was too young to have vivid memories, he keeps your picture in a place of honor in his living room. And Peter has never forgotten you. Though his life is filled with joy and fulfillment, he carries within him a core of sadness which I feel certain developed the moment he said "good-bye" to you at the train station, the moment he knew at that tender age he would never see you again.

And though I never had the privilege of meeting you, I feel in my very being that I know you, that our hearts are somehow touching across the silence of the years. Your presence has never left us, dear Lotte. Rest in peace.

Nancy

Lotte learned about the arrival of Werner and me in the United States from a letter she had received from her cousin, Lucy Lewy, who was working as a chemist in Tarrytown, New York, as indicated in her last letter to her children dated November 10, 1941.

On December 7, 1941, the Japanese attacked Pearl Harbor and the United States entered a state of war against Japan and Nazi Germany. Ordinary mail between the two countries ceased.

Sometime thereafter, Lotte and Hilde were compelled to work at the following factories: Lotte worked at "Deuta Werke", which made railroad communications equipment at that time, and Hilde was compelled to work at "A.E.G. Fernmeldekabel-und Apparatenfabrik Oberspree", a company that may have made telecommunications equipment.

Lina was deported to the concentration camp at Theresienstadt (Terezin) in Czechoslovakia on April 4, 1942. Lotte suffered a nervous breakdown when Lina was abducted, which afflicted her for a long time, even though she may have obtained permission to travel to Switzerland at that time.

Lina died at Terezin on November 23, 1942.

On Saturday, February 27, 1943, Hilde was taken from her home and subsequently put on a train bound for Auschwitz. Lotte was deported the following day. She took luggage along for Hilde.

According to the records we obtained from the archives, neither Hilde nor Lotte were given a number when they arrived at Auschwitz on March 1 and March 2 respectively, indicating they were murdered there shortly after their arrival. Our Mutti was thirty-nine years old.

That same day, March 2, 1943, the Sixth German Army surrendered to the Russians at Stalingrad, marking the beginning of the end of the Nazi regime.

ČESKOSLOVENSKÁ UMĚLECKÁ AGENTURA

MALTÉZSKÉ NÁM. 1, 118 13 PRAHA 1 • TELEFON: 533441-9 • TELEGRAM: PRAGOKONCERT PRAHA • TELEX: PRAGOKONCERT 12181C

VAŠE ZN.:
NAŠE ZN.:

Mr.C.Peter R.Gossels
ATTORNEY AT LAW
84 State Street
BOSTON
MA 02109

PRAHA 23.IX.1992.

Dear Peter,

I am answering your fax from the 16.IX.1992. I hope, that this time it will be in order.

Some explanations to the copy of the register card which I have found in the card index from Terezin - ghetto :

The number I/71 is the number of the transport which was send on the 4.IV.-1942 from Berlin to Terezin.
The second part - 8484, was the personal number of Mrs.Lewy.
[redacted]
of the Card.
12907 is the number of the coffin. The body of Mrs.Lewy was crematised, because in that time the crematorium was already working. When it happend I could not find out.

I hope that this is what you wanted.

With friendly regards to you, and your family.

Your

Jiří Vrba
Advisor to the General-Director
Pragokoncert

VYŘIZUJE:

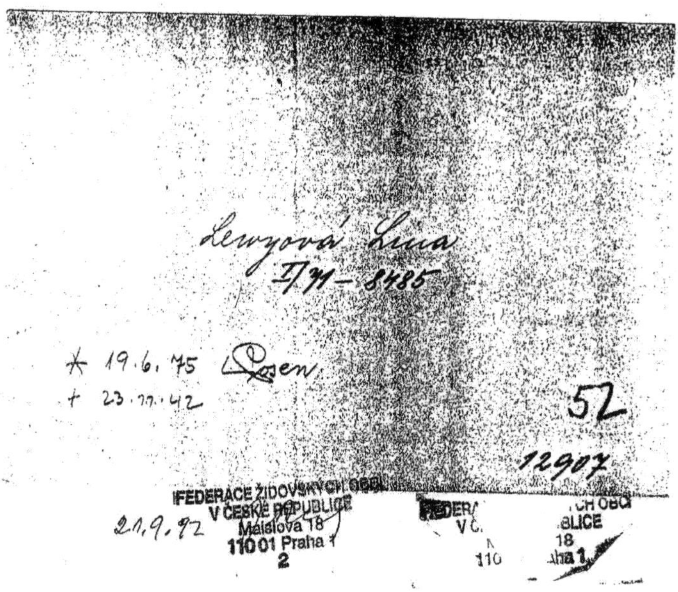
Lewyová Lina
I/71 - 8485
* 19.6.75 Posen
+ 23.11.42
52
12907
21.9.92
FEDERACE ŽIDOVSKÝCH OBCÍ
V ČESKÉ REPUBLICE
Maislova 18
110 01 Praha 1
2

A copy of the register card for Lena Lewy found
in the card index from Terezin

Oświęcim — Brzezinka, dn. 25 stycznia 1994 r.

L. dz. IV-8521/5601-5602/4715/93

PAŃSTWOWE
MUZEUM
OŚWIĘCIM
BRZEZINKA

BPH OŚWIĘCIM
KONTO 320629-5177-131

CENTRALA TELEF.
320-22 lub 320-77

MUZEUM CZYNNE
CODZIENNIE
W GODZ. 8—15

PRZYJAZD
ZWIEDZAJĄCYCH
NALEŻY
WCZEŚNIEJ
ZGŁOSIĆ

C. Peter R. Gossels
ATTORNEY AT LAW
84 State Street
BOSTON, MASS 02109
USA

Panstwowe Muzeum w Oświęcimiu informuje, że

GOSSELS Lotte zd. LEWY ur.7.9 1903 r Berlin, figuruje na spisie osob deportowanych w dniu 2.3 1943 r. 32 transportem RSHA Żydow z Berlina.

LEWY Hildegard ur.24.9.1901 r. Berlin, figuruje na spisie osob deportowanych w dniu 1.3.1943 r. 31 transportem RSHA Żydow z Berlina.

Zachowanę w stanie szczątkowym archiwalia KL Auschwitz-Birkenau nie pozwalają na ustalenie czy wymienione przybył do obozu i jakie były ich dalsze losy.

PODSTAWA informacji:

nazwiskowe spisy osob deportowanych z Berlina do KL Auschwitz-Birkenau.

W dalszych poszukiwaniach Muzeum radzi zwrócić się na adres:
INTERNATIONALER SUCHDIENST
Grosse Allee 5 - 9
D - 34444 A R O L S E N
D E U T S C H L A N D

D Y R E K T O R
/mgr Jerzy Wróblewski/

AL

Information in Polish from the authorities at Auschwitz concerning Lotte (Lewy) Gossels and Hildegard Lewy

Information in Polish from the authorities at Auschwitz concerning Lotte (Lewy) Gossels and Hildegard Lewy

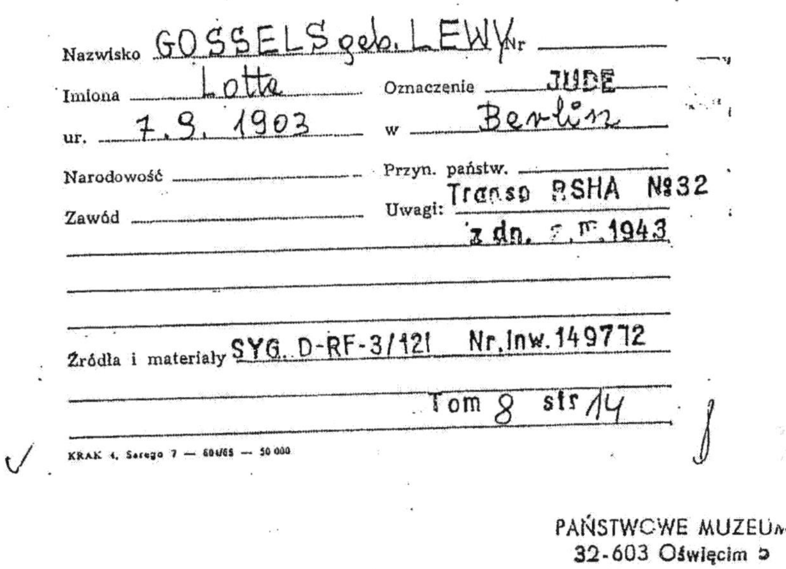

Nazwisko GOSSELS geb. LEWY Nr

Imiona Lotta Oznaczenie JUDE

ur. 7.9.1903 w Berlin

Narodowość Przyn. państw.

Zawód Uwagi: Transp RSHA №32 z dn. 2.III.1943

Źródła i materiały SYG. D-RF-3/121 Nr.Inw.149772

Tom 8 str 14

KRAK 4, Sarego 7 — 604/65 — 50 000

PAŃSTWOWE MUZEUM
32-603 Oświęcim 5

A copy of the register card for Lotte (Lewy) Gossels received from the authorities at Auschwitz

THE STORY CONTINUES

Peter's Story

After living two and a half years with the Singal family in South Brookline, Massachusetts, I was sent to a group home in the Mattapan section of Boston owned by Pauline Perlman, thereby becoming the first Jewish boy to do so, as the Jewish community of Mattapan gradually moved to the upscale communities of Brookline and Newton. The move proved to be a blessing for me, however, because, as a resident of Mattapan, I became eligible to attend Boston Latin School, which ultimately opened the doors of Harvard University for me. While living in Mattapan, I worked after school as a soda jerk, a movie usher, as a clerk in a candy store and in a book store to help support myself.

After graduating from Boston Latin School, I obtained my A.B. degree from Harvard College with honors in three years. I studied law at Harvard Law School, obtained my LL.B. degree in 1954 and served in the U.S. Army from October 1954 to July 1956.

In 1955 I was admitted to the Massachusetts Bar. I was subsequently admitted to the Bar of the U.S. District Court for the District of Massachusetts in 1957, the Bar of the U.S. Court of Appeals for the First Circuit in 1957 and the Supreme Court of the United States in 1965.

Upon my discharge from the Army in 1956, I joined the Boston law firm of Sullivan and Worcester where I spent most of my time as a trial lawyer. In 1965, I joined the law firm of Zelman, Gossels and Alexander.

I married Nancy Lee Tuber on June 29, 1958 in Brookline, Massachusetts. We moved to Wayland, Massachusetts in 1961. After serving as a member of the Finance Committee of the Town of Wayland, Massachusetts between 1966 and 1968, and as Wayland's Town Counsel for eleven years. I was elected Moderator of the Town of Wayland in 1982 and served Wayland as its Moderator until 2011. During this time, I implemented the first system of electronic voting to be used at New England town meetings.

As a member of the Boston Bar Association, I served as Chair of the Section on International Legal Practice between 1962 and 1967. In that capacity, I organized and produced *The New England Conference on Legal Problems on Doing Business Abroad*, which attracted large audiences each year. In 1970, I worked with Michael Dukakis, soon-to-be-Governor of Massachusetts, to create and enact the first system of no-fault automobile insurance protection in the United States. I also helped to draft G.L. c. 183A, the statute that authorized the creation of condominiums in Massachusetts, the second state after Hawaii to do so.

Between 1965 and 1970, I served as Adjunct Professor of International Business Law at Boston University.

In 1966, I was appointed to Wayland's Finance Committee.

In 1968, I was appointed Town Counsel of the Town of Wayland.

In 1972, I joined the Boston law firm of Weston Patrick and have worked there ever since.

In 1974, I was appointed Town Counsel of the Town of Boxborough. I also served the Towns of Needham and Franklin as Special Counsel at a later date.

While serving as president of Congregation Beth El of the Sudbury River Valley in Sudbury, Massachusetts (1977-1979), I also worked as co-editor with my wife Nancy Lee Gossels and Joan S. Kaye of the first egalitarian Jewish prayer book (or siddur) *Vetaher Libenu* published in 1980. The book featured nonsexist, inclusive language and revised the traditional Hebrew translation of "Baruch attah Adonai Eloheinu, melech ha'olam", or "Praised are You, Lord, our God, King of the Universe" to "Holy One of Blessing, Your Presence Fills Creation". I also served as co-editor of *Chadesh Yamenu*, an egalitarian machzor for Rosh HaShanah (1997) and *Kanfay HaShachar* (2003), a siddur for weekday morning prayer.

Between 1976 and 1981, Nancy and I served on the National Commission on Worship of the Union for Reform Judaism.

I co-authored the report of the Boston Bar Association's Work Group on Cost and Time Efficiencies in the Massachusetts Courts in 2005. I have published articles in the Boston Bar Journal and Massachusetts Lawyers Weekly, which may be found at my website, www.gosselslaw.com. I served as Chair of the Fee Disputes Committee of the Boston Bar Association from 2000 to 2010 and as a hearing officer for the Massachusetts Board of Bar Overseers from 2006 to 2012. I have earned the highest "A.V." rating from the publishers of the *Martindale Hubbell Law Directory* and was included among Boston's Top Rated Lawyers, according to the Boston Globe 2012 and 2014 ratings.

Since 1998, I have hosted an annual two-hour cable television program in Wayland, Massachusetts, "Ask the Candidates Live!", which allows voters to ask questions to candidates for public office in Wayland, Massachusetts.

I retired from the practice of law on September 30, 2019 after 63 years of practicing law.

Nancy's Story

NANCY LEE GOSSELS was born in Norwich, Connecticut. She was raised in Putnam, Connecticut by her parents, Benjamin Michael and Sadie Pearl Tuber (nee Zaltas) and received a Bachelor of Arts degree (magna cum laude) from Pembroke College (Brown University) and was elected into the Phi Beta Kappa Society.

Nancy married C. Peter R. Gossels in 1958. They have three children born in Boston: Lisa R. (b. 1960), Amy D. (b. 1962) and Daniel J. Gossels (b. 1967), who married Jackie Chae in 2015 and gave birth to Sophia Rose on March 16, 2017.

Nancy worked at *The Atlantic Monthly* from 1956 to 1958 and subsequently served as associate editor of *Child Life Magazine* from 1958 to 1960. Between 1962 and 1964, Nancy worked as a reporter and columnist for the *Cochituate/Wayland/Weston Town Crier*. From 1976 to 1977, Nancy served as chair of the building committee of Congregation Beth El of the Sudbury River Valley. In this capacity, she oversaw the enlargement of the temple building.

Nancy began her artistic career as a painter, but over time found that her painting was becoming more and more sculptural. In 1986 she and her cousin, Brenda Zaltas, exchanged ideas about designing outdoor sculptures from found metal, discovered that the metal shapes reminded them of chanukiot and embarked on a new career. Although they work separately, they shared a vision and often showed their work together at art exhibits and galleries.

Since the late 1980s, Nancy has received national attention for her unique "found metal" sculptures, both religious and non-religious, which "have been shown in museums, galleries and selected juried exhibitions" across the U.S., including the Bronx Museum of the Arts, Yeshiva University Museum, the National Museum of American Jewish History in Philadelphia, Mizel Museum in Denver and the Flagler Museum in Palm Beach.

In 1988, the "In the Spirit Studio/Gallery" in New York City featured her aluminum and brass menorah titled "*Brave New World*". McCalls featured Nancy's *Reflections*, a Chanukah lamp with bronze mirror back, in its December 1990 article, "The Art of the Menorah". The General Assembly of the Council of Jewish Federations, Combined Jewish Philanthropies included a gift shop that displayed "unique Jewish artworks from throughout the world" including Nancy's menorah works created from industrial metals.

In 1996, Nancy was named a "Copley Artist" by the Copley Society of Art, the oldest art association in America. In order to qualify for this honor, an artist must meet the demanding standards for membership in the society and must have his or her work accepted into five different juried shows produced by the society. Nancy received her art training at the DeCordova Museum School in Lincoln, Massachusetts. She also took classes with Boston area artists Glenda Tall and George Dergalis. Her works are also represented in a growing number of private collectors.

In addition to her sculpture, Nancy is a poet. According to an interview in the *Wayland Town Crier*, designing sculptural pieces made her realize "the connection between the written word and the visual piece."

While serving as a member of the National Commission on Worship of the Jewish reform movement between 1976 and 1980 and as Vice President of Congregation Beth El of the Sudbury River Valley in Sudbury, Massachusetts, Nancy composed and edited (with Joan S. Kaye and her husband, C. Peter R. Gossels) the first egalitarian Jewish prayer book for the Sabbath and Festivals, *Vetaher Libenu*, which was published in 1980. Among the many innovations contained in *Vetaher Libenu*, Nancy and Joan revised the traditional Hebrew translation of "Baruch attah Adonai Eloheinu, melech ha'olam", or "Praised are You, Lord, our God, King of the Universe" to "Holy One of Blessing, Your Presence Fills Creation". They also included the matriarchs in the Tefilah (the Amidah), a practice that has been followed by the new siddurim and machzorim published by the Central Conference of American Rabbis.

This siddur, which has sold more than 10,000 copies worldwide, contains many liturgical poems written by Nancy (including her well-known poem, "*Somewhere Out of Time*"), which have been widely republished, translated into German, anthologized and included in the Singing the Living Tradition hymnal of the Unitarian Universalism Association.

Nancy's poetry has also been included in the anthologies *"Sarah's Daughters Sing", "Esther erhebt ihre Stimme", "Kol HaNeshamah, Celebrating the New Moon", "The Torah: A Woman's Commentary", "Covenant of the Generations"* and *"Gates of Shabbat: A Guide for Observing Shabbat"*. Nancy also served as the editor of *Chadesh Yamenu (Renew Our Days)*, an Egalitarian machzor for Rosh HaShanah, published in 1997, and *Kanfay HaShachar (Wings of Dawn)*, a siddur for weekly morning worship published in 2003.

In 2011, Nancy co-edited *Veha'er Eyneynu (Enlighten Our Eyes)* with Michael Mirman, Harry Abadi and Sheila R. Deitchman.

In 2005, Nancy and Peter were honored by the Massachusetts Association of School Committees for their commitment to public education and their generosity of time, energy and support to enhance the educational opportunities of students at Wayland High School by creating and endowing (with Peter's brother, Werner F. Gossels, and Elaine Gossels) the Gossels Fund for Academic Excellence and the Gossels Fund for Human Dignity.

Nancy served as a trustee of the Exploration School from 2001 to 2011, a summer enrichment program for approximately 3,000 students from Grade 4 through high school on the campuses of the St. Mark's School (Massachusetts), Wellesley College and Yale University.

Nancy currently serves as a member of the board of directors of the Boston Jewish Film.

קריאת התורה

Reading the Torah

Somewhere out of time
In the mystery of time
Somewhere between memory and forgetfulness,
Dimly though
I remember how once I stood
At Your mountain trembling
Amid the fire and the thunder.
How I stood there, out of bondage
In a strange land and afraid.
And You loved me and You fed me
And I feasted on Your words.
And, yes, I can remember
How the thunder was my heart
And the fire was my soul.
O God, I do remember.
The fire burns in me anew.
And here I am, once more
A witness to that timeless moment.
Present now in the light of Your Torah
I am reborn.

Peter (on the far right) at a Boston Quiz Kid on the WHDH national radio program December 1944

Pvt. C. Peter Gossels, Fort Bragg, North Carolina in November, 1954

The Commonwealth of Massachusetts
EDWARD J. CRONIN
SECRETARY OF THE COMMONWEALTH
DIVISION OF VITAL STATISTICS

450

COPY OF CERTIFICATE OF MARRIAGE
For the use of Clergyman or magistrate solemnizing marriage
(SEE INSTRUCTIONS ON MARGIN)

BROOKLINE
(City or town making return)

Registered No. 425

PLACE OF MARRIAGE (City or town) BROOKLINE
(Do not enter name of village or section of city or town)

DATE OF MARRIAGE June 29, 1958
(Month) (Day) (Year)

GROOM		BRIDE	
FULL NAME	Claus Peter R. Gossels	13 FULL NAME (Also maiden name, if widowed or divorced)	Nancy L. Tuber
AGE AT LAST BIRTHDAY (Years)	27	14 AGE AT LAST BIRTHDAY (Years)	23
5 COLOR	White	15 COLOR	White
RESIDENCE	Boston, Mass.	16 RESIDENCE	Boston, Mass.
NUMBER OF MARRIAGE (1st, 2d, 3d, etc.)	1st	17 NUMBER OF MARRIAGE (1st, 2d, 3d, etc.)	1st
8 WIDOWED OR DIVORCED	single	18 WIDOWED OR DIVORCED	single
OCCUPATION	Attorney	19 OCCUPATION	----
BIRTHPLACE (City or town) (State or country)	Germany	20 BIRTHPLACE (City or town) (State or country)	Norwich Conn.
NAME OF FATHER	Max Gossels	21 NAME OF FATHER	Benjamin M. Tuber
MAIDEN NAME OF MOTHER	Charlotte Lewy	22 MAIDEN NAME OF MOTHER	Sadie P. Zaltas

The Town Clerk of BROOKLINE (City or town) HEREBY CERTIFY that the foregoing is a true copy of the Certificate of Marriage issued June 23, 1958 (Month) (Day) (Year) by Charles H. Mackie (Name of clerk) Clerk of the city (or town) of Boston Massachusetts, and the persons named therein were joined in marriage by me, at No. Temple Emeth St. (If marriage was solemnized in a church, give its NAME instead of street and number) BROOKLINE on June 29, 1958 (Month) (Day) (Year) in the city (or town) of

Zev K. Nelson Official station Rabbi (Minister of the Gospel, Clergyman, Priest, Rabbi, or Justice of the Peace)

Residence No. 258 Russett Road St., City or Town of Brookline

Received by city or town clerk July 7, 1958 [signature] REGISTRAR

I, the undersigned, hereby certify that I am the Registrar of Vital Records and Statistics; that as such I have custody of the records of birth, marriage and death required by law to be kept in my office; and I do hereby certify that the above is a true copy from said records. WITNESS my hand and the SEAL OF THE DEPARTMENT OF PUBLIC HEALTH at Boston on the date inscribed hereon. SEPTEMBER 21, 2000

Elaine B. Trudeau
ELAINE B. TRUDEAU
Registrar

IT IS ILLEGAL TO ALTER OR REPRODUCE THIS DOCUMENT IN ANY MANNER

THE NEW ENGLAND CONFERENCE

on

LEGAL PROBLEMS of DOING BUSINESS ABROAD

1964

Sponsored by the
Boston Bar Association Through Its
Committee on International Legal Practice*

April 25, 1964
Sheraton Plaza Hotel
Boston, Massachusetts

COMMITTEE ON INTERNATIONAL LEGAL PRACTICE

C. Peter R. Gossels, *Committee Chairman*
Sullivan & Worcester

Robert B. Fraser, *Conference Chairman*
Goodwin, Procter & Hoar

Donald Baker
Nutter, McLennen & Fish
Michael Baram
Massachusetts Institute of Technology
William S. Barnes
Harvard Law School
Prof. Richard R. Baxter
Harvard Law School
John F. Cogan, Jr.
Hale & Dorr
Walker B. Comegys
Goodwin, Procter & Hoar
Bryan E. Concannon
Choate, Hall & Stewart
Frederic G. Corneel
Sullivan & Worcester
Belden Hull Daniels
The First National Bank of Boston
Jean E. deValpine
Powers, Hall, Montgomery & Weston
Jose DeVaron
Eastern Gas & Fuel Associates
Patricia Foley
John Hancock Mutual Life Ins. Co.

Walter F. Greeley
Cabot Corporation
June D. Hawker
Choate, Hall & Stewart
Robert Haydock, Jr.
Bingham, Dana & Gould
Martha Henissart
Raytheon Company
Charles E. Holly
Weston, Patrick & Stevens
Sheldon Z. Kaplan
Herbert S. Kassman
Polaroid Corporation
William A. Krebs, Jr.
Arthur D. Little, Inc.
Hans F. Loeser
Foley, Hoag & Eliot
Robert W. Maynard
United Shoe Machinery Corporation
William C. Munroe
United Shoe Machinery Corporation
Richard T. Murphy, Jr.
Arthur D. Little, Inc.

Conrad W. Oberdorfer
Choate, Hall & Stewart
Arthur H. Phillips
Cabot Corporation
Peter W. Princi
Roy S. Remar
Anthony O. Shallna
Shallna & Shallna
Henry B. Shepard, Jr.
Goodwin, Procter & Hoar
Russell Simpson
Goodwin, Procter & Hoar
Irwin Springer
Springer & Krock
Robert P. Springer
Springer & Goldberg
Charles H. Stockton
Choate, Hall & Stewart
Joseph B. Szabo
John Vincent, Jr.
Peabody, Koufman & Brewer
Richard A. Wiley
Bingham, Dana & Gould

**with the cooperation and support of*

Greater Boston Chamber of Commerce
International Trade Association of New England, Inc.
Massachusetts Society of Certified Public Accountants
U. S. Department of Commerce
World Affairs Council
World Trade Center of New England, Inc.

Top left photo, left to right: *Robert Fraser, Senator Saltonstall, Peter Gossels, Wolfgang Friedman.*

Bottom photo, left to right: *Henry Shepard, Albert Redway, Henry Sheehy, Charles Warden.*

International Legal Practice

ON April 13, 1963, the Boston Bar Association through its Committee on International Legal Practice, produced and sponsored the New England Conference on Legal Problems of Doing Business Abroad — 1963 at the Statler Hilton Hotel in Boston. The purpose of the Conference, like the Conference held last year, was to make available to the Bar and the business community of New England, if only for one day, the experience and learning of some of the more distinguished practitioners in the field in international legal and commercial practice.

The Committee, under the chairmanship of C. Peter R. Gossels, Esq., of the firm of Sullivan & Worcester, received support and cooperation from many leading organizations including: American Society of International Law, Greater Boston Chamber of Commerce, International Trade Association of New England, Inc., Massachusetts Society of Certified Public Accountants, New England Council, U.S. Department of Commerce, World Affairs Council, World Trade Center of New England, Inc.

Thus, although a beautiful Saturday before Easter was chosen for the Conference, more than one hundred and thirty persons attended, nearly one-half of them being non-lawyers.

The program, planned and organized by a subcommittee, under the direction of Robert B. Fraser, Esq., of the firm of Goodwin, Procter & Hoar consisted of four sessions which were devoted to the following topics:

Legal Aspects of Foreign Investment were discussed by Wolfgang G. Friedmann, Esq., Professor of International Law and Director of International Legal Research, Columbia Law School, New York;

Tax Aspects of Doing Business Abroad were explained by a panel consisting of Robert B. Fraser, Esq., Goodwin, Procter & Hoar, Frederic G. Corneel, Esq., Sullivan & Worcester, Champe A. Fisher, Esq., Ropes & Gray, Carl A. Horne, Esq., United Shoe Machinery Corp.

The luncheon, graced by amber bottles of Vouvray, was crowned by a most interesting talk on Military Diplomacy and Business by the Senior Senator from Massachusetts, Leverett Saltonstall, a fellow member of the Association.

Common Market Antitrust Problems was the topic of the first afternoon panel composed of Jean E. deValpine, Esq., Powers, Hall, Montgomery & Weston, Conrad W. Oberdorfer, Esq., Choate, Hall & Stewart, Louis Schwartz, Esq., Professor of Law, University of Pennsylvania Law School; Visiting Professor of Law, Harvard Law School, and Richard A. Wiley, Esq., Bingham, Dana & Gould.

Ending on a spirited note the panel consisting of Henry G. Sheehy, President, Foreign Credit Insurance Association, Henry B. Shepard, Esq., Goodwin, Procter & Hoar, Mr. Charles B. Warden, Chief, Investment Guranties Division Agency for International Development, Department of State, and Mr. Albert J. Redway, Chief, Business Liaison Division, Export-Import Bank, and Edward G. Dineen, International Officer, First National Bank of Boston, brought the Conference to a close with a stimulating discussion of the sources and procedures for obtaining "Governmental Assistance to Companies Doing Business Abroad."

A printed outline of the Conference was distributed.

The Committee believes that the warm response to the Conference from those in attendance reflects a growing awareness in New England, indeed throughout the country, of the need for more vigorous competition by our exporters in the field of international trade.

To assist in this effort, the Committee on International Legal Practice will continue to cooperate with industry and the educational institutions of this area to raise the general level of competence among those engaged in doing business abroad.

C. Peter R. Gossels (second from right) with Massachusetts Governor John A. Volpe (seated) and others – April 1966

C. Peter R. Gossels with Massachusetts Governor Francis Sargent

Vetaher Libenu: The first egalitarian Jewish prayer book

See the article on www.wikipedia.org.

Chadesh Yamenu: An egalitarian Jewish prayer book for Rosh HaShanah

Kanfay HaShachar: An egalitarian prayer book
for morning worship

Min HaShamayim Tenuchmu: An egalitarian prayer book for the House of Mourning

JANUARY 24, 1991 • WAYLAND/WESTON TOWN CRIER • PAGE 5

WAYLAND NEWS

FY '92 budgets

Fire chief worried

BY JEFF ADAIR
TOWN CRIER STAFF

WAYLAND — Unless the fire department's budget is increased for FY '92 the fire department will run one person short and the Cochituate fire station may have to close at some point, warns Fire Chief Michael Murphy.

The fire department has submitted a no-increase budget under the guidelines set for it by the Finance Committee. The budget approved for this fiscal year is for $1,018,891. The budget submitted for FY '92 is for $1,015,594.

Among the items in the budget which bother Murphy is the fact that there is no increase in the overtime budget. Murphy fears that his department will face the same situation it has this year when the overtime account dried up six months into the fiscal year. "Given the cutback in the budget we will run out of overtime during the year. We will face the potential of having to close down a station," he said.

Even though the Finance Committee recently allowed him to transfer money into the overtime account for this fiscal year, he said, by May or June he may have no choice but to close a station.

The minimum increase in the overtime account should equal the same percentage of pay increase which the fire fighters receive, he said.

There's no provision in the budget should a fire fighter be out because of an injury and there's no increase in the callback account, he said. "One incident will drain me. It will cost a lot of money," he said.

The personnel shortage will come because a fire fighter has retired and the department has been told it may not be able to hire a replacement.

The town will face "a severe situation" should there be no increase, he said. "One, there won't be enough personnel to effectively handle a fire incident. There's not enough money to handle a major emergency," he explained.

Since other area fire departments are facing the same budget constraints, Wayland cannot rely on them to take up the slack during a fire, he said. As a long-term measure regionalizing fire departments "is the only solution to the problem," Murphy said.

SEE PAGE 6

Police chief content

BY JEFF ADAIR
TOWN CRIER STAFF

WAYLAND — "At this point I don't foresee any problems," said Police Chief Tom O'Loughlin speaking about the three budgets under his department which he has submitted for FY '92.

Under the guidelines set by the Finance Committee town departments have been asked to submit zero-based budgets for FY '92. In the current fiscal year, excluding capital items, the budgets for the police, the joint communications center, and the auxiliary police total $1,404,481. For FY '92 the total of the three is $1,429,634.

O'Loughlin noted that problems could arise depending on the amount which the police receive in raises. The police union is currently negotiating for a contract. If raises are higher than four percent, O'Loughlin said, he will have to find the money somewhere. He did not rule out laying off personnel should he have to make cuts.

Under capital items the police department is seeking money to purchase a new tape machine for the Joint Communications Center. The machine which records all incoming calls to the station "works sometimes, rarely," said O'Loughlin.

NANCY LEE GOSSELS has received national attention for the unique sculptures which she has created out of found metal. PHOTO BY JEFF ADAIR

Artist creates unique menorahs

BY JEFF ADAIR
TOWN CRIER STAFF

WAYLAND — Wayland artist Nancy Lee Gossels has received national attention in the past few years for her unique "found metal" sculptures. Having been an artist for more than 25 years, Gossels came to the medium of sculpturing all by accident.

Gossels constructs Jewish ceremonial pieces, many of which are menorahs, and non-religious sculptures. Her menorahs have been shown in museums, galleries and selected juried exhibitions in cities as far west as Denver and as far south as Miami.

"I've seen wonderful menorahs but I've never seen anything like this," said Gossels, speaking of her menorahs. "They really are unusual. A lot of people have been excited to see that because they are not in any way traditional looking."

Gossels uses a lot of symbols in her pieces. In one menorah called "Out of Bondage" there is a loose chain on it, and various levels which represent climbing Mount Sinai. She mentioned that she uses mirrors and circles in a lot of her pieces. "The mirror I think of reflecting God's light," she said. "I use a lot of circles and that to me has spiritual meaning too. I think of that as being the universe — God's creation."

All of the menorahs which she constructs are functional. She also does limited edition pieces of menorahs, mezuzots and other sculptures.

To find the pieces which she uses in her sculptures Gossels said she goes to all kinds of places foraging for used metal. Salvage yards, hardware stores, and antique places, she said, are wonderful places to find all kinds of interesting shapes.

Gossels received her art training at the DeCordova Museum School in Lincoln. She has also taken classes with Boston area artists Glenda Tall and George Dergalis.

Not satisfied

During her early years as an artist Gossels was mainly a painter. Because she was not satisfied with the direction she was taking as an artist she stopped doing it altogether for 12 years. Explaining why she quit Gossels said, "I think my interest just changed. I think I just became not quite so excited about art. As I said the last piece I did just wasn't satisfactory and I kept trying. I just hadn't found the right media."

During the years when she was absent from art Gossels wrote several prayer books for her congregation, Congregation Beth El in Sudbury.

A few years ago, she said, she ran into Brenda Zaltas, a sculpturalist

SEE PAGE 16

PAGE 16 • WAYLAND/WESTON TOWN CRIER • JANUARY 24, 1991

Menorahs

CONTINUED FROM PAGE 5

who does similar work. Zaltas, Gossels said, had the idea of designing outdoor sculptures from found metal. After their first trip together to a salvage yard the two came back with all kinds of rusty metal and aluminum in various shapes. "We began actually by working together. And we thought we were designing something for outside when all of a sudden the shapes reminded us that this could be a menorah," Gossels commented.

It can take weeks, even months, Gossels said, to produce a sculpture. She said it's a three-step process of finding the material, designing the work and putting it together. To put the pieces together, she said, she goes to a machine shop. Each of the pieces are buffed, and individually screwed together.

Gossels said her inspiration for her designs comes from within. "But I'm not sure how. I've been involved in my congregation and I have written a lot of prayers. I like to think these are in a way my kind of prayer," she said.

Gossels said she doesn't have a favorite among the many pieces which she has created.

Asked why she does what she does Gossels answered, "I don't do it for money, I don't think any artist or writer does — I hope people love the work and want to own it. It's very exciting."

She said that this past Chanukah she and Brenda were thinking as they were lighting their own candles "how many people in this country are lighting our menorahs — that's kind of a wonderful thing. I would like to share that and have people love the work enough to want to buy it."

One of Gossels' menorahs was featured in the December issue of McCall's magazine. One of her pieces can currently be seen in Boston at The Copley Society's Winter Show until Feb. 2.

THIS ONE-OF-A-KIND MENORAH created by Nancy Lee Gossels is called "Out of Bondage." It is made of aluminum, brass, bronze, mirror and stainless steel.

Obituaries 5
Accent 7
Opinion 10
Travel 12
B

IDDLESEX NEWS Sunday, Dec. 29, 1985

Wayland brothers honor mother's memory with gift

By DAVID GILLIS
News Staff Writer

WAYLAND — Like millions of others, Charlotte Lewy Gossels died at the hands of brutal men who had no regard for human life.

Her family does not know how or when she died, only that she was one of the nameless men, women and children killed at the Nazi death camp at Auschwitz.

But Peter and Werner Gossels, who last heard from their mother in November 1941 and later learned she was taken to Auschwitz in 1943, said they could never allow their mother's memory to fade.

Now, more than 40 years after her death, the two men have donated $20,000 in her memory to the library Building Fund.

The Nazis tried to destroy an entire people and with them truth and justice, Peter Gossels said. His family hopes their gift will encourage "respect for peaceful study and thought" and promote "the pursuit of freedom and dignity for all people."

The two men, however, are not seeking recognition for their mother's deeds, Peter said. They simply want to honor the woman who gave them life and twice saved them from death.

"She was a very special woman," Peter said. "She was warm and generous — a very brave woman."

He said his mother was able to arrange the two boys' escape from Germany in July 1939, when Peter was 8 years old, and Werner, 5. That was two months before Hitler's army invaded Poland and World War II began. Thirty

CHARLOTTE LEWY GOSSELS
...Auschwitz victim

children were able to flee to France because of his mother's efforts, Peter said.

"She managed to get us on that train," he said. "She made that possible."

But she decided to remain in Berlin to care for her ailing mother, and in 1942 refused an opportunity to escape to Switzerland, he said. It was her last chance to join her two boys, who had just arrived in the United States.

Their mother had also saved their lives while the family was still living in Berlin, Peter said. He said he and his brother were surrounded by a gang of Hitler Youth armed with knives supplied by the Nazi Party.

But their mother, who saw their danger, waded through the crowd of youths, took her boys by the hand "and walked us out," Peter said.

After years of searching for a way to honor their mother, both men decided to help support the library's plan to build an addition to the existing building and nearly double its space.

"We feel that the public library helps to foster contemplation and peace and concern for other people," he said. "We're hoping to encourage other people" to also donate to the library Building Fund.

Peter, an attorney, serves as town moderator, and Werner is a real estate investor and developer.

Peter Gossels said his family, as well as his brother's, has lived in Wayland for more than 20 years and wanted to show its appreciation to the town by making the donation.

Library Director Louise R. Brown said the donation is a "tribute to the library."

"Everyone is delighted with this gift and very moved by the idea behind it," Brown said. "We feel very honored."

Although the library has raised more than $50,000, including a $20,000 grant from Raytheon Co. and $5,000 from Dow Chemical Co., Brown said she was recently notified that the library is no longer eligible for a $25,000 National Endowment for the Humanities matching grant.

She said NEH officials did not say why the library would not receive the grant.

The Gossels brothers at the dedication of the plaque
at the Wayland Public Library in 1988

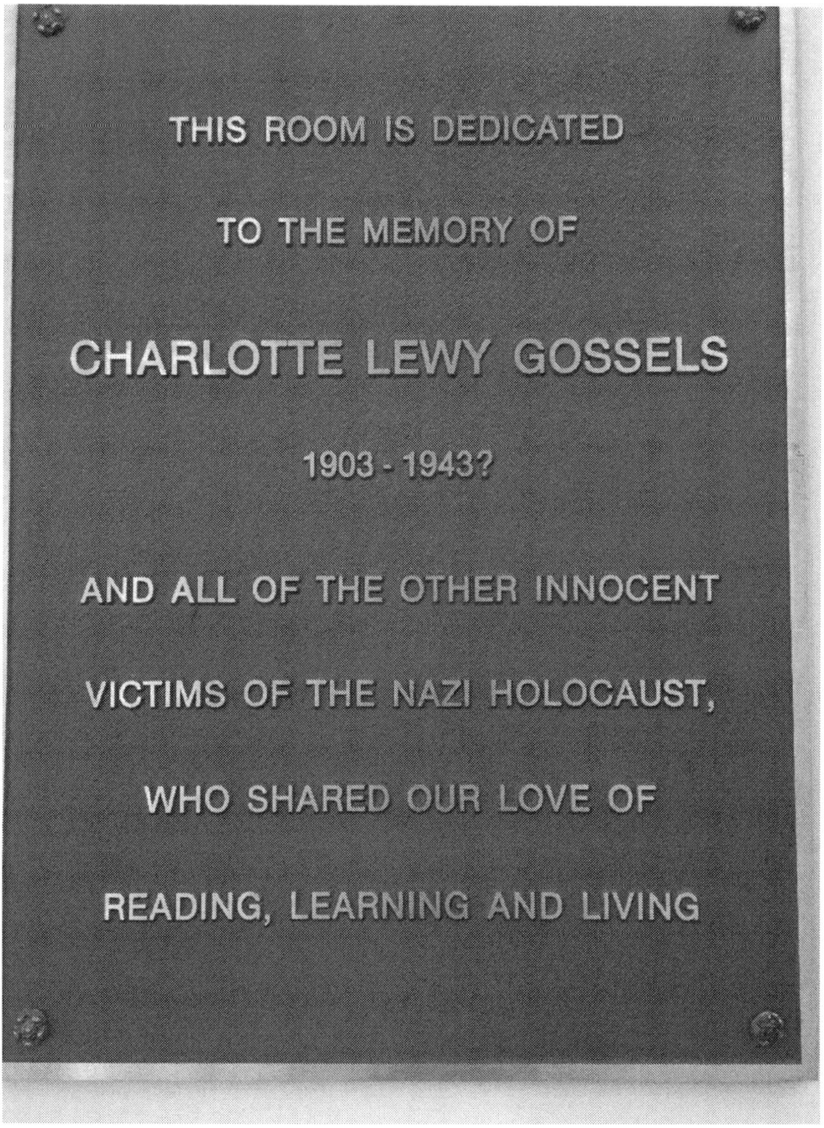

The plaque was installed at the Wayland,
Massachusetts Public Library in 1988

C. Peter R. Gossels presiding as Moderator at the
Wayland Town Meeting – 1984

C. Peter R. Gossels presiding as Moderator at the Wayland Town Meeting – 2005

C. Peter R. Gossels marching with other Wayland town officials in the 1995 Memorial Day Parade

April 18, 2002 The Wayland Town Crier

Gossels is the man in charge

Town moderator has been at his post for 20 years

By Melissa Beecher
STAFF WRITER

Peter Gossels has been the moderator in Wayland for the past 20 years, something that he simply looks at as a way to give back to his town.

"I loved the idea of contributing to a town that has been so good to my family and I," he said. "This is how I decided to volunteer and make a small contribution to Wayland.

"When I first started, I wanted to make town meeting more of a conversation, a congenial gathering for residents to discuss important issues, rather then emotional debate among factions like it is in some other towns."

Gossels' service in local government dates back to 1962, when helped establish the Taxpayers of Wayland Association, a coalition of over 100 residents that attempted to act as a watchdog over local government.

An elected member of the Finance Committee in 1966, he served a two-year term before becoming Wayland's town counsel in 1968. Gossels' resigned from the position in 1979, but continued to work in the capacity of assistant to town counsel for the next two years.

While working as counsel for both Wayland and Boxborough, Gossels was exposed to the proceeding of Town Meeting.

"In Boxborough, I sat next to the moderator and

GOSSELS, see page 5

PHOTO BY JEFF GAHRES

Wayland Town Moderator Peter Gossels has been on the job for 20 years, although he has been in local government since he helped establish the taxpayers of Wayland Association.

Gossels bangs the gavel April 25

GOSSELS, from page 1

learned quite a bit on how to conduct a managed town meeting. That, basically, advanced my ambitions to become moderator of Wayland," he said.

"It (town meeting) is the opportunity that allows people to conduct debate of serious, important and sometimes expensive issues in a well modulated way," said Gossels. "I am very proud of the way that I conduct business."

Gossels has worked as a trial lawyer at the Weston, Patrick, Willard & Redding law firm in Boston since the 1970s. Prior to his 40-year practice, he graduated from Harvard Law School. Gossels also served in the United States Army during the Korean War. He was trained as a trial lawyer at Sullivan & Worcester and taught international business law at Boston University.

He and his wife, Nancy Lee Gossels, have been married for 44 years. In her own right, she is renowned artist, poet and author. The two have three children, Amy, Lisa and Daniel, who are each involved in various aspects of film production.

"I have been very fortunate to have such a wonderful family," said Gossels.

Gossels will bang the gavel and begin Town Meeting on April 25, something he says he looks forward to every year.

Nancy and Peter Gossels

Lisa Gossels

Daniel, Jackie and Sophia Gossels

Amy Gossels

Daniel, Jackie & Sophia Gossels, Peter and Mirae Chae, Lisa Gossels and Amy Gossels, Nancy and Peter Gossels – June 29, 2018 – Nancy and Peter Gossels' 60th Wedding Anniversary

Werner's Story

We arrived in New York on September 27, 1941; spent two weeks on Ellis Island; then I was driven to Boston where a wonderful family welcomed me. Israel Glaser & Ethel Glaser, their daughter Mary and son-in-law Louis Gordon and 2 ½ year old Robert Gordon became my family (younger brothers Clifford and Fred Gordon were born May 29, 1942 and March 10, 1945, respectively): we lived in South Brookline, Massachusetts, where I attended the Edith C. Baker Grammar School, graduating as Class President in 1948. Simultaneously with attending Public School, I went to the South Brookline Community Center Hebrew School, culminating in my Bar Mitzvah in 1946.

By 1948, the South Brookline Community Center congregation built Temple Emeth. Israel Glaser and his family had been instrumental in the founding of the SBCC and ultimately in the construction of the Temple. His daughter, Mary Gordon, as President of the Sisterhood and I, as head of the Junior Congregation, both spoke at the cornerstone laying of the Temple.

I graduated from Brookline High School in 1952. Four years of conscientious academic effort, plus participation in student government, sports, year book, and other miscellaneous extra-curricular activities prepared me for college. When I applied to colleges, I expected to live at home and commute to a local university. I applied to and was admitted to Harvard, Massachusetts Institute of Technology, Tufts and Northeastern University. Fortunately, Peter suggested that I apply to Yale. Daniel Tyler, a Brookline Selectman and Yale Graduate, interviewed me one night and somehow talked the admissions office into accepting me and granting me sufficient scholarship aid to allow me to live at college in New Haven. Part of the scholarship aid was a requirement that I work fourteen hours per week to earn $400 of the scholarship. Freshman year, I ran the milk machine for the lunch cafeteria line in Commons. The next two years, I helped two geology professors, and Senior year I worked in the University library.

In 1956, as I was about to graduate from the school of Engineering with my 1st degree in Industrial Administration, Yale decided to begin a Masters Program in Industrial Administration. The Department Chairman, Thomas Holmes, invited us to apply for admission to the new program. I applied and was accepted and awarded a fellowship that paid for my tuition for the next two years, leading to my Masters degree in Industrial Administration [MIA] from the School of Engineering in 1958. From the beginning, we thought of our Industrial Administration Graduate Program as Yale University's first business school class.

Elaine Furman and I dated throughout my college years and married on June 14, 1956, three days after graduating from Yale. Elaine commuted from New Haven to Smith College in Northampton, Massachusetts during her Senior year, graduating with honors in 1957.

Our first child, Jeffrey Howard Charles Gossels, was born on May 21, 1957, in Boston. Unfortunately, he died on August 3, 1957 of sudden crib death while we were visiting with Elaine's parents in Newton. Stuart Daniel Gossels was born in Cincinnati, Ohio on October 24, 1958. Jonathan Gordon Gossels was born in Syracuse, New York, on March 7, 1960. Bonnie Lynne Gossels was born in Syracuse, New York, on March 14, 1962. Warren Joseph Gossels was born in Boston on August 23, 1963, and Elizabeth Louise Gossels was born in Boston on May 30, 1967.

A month before graduating from Yale with my MIA, I received a job offer from General Electric Company [GE] to join their 3-year Manufacturing Training Program with my initial assignment in Evendale, Ohio (outside Cincinnati). Two 6-month assignments (plus after-hours classes) in Jet Engine Manufacturing were followed by two 6-month assignments in Semi-Conductor Manufacturing at Electronics Park, Syracuse, New York, and one 6-month assignment renovating the old factory building housing the Watt Hour Meter Department in Somersworth, New Hampshire. My next and final assignment in the Instrument Department in West Lynn, Massachusetts was cut short by an invitation to return to Syracuse to join eleven other young manufacturing engineering people from within General Electric Company to study diffusion technology for Semi-Conductor Manufacturing full-time for three months.

When I graduated from both the Manufacturing Training Program, and the Diffusion Technology Program in June 1961, I accepted permanent assignment as a Quality Control Engineer on the Silicon Diode Line at the Semiconductor Products Departement in Electronic Park, Syracuse, New York. Because the enormous advance in technology of semi-conductor manufacture, that we learned in our three months of intense study, resulted in dramatic price reductions in products being sold, *General Electric Company* declared a 2-year freeze in salaries at the Semiconductor Product Departement because product selling price reduction overnight were so severe that cutting cost was paramount.

In the spring of **1962**, Elaine and I decided that we could take the opportunity to return to live in the Boston area. I accepted a job with Transitron Semi-Conductor Corporation and worked there (in Melrose, Wakefield and East Boston) for three years until 1965.

In June of 1965, I accepted a job offer from Dr. An Wang, Founder and Owner of Wang Laboratories, Inc. in Tewksbury, Massachusetts, to head up their manufacturing operation. When Wang Laboratories went public in August of **1967**, I was named Vice President of Manufacturing. In November of 1970, I was named Vice President of Sales/Marketing: during these seven years (1965-1972), I participated in the transformation of Wang Laboratories from a successful small, high-technology company making custom digital equipment primarily sold under other company's names, into a successful middle-size company selling innovative digital technological products under its own name; through its own sales force; servicing its own products with its own technicians, throughout the entire United States.

When I started, there were 72 employees and when I left in 1972, there were over 1,400 employees; dollar output grew from $1.8 million in fiscal year 1965 to $ 40 million in fiscal 1972; productivity improved 75%; costs of products and services sold declined from 60.6% to 39.6% over the 5.5 year period I ran Manufacturing. Productivity per salesman increased 16.4% and cost of sales declined during the 2-year period I was in charge of marketing and sales.

In addition to my work activities, I have volunteered for years on Town of Wayland boards and committees – including the Joint Wayland-Sudbury Septage Treatment Facility, the Planning Board, the Beautification Committee, etc. My recent athletic activities include tennis, biking and playing in the Eastern Mass Senior Softball league. From 1972 to the present time, Elaine and I have developed and run our own business. We converted our Wang Laboratories stock options into the capital that enabled us to purchase commercial real estate in the Greater Boston area. Elaine's father, Jack Furman, had similarly shifted to investing in real estate when the poultry business moved south in the late 1950s.

Elaine's Story

I was born October 15, 1935 to Anne Shapiro Furman and Jacob (Jack) Furman and in Boston, Massachusetts. Our family initially lived in Boston and then moved to Hammond Street in Chestnut Hill [Newton] Massachusetts. The house is at the top of Heartbreak Hill on the Boston Marathon course.

I went to Smith College in Northampton MA and received a Bachelor of Arts Cum Laude. My father Jack and mother Anne were natural entrepreneurs. Jack was born in Lechovitz Volin, Russia and arrived at Ellis Island onboard the ship America on August 21, 1921. He rose from selling and dressing live chickens on the street in the North End of Boston as a child to owning the largest turkey farm (Lake Shore Turkey Farm in Swanson, Vermont on the shore of Lake Champlain) in the eastern United States by 1943. After the War, he transitioned to the real estate business.

None of this would have been possible without Anne, making everything work at the highest professional level behind the scenes. Besides business acumen, my mother's true gift was with people; she made friends with everyone everywhere she went. Werner Gossels and I were married in 1956 at Temple Emmanuel in Newton. I completed college while Werner was starting his Master's degree at Yale. After that, we moved frequently as Werner was in the General Electric Manufacturers Training Program. We moved a growing family to Cincinnati, Syracuse, Dover New Hampshire, back to Syracuse and then to Natick at essentially six month intervals.

As the children grew up, I became active in community activities including school related drama, music programs (establishing the Committee for the Advancement of the Performing Arts), sports (establishing the first running club in Wayland –"Wayfarers" and establishing a food concession for the Dual County League Winter Track meets to raise money initially to provide money for Alberto Salazar's travel costs and later to support the Wayland Track program.

I have always been interested in education and Jewish education in particular. Life-long Jewish learning is key, but I only like to study with teachers who can offer genuine insight and an intellectual challenge. I was fortunate to have Rabbi Harold Kushner as our congregational leader and he is an extraordinary teacher. I studied regularly in his classes.

Our Bennett Road neighborhood was a remarkable place in the 1970s and 1980s. Our children grew up interacting daily with their friends from the Martin, Hagenstein, McVicker, and Donahue families. It was a close knit community and the parents were friends as well.

For many years, Ann Hagenstein and I played tennis every morning on the court between our two homes [Bonnie bought and renovated the Hagenstein house]. Each Labor Day, there was and continues to be an extensive "block party" encompassing not just Bennett Road, but the larger Wayland Center neighborhood.

Werner I and truly enjoy watching our family compete in an endless array of sports. Often multiple times a week, I can be seen with my floppy yellow hat and warm coat focusing on Little League and Youth Soccer, Middle School Cross Country and Basketball, High School Field Hockey, Softball, Ice Hockey, Cross Country and Track and tennis, and local and not so local intercollegiate events as well as assorted road races and marathons.

When Werner left Wang Laboratories, we focused on growing our small commercial real estate holdings into a real business. Eventually, I took over management of my parent's real estate business too and continue to run a significant portion of it. Bonnie, Warren and Liz work with Werner and me running the family real estate business.

Elaine, Werner and Bonnie Gossels

Peter, Stuart, Maria, Eric and Nicholas Gossels

Daniel, Jennifer, Jon, Jamie and Benjamin Gossels

Michael, Jane, Neil, Elizabeth and Matthew Blicher

Andrea, Lisa, Warren and Leanne Gossels

MISCELLANEOUS DOCUMENTS

WIKIPEDIA

RMS *Ebro*

RMS *Ebro* was an ocean liner built in 1914 for the Royal Mail Steam Packet Company. She was later owned and operated by the Pacific Steam Navigation Company, *Jugoslavenska Lloyd* and finally by *Companhia Colonial de Navegação*. In her last incarnation, under the name ***Serpa Pinto***, she made more crossings of the Atlantic during the Second World War than any other civilian vessel, leading to her being termed the *Friendship vessel* or *Destiny ship*.[1] She was scrapped in 1954.

Serpa Pinto during the Second World War

History

United Kingdom

Name:	RMS *Ebro*
Owner:	Royal Mail Steam Packet Company: 1914-1922 PSNC: 1922-1935
Operator:	Royal Mail Steam Packet Company: 1914-1922 PSNC: 1922-1935
Port of registry:	
Route:	West Indies and New York City-Chile
Builder:	Workman, Clark and Company, Belfast
Launched:	September 1914
Maiden voyage:	April 1915
Fate:	Sold to *Jugoslavenska Lloyd*, 1935

Yugoslavia

Name:	*Princess Olga*
Owner:	*Jugoslavenska Lloyd*
Operator:	*Jugoslavenska Lloyd*

Contents

Construction

The *Ebro* was ordered by the Royal Mail Steam Packet Company from the Belfast shipbuilders Workman, Clark and Company. She was launched in September 1914, and was 468 ft long with a beam of 55.8 ft.

British service

The Royal Mail Steam Packet Company initially planned for *Ebro* to operate on the West Indies service in the Caribbean, but due to the start of the First World War, she made only a single voyage on this service, in April 1915. She was then requisitioned, together with her sister ship RMS *Essequibo* and four other liners of the company, by the Royal Navy to serve as auxiliary cruisers armed with eight 6-inch guns, depth charges and mines. The ships were integrated in the 10th Auxiliary cruiser squadron, where they served as convoy escorts throughout the war.

After the war *Ebro* was returned to the Royal Mail Steam Packet Company. The company decided to sell her to the Pacific Steam Navigation Company, which refitted her and then placed her on the New York – Chile service, sailing through the Panama Canal. She carried out this service until the 1929 Wall Street crash forced the company into bankruptcy in 1930. *Ebro* was then moored at Avonmouth until 1935.[2]

Yugoslav service

In 1935 *Ebro* was sold to *Yugoslavenska Lloyd* and re-named *Princess Olga*. Under Yugoslav ownership, *Princess Olga* was used on the Dubrovnik – Haifa route, transporting passengers and general cargo. In 1940 *Princess Olga* was bought by the Portuguese company *Companhia Colonial de Navegação*.

Portuguese service

By 1940 the Second World War had greatly increased the numbers of people seeking to leave Europe for the Americas. *Companhia Colonial de Navegação* operated the small and underpowered *Colonial* on the Lisbon – Rio de Janeiro route. During 1940 *Colonial* transported around 2000 people to Brazil. With the increased demand, and already overstretched with passenger routes from Lisbon to Angola and Mozambique, to the Portuguese State of India, Macau and East Timor, in 1940 *Companhia Colonial de Navegação* decided to purchase *Princess Olga* to carry greater numbers of passengers between Portugal and its colonies. Prior to this, the service had been carried out by pre-First World War liners, like *Colonial* and her sister ship *Mouzinho*, the former SS *Corcovado*. The *Princess Olga* was bought in April 1940, re-named *Serpa Pinto* and sailed to Lisbon. Her first voyage under the Portuguese flag was carried out soon after her arrival in Lisbon in May 1940, sailing to Lourenço Marques.

When Italy declared war on the Allies in June 1940, all Italian shipping routes were closed. Only three companies from neutral countries maintained their transatlantic routes. These were the Portuguese *Companhia Nacional de Navegação* and *Companhia Colonial de Navegação* and the

Port of registry:	
Route:	Dubrovnik-Haifa
Out of service:	1940
Fate:	Sold to *Companhia Colonial de Navegação*, 1940
Portugal	
Name:	*Serpa Pinto*
Owner:	*Companhia Colonial de Navegação*
Operator:	*Companhia Colonial de Navegação*
Port of registry:	Lisbon, G-407
Route:	Lisbon to Rio de Janeiro, Philadelphia, New York City and Havana
Maiden voyage:	May 1940 to Beira
Out of service:	7 August 1954
Identification:	CSBA
Fate:	Scrapped at Antwerp, 1954
General characteristics	
Type:	Ocean liner
Tonnage:	8,267 tons
Length:	142.47 m (467.4 ft)
Beam:	17.0 m (55.8 ft)
Draught:	6.85 m (22.5 ft)
Installed power:	6,000 hp
Propulsion:	2 beams
Crew:	160
Notes:	600 250 First Class 350 Third Class

Spanish *Ybarra*, from Seville. The Spanish company, however, did not have enough ships to best utilize the transatlantic routes.

From August 1940 *Serpa Pinto* began her service on the transatlantic routes between Lisbon, and Rio de Janeiro and North America (Philadelphia and New York).

She was repeatedly stopped in mid-Atlantic by German submarines and US Navy and Royal Navy ships for inspections. On 26 May 1944, on its way from Lisbon (departure 16 May 1944) to Port Richmond, Philadelphia, USA (arrival 30 May 1944), the *Serpa Pinto* was stopped in the mid-Atlantic by the German U-boat U-541.[3] The U-boat's captain ordered the *Serpa Pinto*'s crew and passengers to abandon the ship in the lifeboats, and requested permission from Kriegsmarine headquarters to torpedo the ship. The passengers and crew, with the exception of the captain who decided to remain on board whatever the German decision, duly left the ship in the lifeboats. There they were forced to wait all night while the German U-boat awaited a reply to its request. By dawn an answer had arrived from Admiral Karl Dönitz, who refused permission to sink the ship. The U-boat then departed the area and the lifeboats returned to the ship. Three passengers were drowned during this incident.[4]

During the Second World War *Serpa Pinto* made ten voyages between Lisbon and Rio de Janeiro, and ten between Lisbon and Philadelphia and New York. Since it was one of the few ships making transatlantic voyages in this period, many of the refugees from Nazi Europe who reached the United States and Brazil in this period traveled on the ship. (The other important but smaller ships were the *Mouzinho* and the *Nyassa*.) Some of the more notable refugees, most of whom were of Jewish background, included Marcel Duchamp,[1] Simone Weil,[1] Pierre Dreyfus (son of Alfred Dreyfus),[1] Menachem Mendel Schneerson,[5] Marc Rich,[6] and Naoum Aronson.[7]

Also in this group were many children who came unaccompanied, without their parents, some of whom had been killed by the Nazis (see One Thousand Children). Many of these unaccompanied children were aided in Europe and in transit by the American Jewish Joint Distribution Committee (the "Joint"),[8], the French Jewish organization Œuvre de secours aux enfants, and the Hebrew Immigrant Aid Society (HIAS). One of these children became the rock impresario Bill Graham.[9]

After the war *Serpa Pinto* remained on the Lisbon – Rio de Janeiro – Santos route until the company's new ocean liners *Vera Cruz* and *Santa Maria* entered service. Her last voyage to Brazil took place in July 1953. Afterwards she was placed on the Caribbean route (Lisbon – Havana) making 12 round trips to Havana, with stops at Vigo, Funchal, La Guaira and Curacao.[2]

On 9 July 1954, *Serpa Pinto* sailed from Lisbon on her last voyage, São Vicente – Rio de Janeiro and Santos.[10]

Scrapping

After her last voyage, *Serpa Pinto* remain moored in Lisbon until 5 September 1954, when she departed under tow for Antwerp, Belgium, to be scrapped.

References

1. Eckl, Marlen. "Review: Serpa Pinto, the Ship of Destiny" (http://www.casastefanzweig.org/sec_news_list.php?language=en&id=65). Casa Stefan Zweig.
2. Rossini, José Carlos (5 January 1992). "Navios: o Serpa Pinto" (http://www.novomilenio.inf.br/rossini/serpapin.htm) (in Portuguese). A Tribuna de Santos.

LETTER Nº 35

9th September 1941

Mr. Robert Lang,
USCOM
215 Fourth Avenue,
NEW YORK CITY

Dear Sir,

The American Friends Service Committee, Philadelphia has instructed us to forward these fiches directly to you.

The children left today by the "Serpa Pinto" well and happy, and we hope they will arrive there in due time.

Yours sincerely,

PHILIP A. CONARD

PAC/DIT

THIRD CONVOY USCOM CHILDREN SAILING ON S.S.SER. PINTO" SEPT. 9, 1941

Nº	Name and Surname	Nationality & Religion	Date and place of birth	Languages spoken
46	Mildrut Straahs	German Israelite	9 Aug. 1929 Kaiserslautern.	French and German
47	Edith Roth	Ex-Austrian Israelite	9 Dec. 1930 Vienna.	French and German
48	Felix Roth	Ex-Austrian Israelite	23 Sept. 1926 Vienna	French and German
49	Gertrude Mane	German Israelite	17 Sept. 1931 Waxhenheim	French and German
50	Manfred Mane	German Israelite	15 Mar. 1929 Wachenheim	French and German
51	Werner Goldschmidt	German Izraelite	13 Nov. 1928 Erfurt.	French and German
52	Hans Hanauer	German Israelite	9 Aug. 1930 Karlsruhe	French and German
53	Dieter Hanauer	German Israelite	16 Apr. 1932 Karlsruhe	French and German
54	Thomas Mertens	Ex-Czech Israelite	7 Mar. 1928 Prague.	French, German Czech and Polish
55	Henri Pasch	Ex-Czech Israelite	13 Apr. 1928 Prague	French a little German and Czech
56	Heinz Sinashhn	German Israelite	26 Aug. 1925 Berlin	French, Germand and a little English
57	Erika Glaser	Ex-Austrian Israelite Ort.	27 Dec. 1930 Vienna	French and German
58	Norbert Rosenblum	Undetermined Israelite Ort.	29 June 1926 Strasbourg	French and German a little English
59	Erich Thorn	Ex-Austrian Israelite	30 Nov. 1929 Vienna	French and German
60	Eduard Goldschmied	Ex-Austrian Israelite	3 Dec. 1931 Vienna	French and German
61	Otto Berg	German Israelite	22 Feb. 1934 Rockenhausen	French and German
62	Alfred Berg	German Israelite	11 Dec. 1930 Rockenhausen	French and German
63	Ralph Moratz	German Israelite	10 Oct. 1931 Berlin	French and German

Nº	Name and Surname	Nationality & Religion	Date and Place of birth	Languages spoken
64	Martin Lewin	Underterrined Israelite	27 July 1931 Loitz	French and German
65	Joachim Lewin	Undetermined Israelite	9 May 1930 Baruth	French and German
66	Wolodia Grajonca	German Israelite	8 Jan 1931	French and German
67	Benjamin Plat	Heimatlos Israelite	27 Feb. 1933 Brussels	French
68	Henri Plat	Heimatlos Israelite	8 Sept. 1931 Brussels	French
69	Jacques Plat	Pole Israelite	6 Dec. 1927 Lodz	French
70	Siedmund Cige	Heimatlos Israelite Ort.	11 Nov. 1930 Berlin	French and German
71	Manfred Cige	Heimatlos Israelite Ort.	31 Oct. 1929 Berlin	French and German
72	HOrst Nathan	German Israelite	7 Nov. 1929 Mannheim	French and German
73	Elie Hirsch	German Israelite Ort.	20 Sept. 1934 Ladenburg	Germand and a little French
74	Jacob Hirsch	German Israelite Ort.	13 June 1930 Ladenburg	German and a little French
75	Werner Gossels	German Israelite	23 July 1933 Berlin	French and German
76	Claus Gossels	German Israelite	11 Aug. 1930 Berlin	French and German
77	Samuel Stuck	Heimatlos Israelite	17 Aug. 1929 Berlin	French and German
78	Heinz Grunberg) twins	Heimatlos Israelite Ort.	10 June 1929 Speyer	German little French and English
79	Margit Grunberg)	Heimatlos Israelite Ort.	10 June 1929 Speyer	German little French and English
80	Kurt Berg	German Israelite	20 Jan 1934 Ludwigshafen	French, Little German
81	Rosa Krolik	Pole Israelite Ort.	24 Aug. 1931 Berlin	French

Nº	Name and Surname	Nationality & Religion	Date and Place of birth	Languages spoken
82	Manfred Tidor	Pole Israelite	18 Mar. 1932 Francfort	French and German
83	Camilla Tidor	Pole Israelite	11 Dec. 1930 Francfort	French and German
84	Alice Grunewald	German Israelite	27 Sept. 1931 Waldfischbach	French and German
85	Inge Grunewald	German Israelite) Twins	22 Aug. 1929 Walfischbach	French and German
86	Lilly Grunewald	German Israelite) Twins	22 Aug. 1929 Walfischbach	French and German
87	Edith Moses	German Israelite Ort.	20 Sept. 1929 Glanmunchweiller	French and German
88	Max Krolik	Pole Israelite Ort.	10 Nov. 1928 Leipzig	French and German
89	Rudolphe Weinmann	German Israelite Ort.	13 May 1931 Bielefeld	French and German
90	Irma Stermer	Ex-Austrian Israelite Ort.	7 Nov. 1929 Gmunden	French and German
91	Helene Hoch	Ex-Austrian Israelite	18 Apr. 1930 Vienna	French and German
92	Eva Mayer	Palestinean Israelite	14 Jan. 1931 Berlin	French
93	Ruth-Marianne Mayer	Palestinean Israelite	28 Feb. 1929 Berlin	French a little German
94	Joseph Findling	Pole Israelite	21 June 1928 Cologne	French and German
95	Siegfried Findling	Pole Israelite	4 Dec. 1930 Cologne	French and German
96	Martin Findling	Pole Israelite	8 Aug 1932 Cologne	French

October 15, 1941

Mr. Robert Lang, Executive Director
U.S. Committee for the Care of European Children
215 - 4th Avenue
New York City

My dear Mr. Lang:

I am enclosing herewith forms CC2 and CC4 for Werner Gossels, which I should like to supplement as follows:

9-24-41 Werner Gossels arrived on the SS Serpa Pinto but was detained at Ellis Island because he had a fever.

9-26-41 Werner was discharged from Ellis Island and was accepted into Pleasantville Cottage School, Pleasantville, NY, for reception care.

10-9-41 Escorted to Boston and placed in care of the Jewish Child Welfare Association, 6 North Russell Street, Boston, Mass. Placed in home of Mr. and Mrs. Louis Gordon, as per attached report.

Sincerely yours,

Lotte Marcuse
Director of Placements

LM:EK
Encs.

Dr. Lucy Lewy

835 Riverside Drive
Apt. 4 E, c/o Tuchler
New York City
October 24th, 1941

Miss Lotte Marcuse
German-Jewish Children's Aid
165 West 46th Street
New York.

OCT 27 194

Dear Miss Marcuse:

I got your letter of October 22, 1941. Many thanks. I am sorry you did not let me know the new address of Werner Gossels. You wrote me that you placed him finally but not where.

The children have other distant relatives at Hartford and they also should like to know the address. They sent the two boys some money to Pleasantville Cottage School and are now afraid that they did not get it.

I really tried very hard when the children arrived to meet them, because I know how the mother feels and she asked me so urgently to do so. But you did not give me a chance. I work the whole day and it is very hard for me to arrange all this. Till I got the permission of the hospital here to see Claus at any time I want he was gone already. I think perhaps the Committee should have been able to get me this permission sooner. Now I wrote to Far Rockaway and they told me that only every first and third Sunday in the month are visiting days. I asked them how I could come there, but they did not answer me.

So you see I did every thing in my power to get in touch with the children, but unfortunately the organisations did not work with me but against my efforts. I am awfully sorry because I like the children and their mother very much. I really don't know what to write the mother, because nobody will believe me, that it was impossible to meet the children on their arrival here. I too would not believe it.

I can't call you at 9 o'clock in the morning, because I am just in the subway on my way to work. But you can reach me every day from 10 to 6 o'clock under the number Shore Road 8-4666, M.M. Laboratories, 6805 Fifth Avenue, Brooklyn.

I wrote the children and asked them to answer me, but they did not do so. I told them also to write to their mother direct, because she asked me to see to it, and I hope they did so.

I should be very thankful if you would let me know: when can I visit Claus in Rockaway, how can I come there best, do you think he wants somethingm, chocolate, fruit etc. ? Where is Werner. I will write to the mother, but I should like first to know all and perhaps to see at least one of the children.

With many thanks and kindest regards,

Sincerely yours,

Lucy Lewy

October 31, 1941

Mrs. Eva Cohen Berlin
Jewish Child Welfare Association
6 North Russell Street
Boston, Massachusetts

re: Claus and Werner Gossels

My dear Mrs. Berlin:

Thank you very much for your report on the home in which Werner is placed.

I have encouraging reports about Claus. His jaundice has cleared up and the orthopedic surgeon plans to remove the cast on Monday. He could therefore leave sometime during the week and we are naturally very anxious to have him settled. I assume he will join Werner in his home and that he would therefore be welcome at any time at which he can be taken to Boston.

I wrote to Miss Margolis earlier this week, telling her that I was planning to spend the weekend of November 8th in Boston. That is still possible and now that Claus is ready to leave for Boston, I would combine these two things. This would mean that I would either arrive in Boston Friday late or Saturday: the latter would be better for me.

Would you please let me know whether the foster home will be ready for Claus at that time.

Claus surprises everybody with his really unusual intelligence and his charming manner. These children really had excellent upbringing in the home of their parents, while that was still in tact and I hope that you will derive as much satisfaction from the placement of Claus as you do from Werner's placement.

There is just another thing that I wanted to bring to your attention. Mrs. Gossels has been writing to innumerable people in different parts of the United States, in an effort to obtain from them some kind of indirect statement about the boys. One of these people, of course, is the aunt in Hartford, who seems to be corresponding all along with Claus. One seems to be a member of the Friends, who met Mrs. Gossels in Germany. Another is a

To: Mrs. Berlin -2- October 31, 1941

Board member in St. Louis who has a child in h r home, who at one time knew these two boys in France. She, too, claims to have a request from the mother to "report" on the boys' placement. The fourth is a refugee physician in New York who is about to establish herself here and who has been a little difficult to handle because of her own inability to find the time to visit Claus and to see Werner before he left.

Claus himself has asked me to do everything in my power so that his mother would not find out he is ill and that is why I haven't written to Mrs. Gossels direct, as I sometimes do in such situations. Since Werner is so young, I wonder whether he has written to his parents or whether his foster parents have, and whether there was something in his letters that may make the mother wonder why Claus was not mentioned. If you could let me know about it, I would know how to write to Mrs. Gossels in order to give her a little comfort. I am sure that you can well understand how worried she would be knowing that the children left France and yet not know exactly where they are and what happened to them.

I would appreciate hearing from you at your earliest convenience.

With kind regards,

Sincerely yours,

Lotte Marcuse
Director of Placements

LM:HK

Translation of Escort's Notes

G o s s e l s , Werner

born on 7/23/1933

Father - City Councillor in Berlin, mother - beautician (cosmetics). Spacious apartment. Comfortable circumstances. Orthodox family. After his dismissal, the father finds a position with the Jewish Community. Divorced in 1936, the two boys are given into the mother's care.

They live with her until their departure for France on July 7, 1939. The father has married again in Belgium and goes to France after the German invasion, interned at Gurs. He has seen his children in France.*

The boys lived at the Chateau de Quincy (see Stuck, Grajonca, Werner Goldschmidt). From Quincy to Varennes (OSE) and from there, after 3 months, to the Chateau de Chabannes (7 months). He liked life in all the homes.

No school attendance in Germany (he was too young at the time of his departure).
French schools in the homes.

Positive attitude towards his emigration to the U.S.A.

Like his older brother, he is a bright child, frolicsome, gay, proved bis his robust mental stamina; for, he has experienced all the horrors and dangers of the terrible battle of Fontainebleau. Perhaps some kind of slight impudence reminds of these premature experiences, as if he would say to adults trying to guide him: I have seen other things!

*
Mother remained in Germany where she must work in a factory. Is in contact with her Children.

RFC

-2-

Claus is an attractive boy, with light complexion, brown eyes and brown hair; his impression is that of a "light brown" child. He has some freckles, an straight nose and well cut features. He looks quite mature, really for his 11 years. He talks German still quite well, though once in a while he has to use a French word. He has had many changes in France and was at times separated from his best friend, a boy whom he hopes to find somewhere at some future time to meet here again. He refers to the other children as "Kameraden" which is rather typical for the children in group care, a concept intrdduced by their teachers in an appeal to their loyalty to others in the group. He said he made no new friendships in the group with which he travelled, though he liked some.

Werner is a little "imp", charming, bright and appealing. He is most attractive, has fine colorng and dimples. He does not seem worried about what we are going to do about him, but he would like to go into a family and go before his brother will be able to leave the hospital. This plan was most pleasing to Claus, and he too, was not troubled about our plans. The two boys look out one for the other, and Claus seems to take responsibility as far as any boy of his age can be expected to.

A friend of the mother's called us up the other day; she is a newcomer who is trying to establish herself; she would like to see the boys before they leave town, but has little time to do so. She explained that she understands our plans. There is also a cousin to the mother, a Mrs. Lewis who lives in Hartford Connecticut, but has not found her adjustment there. The agency in Hartford found that she had no plan to offer and did not expect the agency to place the boys in Hartford; the agency, nevertheless mighth have tried to work out a placement, but as you probably know, they started very recently only on development of their foster home program and they have made many efforts, without success to make a plan for these boys. Their efforts have discovrred some adoption or quasi-adoption applications, as always happens during that stage of te foster home development. We have gone into this, quite in detail, in telephone conversations and in correspondence, and Mr. Kopel very frankly stated that he did not know when he would be ready to make the type of placement-- if ever-- which a situation such as the one concerning these boys-- demands.

It seems to me therefore, that you have here two brothers of 11 and 8 from a middle class family in Berlin; parents are divorced, each has poor prospects for a reunion with the children. The boys are "good material" as to background and personality.

We would not have obtained the consent from the Immigration authorities to transfer Claus to another city, and we are therefore ready to have him remain here until he is ready for discharge from hospital care. We would appreciate it very much if you would accept Werner now, with the plan of havig his brother follow. Will you 'phone me to-morrow, if possible, whether we may have him accompany the Roth children?

Sincerely yours,

background NOV 1 1941

MEETING HELD AT U.S.COMMITTEE
IN ROOM 1707, 215 Fourth
Avenue, New York City
at 3 P.M.

(58)

PRESENT: Dr. Paul Amann
Mrs. Paul Amann
Mr. Meltz
Dr. Polizer
Miss Marcuse
Mrs. Stein
Mrs. Slawson
Miss Lowy
Mr. Lang

Dr. Amann and Mr. Meltz discussed the problems and difficulties of their voyage from Marseilles to New York with the transport of 51 children who arrived on the Serpa Pinto. Neither of the escorts had been given any preparation or instructions about the children and they were all put on the train leaving Marseilles at 3 o'clock in the morning.

Mr. Meltz, who had been working with the Friends Service Committee in Marseilles knew something of the procedures and responsibilities of the U.S.Committee and had been told by Mr. Champenois of the Friends to take notes on each one of the children during the voyage. This was all general information and no specifid items were mentioned. It was only after the voyage was begun that the escorts discovered that certain of the children who were orthodox would not eat meat or fish. Also, they discovered that the children were without change of clothing, either underclothing or night clothes; that they literally were travelling in the clothes on their backs. They had no soap or towels and before the journey was completed were sadly in need of all these things.

Dr. Amann wrote Mr. Champenois a long letter from Lisbon in which he told him about all of these things and said that he hoped that the next transport would be better equipped.

When they arrived in Madrid they were extremely well treated by a group of Sisters at a Catholic Convent, where the children had their first real meal. When the changed trains at the Spanish border at Saragosse, they had only ten minutes in which theeffect the transfer and there was a great deal of confusion and unrest. Dr. Amann said that it was a miracle that the children were not all injured. He said it was absolutely essential that a longer period of time be allotted for the journey from Marseilles to Lisbon so that in the event that one train is missed, arrangements could be made for taking another. When they arrived in Lisbon they were very cordially greeted by the editor of the O'Seculo. The children were all taken for a day's outing and also to the cinema. They stayed at a boy's college where they had very good food. Both escorts agreed that customs officials, government officials, etc. treated them extremely well and they were cordially taken care of wherever they stopped. Their suggestions for the trip from Marseilles to Lisbon are:

Planning for carrying food; longer period of time for the journey and a much fuller preparation of the escorts, that is, telling them about the children, abo the U.S.Committee, etc. The journey from Lisbon to New York was interrupted at 2 points: 1. when the boat stopped at Casablanca and 2. when the boat stopped at Bermud. In Bermuda the escorts were separated from the children by the British Government officials and it was during this separation that Klaus Gossels slipped on the deck an

-4-

(59)

had wooden shlesshoes, stepped off a stairway or some step, slip on the deck and broke his leg. The leg was put in a plaster case by a Bermuda doctor , with the help of the ship's doctor and Klaus spend the remainder of the voyage in the ship's hospital

Dr. Amann reported that the two things that were lacking on the boat trip were, sufficient fruit for the children and sufficient games and books. He said that fortunately the weather had been very good but that when it rained, the children could not be kept below because it was very damp and they were not allowed to go up to first class and he thinks that some of the children probably got fever because their feet got wet and they had no shoes or socks in which to change. Dr. Amann said that all the children were of very high standing and intelligence and that many were extremely gifted. Dr. Amann said he made notes on each child during the voyage and had given these to Miss Marcuse. Miss Marcuse questioned him about one boy, Ralph Weinman who seemed a little sub-normal, but both Dr. Amann and Mr. Meltz were very enthusiastic in their endorsement of the boy, who it seems had helped the others when they were seasick, had very good marks in his studies and was an extremely affectionate and talkative youngster. Dr. Amann said that the children's wishes were, that boothers and sisters should not be separated, that they be placed in foster homes rather than in instititions.

Mr. Conard of the Friends Service Committee gave the escorts $2. for each child and $20. each for Dr. Amann and Mr. Meltz. Both escorts felt that this was not enough money for the voyage and had to use some of their own money. Although Dr. Amann stated that he expected no honorarium because the American Friends had arranged for his transportation, Mr. Lang told him that both he and Mr. Meltz had done such a splendid job that he felt that the U.S. Committee could show its appreciation only by paying them an honorarium, although he said that he knew the Committee could never repay with any amount of money, the care and kindness which Dr. Amann and Mr. Meltz had exhibited toward the children.

This is a brief account of my efforts to fill in some of the blanks in the story of your escape from unoccupied France in 1941. I am neither an archivist nor an historian; nevertheless, I have been able to uncover in part the role played by the American Friends Service Committee.

My search for documentation of the presumed roles of Clarence Pickett, Executive Director of the Service Committee, and Eleanor Roosevelt in persuading the President to have the Department of State issue your visas is not yet complete.[1] I have a request before the curators of Mrs. Roosevelt's papers at the FDR Library in Hyde Park to look for any documentation in that collection that might shed light on the issue. The curator with whom I spoke on the phone knew immediately who Clarence Pickett was and told me that Pickett's name appears regularly in her papers.

I do know that Clarence and Lilly Picket traveled extensively in Europe in September 1938 specifically to learn first-hand the worsening situation for Jews in Germany and later Austria. Upon their return Pickett prepared a lengthy confidential report on his findings. That report was circulated to interested individuals and groups such as Paul Baerwald of the JDC and Mrs. Roosevelt. The report ends, "What can be done, especially by the American Friends Service Committee? That is hard to discuss briefly. Relief is still important. We may feel penitent for our part in the vicious Versailles Treaty and war settlement. But the Jews are the ones on whom now the burden for that war settlement falls hardest. We can do no less than give every aid possible to help those who come to us to make a new and fruitful start. This will be our chief relief work for some time to come." *This will be our chief relief work for some time to come.* In fact, that work lasted in Europe for 11 years; first with Jews and other refugees and later also with displaced Germans after the end of the war. Today it continues in Kosovo, Angola, Florida, and right here in Greater Boston, to name a few places.

On November 9 Pickett had lunch with the President and Mrs. Roosevelt at Hyde Park to report in person on his trip. I know that problems with the Nazis were discussed. It is the specifics that I am still in quest of.

There is no doubt in my mind that Pickett was a key player at the policy level. On the ground, in France, the name Alice Synnestvedt comes up regularly. She is among the righteous listed at Yad Vashem, under her maiden name, which I do not know. Now 92 and nearly blind, she lives in Denmark. She tells us that the Service Committee was involved in selecting the children for transport to the United States. We also know that she was in Chabannes at least once because she has photographs taken there. Was Alice there when you were selected? I don't think we'll ever know.

---

[1] One source cited just such a connection, but referred to events a full year after September 1941.

Richard Weilheimer, who was also brought to the United States as a child, told wonderful stories of Alice at the opening of the "Quiet Helpers" exhibit in Philadelphia. Among them was the time she bought ice skates and taught some children how to skate. Then they waited until the Swiss and French border guards were digesting their lunches and the children just skated over the border to where I assume they were expected.

Richard lives in Port Washington, Long Island, and is very active in the Holocaust Memorial and Educational Center of Nassau County. You would like him.

I have discovered some interesting and some heart-breaking events that accompany your story. For the first part, I learned that it was the two Quakers Roswell McClelland[2] and Lindsley Noble who went directly to Pierre Leval and Marshall Pétian to request exit visas for Jewish children in unoccupied France. One source indicated that the French leaders readily agreed, while another recounts difficulty with Lèval. A minute in the Roosevelt Library prepared for Pope Pius in September 1942 indicates that by then exit visas had been canceled.

Both Pickett and Rufus Jones (a founder of the Service Committee) lobbied the House and Senate for passage of the Wagner-Rogers bill that would have allowed 10,000 Jewish children to enter the United States in 1939 and 1940. These children would be over and above the German quota. The Service Committee was named in the bill to supervise the migration of the children. The bill was withdrawn when it was reported out of committee with the children included in the quota. Those are not times that this nation can look back on without a shudder.

I have enclosed a copy of an article from The Christian Century that I found touching and heart-breaking. It concerns the safe-keeping of valuables literally thrown from train windows by Jews leaving France for the death camps.

Peter sent me a copy of lists of "USCOM children" where both Werner and Peter (or Claus) appear. I found the same list in our archives with a cover letter to USCOM in New York City. As our copy was an old-fashioned carbon copy, there is no letterhead. However, Philip Conrad ran AFSC's Lisbon office in 1941 and 1942. It was he who would go to the U.S. Consul in Lisbon with passports if he had them and receive the visas for entry into the United States. In the case that a child arrived without a passport, as often happened, he would produce an affidavit establishing the child's identity based on research done by the Service Committee.

As it was explained to me by one of our researchers in Philadelphia, USCOM was established at the suggestion of the Service Committee to oversee the safety and placement of the transported children after their arrival in the United States. Clarence

---

[2] McClelland went on to head the War Refugee Board in Switzerland, where he was among its most effective operatives. The WRB, although a US government organization, received most of its funding from private Jewish sources.

Pickett sat on its Board of Directors. USCOM also raised funds to help with the placements.

Since our first meeting back in August I have read quite a few accounts of the peril faced by Jews in the 1930s and 1940s. While I found nothing that related directly to Quaker activities in Chabannes, I did find the presence of Quakers and the Service Committee literally in every source. Some of the volumes I consulted are:

The Abandonment of the Jews
Quakers and Nazis
The Politics of Rescue
Witness for Humanity
Lest Innocent Blood Be Shed
Rescue As Resistance (at Peter's suggestion)

While doing this little bit of research I have had to confront, as anyone would, the inexplicability of those times. That the darkness was not total, that there were small lights burning across Europe is some solace: it helps a little. And yet I find myself weeping time after time.

by Robert Snyder
American Friends Service Committee, Inc.

(188)

United States Committee for the Care of European Children, Inc.

215 FOURTH AVENUE, NEW YORK CITY

Telephone ALgonquin 4-5166

(3)

February 7, 1941.

copy

Mr. Clarence Pickett,
American Friends Service Committee,
20 South 12th Street,
Philadelphia, Pa.

My dear Mr. Pickett:

We have been considering the status of the relationship between the American Friends Service Committee and the United States Committee and are giving herewith our understanding of our present working arrangement.

It is the understanding of the U.S. Committee for the Care of European Children that Miss Frawley of the American Friends Service Committee is coordinating the work of the latter Committee as regards refugee children. As a step toward clarifying committee relationships Miss Frawley has agreed to forward to the U.S. Committee copies of all letters dealing with the children's problem received or sent out by her office.

The U.S. Committee has agreed that for the present they will work through representatives of the American Friends Service Committee in investigating possibilities for the evacuation of children from the continent and in the actual evacuation of any groups of children that the Committee accepts as a responsibility.

The U.S. Committee is most interested in the work that the Unitarian Service Committee is doing and is very sympathetic with the desire of this group to evacuate children. The agreement above has been made in order to simplify the situation abroad since the U. S. Committee has no representative of its own in Europe at this time and since some clearance is necessary on that side. It requests that the representatives appointed by the American Friends Service Committee thoroughly study the situation reported by Mrs. Sharp and if, following their reports, the U.S. Committee determines to assist in the evacuation of these children that these representatives cooperate in every possible way with the Unitarian Service Committee and arrange for such evacuation.

The policy here expressed with respect to the Unitarian Service Committee is also one which should control in relation to information and situations reported by the Joint Distribution Committee, Mr. Lowrie of the Y.M.C.A. and other interested groups since the cooperation of these groups is of the utmost importance in the working out of the U.S. Committee plans.

Mr. Clarence Pickett February 7, 1941

- 2 -

It is understood that the U.S. Committee will refer all requests for aid in the evacuation of children to the American Friends Service Committee in Marseille that they may study the situation in regard to each group and advise the Committee of their findings.

In order that the representative of the American Friends Service Committee may be informed of what the U.S. Committee is willing and able to do the Committee will send as exact a statement as possible to the American Friends Service Committee as decisions are made. It is Miss Frawley's opinion that such a statement should be sent to the American Friends Service Committee office at Marseille immediately stating the present policy of the U.S. Committee in regard to what children they wish to receive. Such a memorandum is attached.

Will you advise us whether the foregoing is in agreement with your understanding.

Sincerely yours,

Marshall Field
President

MF:S
Enc.

"for the Care of European Children, Howard Kershner of the International Commission
COPY February 7, 1941
for the Assistance of Child Refugees and the American Friends Service Committee.

M E M O R A N D U M

(5)

To: Mr. Howard Kershner
From: United States Committee for the Care of European Children.

Miss Frawley of the Philadelphia Committee has suggested that a more amplified statement regarding the position of the United States Committee and the type of child that it wishes to receive would be helpful to you at this time.

The United States Committee is undetermined as to whether it will or will not continue to receive or assist in bringing more children to the United States. At the present time the Committee is analyzing the work it has already done. Immediately following a meeting of the Board which will be held at the earliest possible moment we will advise you by cable what the further policy of the Committee is to be. In the meantime we have agreed that the United States Committee will work on the problems of evacuating children through the representatives appointed by your Committee abroad. We have agreed to refer all requests to you for investigation and earnestly ask your help in co-ordinating the efforts of the various groups to evacuate children. While the representatives of the American Friends Service Committee under this arrangement are acting as our representatives, we trust that other groups interested in this same problem shall find that their projects, if coming within our scope, can be expedited rather than limited by working with our representatives.

We have advised the Unitarian Service Committee of our decision to work through the American Friends Service Committee, and have expressed to them our very real desire that you cooperate in every way with them, particularly with reference to the groups of children reported on by Mrs. Sharp. In order that the situation may be clearly understood by all of us I quote from our letter to Mr. Emerson, Chairman of the Unitarian Service Committee, as follows:

> "We now understand that the Friends have designated to go to Lisbon Mrs. Bennet Schauffler. She, of course, will be under primary obligation to the Friends but by arrangements concluded between that organization and our own she will also serve in a sense as our representative in Lisbon. To the same end we have agreed with the Friends that their representatives in other places shall also represent us to the extent that such joint representation is practicable.
>
> It is, however, part of our agreement with the Friends that other interested groups shall be encouraged in every way to work with the representatives of the Friends, both in France and in Lisbon. In this connection, and having in mind particularly the remarkable achievement of Mrs. Sharp in cooperation with Mrs. Lowrie in regard to the group of children which Mrs. Sharp brought to this country, we have given specific instructions to the Friends that every effort shall be made by their staff abroad to take whatever steps may be necessary to forward the efforts of the Unitarian Service Committee in bringing over the groups of children which Mrs. Sharp mentioned to us when she was here. Indeed, we have gone a step beyond this. Although we expect that the repre-

Mr. Kershner -2- 2/7/41

(6)

sentatives of the Friends will serve as our immediate liaison officers we have advised them in positive terms of our desire to cooperate with all groups working in the field and, particularly, with yours. In other words, while in any given area the representative of the Friends will serve as a sort of Chairman of the "Board" it is our earnest desire - and we have so stated - that the "Board" will include wherever possible representatives of the Unitarian Service Committee."

We have also advised Mrs. Schauffler to survey the possibility of evacuating children now in Lisbon who might precede their parents if passage could be arranged for them.

I should like to call your attention to the following which we have not expressed clearly in our previous memorandum:

1. It is our understanding that the Departments of State and Justice have not yet reached a final decision in relation to whether the children from Southern France can be admitted on temporary visas. That they are admissible on permanent visas is, of course, obvious. Whether or not all of them or some of them can come in on temporary visas is now under discussion in Washington and we hope to give you a final answer in the very near future.

2. The United States Committee has, up to the present time, not agreed to pay return passage for any children.

3. If the child's visa is secured before its sixteenth birthday we have considered it as eligible under our plan.

4. In the memorandum brought to you by Miss Thorndike a statement is made regarding the permanency of the U. S. Committee. We consider this statement somewhat too positive and the Committee should be considered as having more than a temporary status.

May I also call your attention to one other aspect of the situation which we consider important. As you know, the United States Committee is at this time considering its future status and making definitive plans as to how it will handle its problems from here on. Perhaps in view of the uncertainty still existing in regard to its progra it would be wise not to publicize for the present any particular or definite program on evacuating children.

In order to make a decision on which groups of children the U.S. Committee will receive if it continues to service additional children we should appreciate your gathering and transmitting to us information (which should be as definite as possible) on the following questions:

1. What is the volume of children in France desirous of leaving France?

2. What proportion of these children are Jewish? What proportion Gentile?

3. What nationalities do these children represent and in in approximately what proportion?

Mr. Kershner -3- 2/7/41

(7)

4. What is the age distribution of those children apparently eligible for evacuation?

5. What is the attitude of the French Government concerning the evacuation of unaccompanied French children? Is exit permitted only to children going to relatives, or could they go to friends, or to homes unknown to them but selected by the U.S. Committee?

6. Will the French Government issue exit permits to nationals and non-French alike, and would these serve to permit exit to Portugal?

7. Where are these children located? In occupied France, in unoccupied France, or in Lisbon? Is there a group in Marseille?

8. Are the children living in congregate care or are they individual children?

9. If children are in congregate care, could these groups be broken down into smaller groups adaptable to current traveling conditions, or would it be necessary to move an entire group?

10. If children are evacuated, are there facilities for caring for them at the port of embarkation until passage is secured?

11. Are there escorts qualified and available to travel with the children? Would they travel with them from Marseille to the U. S.? Would they remain in the U.S. or return to France? On the subject of escorts consideration should be given to professional services needed enroute, especially on boats which may not have medical care.

12. What particular conditions make necessary the immediate evacuation of a child or a group?

13. Have you any special information concerning approximate costs of travel for each group, i.e. travel to Marseille, Marseille to Lisbon or other port, from port of embarkation to the U. S., care in the U. S.? Any information which you might have as to whether any part of this expense could be borne by individuals or organizations would be useful.

14. To what extent would it be necessary for the U.S. Committee to assist in securing exit permits, transit visas, affidavits, etc. for each group?

15. To what extent and for what kind of children must permanent care in the U. S. be considered.

16. If only a few small groups are available for evacuation what does the American Friends Service Committee recommend?

17. Is it the opinion of the AFSC that within the next three or four months additional groups may be available for evacuation?

18. If a large number of children is not available for evacuation would the AFSC deem advisable a plan to give assistance in evacuating individual cases?

Mr. Kershner -4- 2/7/41 (8)

In compiling information on the above, we would appreciate your considering the following preferences of the United States Committee:

a. Size of group. From our point of view, sailings of from 50 to 100 children at a time would be better. However, we would consider groups as small as 25 at a time or even a full shipload.

b. Make-up of group: We are aware of the great need of Jewish children and the U.S. Committee wishes to make every effort to rescue these children. There is a risk, however, that the plight of this group may obscure the need of other children. In the circumstances, it would seem best, in the interest of fairness and in order to work out with the various groups who have cooperated with us, to work out mixed national groups on any given sailing. If, however, the effort to work out mixed groups results in delay, or appears otherwise impracticable, we would gladly receive sailings of all Jewish, French, Swiss, Dutch, Czech, Polish, Russian or other children. The U.S. Committee has fixed no racial or national proportions.

c. Age distribution of children: It is desirable that the majority of children in a group be between five and twelve years of age. Children under five if traveling with an older sister or brother could be considered. Approximately ten to twelve per cent of children between the age of twelve and sixteen could be accommodated. A preponderance of older children would not be refused, but would require different financing and plans for placement here. If the majority of children in a group are in this higher age range their particularly desperate need should be explained.

Many of the problems presented by groups would require more financing than the United States Committee has considered up to the present time. However, we leave it to the American Friends Service Committee to use its own judgment in proposing such groups for evacuation, and we shall give due consideration to the problems involved.

We realize that hope is stimulated when one makes inquiries about the conditions of any group of children desiring evacuation. We beg that you exercise every precaution in making inquiries, as the plans of the U.S. Committee are much too tentative to be able to hold out much hope. Unless conditions change greatly, it would appear that within the next few months only a limited number of children could be sent here.

With respect to the 175 children, a list of which you have sent us, and in answer to your cables, we greatly appreciate the energy and effort that you have expended in getting this material. It brings to us the more vividly the need for a determination of the United States Committee policy. We will answer your cables in detail as soon as possible.

Rescue in France

This letter was written to Mrs. Roosevelt by Morris C. Troper, Chairman, European Executive Committee of the Joint Distribution Committee.

(40)

Lisbon
June 7, 1941

Dear Mrs. Roosevelt:

Knowing of your deep interest in the work of the United States Committee for the Care of European Children and how greatly our present success in rescuing one hundred and eleven children, many from internment camps in unoccupied France, has been due to your active efforts, I thought the least I could do would be to tell you about the children now that they are here and awaiting departure for the United States aboard the SS Mouzinho early next week.

They are really a fine group of boys and girls and they have endured much in the last year or two. They arrived completely exhausted after a gruelling trip from Marseilles that took four days and five nights.

When they came here they looked like tired, wan, broken little old men and women. None dared to laugh aloud and few smiled — even the youngsters of seven and eight. Their clothes were in tatters. The more fortunate of them clumped around in wooden-soled shoes.

One of the most pathetic sights I have ever seen was that of these children, freed of restraints, trying to learn to play again. They played grimly as though fearing that at any moment the sun, the beach, the food and the new unaccustomed liberty would be snatched from them and they would be thrown back into the misery and distress from which they have just escaped.

Through our Quaker friends we secured some new clothing and shoes. Whatever can be done for them physically is being done. But it will take more than this week of care to erase the imprints of their bitter experiences.

After a few days here they smiled and laughed a little — but apprehensively, as though they might be punished for it. The results of experiences which no child should ever have to go through cannot be shaken off easily. I hesitated to call them over and speak to them individually because of the look of panic that swept their faces when they were singled out.

The memories some of these children must have! They were permitted to say farewell to their families — those still having relatives. The train on which they travelled from Marseilles stopped at the station of Oloron and the fathers and mothers interned at the Gurs Camp were brought to the station under police escort and given a last three minutes with their children. And these kiddies, knowing they were to see their parents, refused to eat their breakfasts on the train that morning but wrapped up bread and rolls and bits of sugar and handed them to their parents when they met.

There is one tot in the group, a wan, undersized girl of seven whom we haven't yet been able to make smile. She had been separated from her mother for over a year. When they met at Oloron for the last time, for it is most unlikely that they will ever meet again, they were unable to converse for the child had forgotten her native German in the effort of learning French and English, and they had no common language except tears.

There is another girl of thirteen, busy mothering her four younger brothers and sisters. Her father died in the Buchenwald concentration camp. Her mother died of pneumonia at Gurs. I found her writing a letter to a woman at Gurs, encouraging her, "because she befriended my mother when she was sick."

I could go on for pages telling you about these children. There is something about each of them — as there is about every child. Bruised in spirit, most of them. Frail in body, many of them. And they are the fortunate ones. I know that in America they will get the sympathy and understanding they need, and I hope that with the passing of time the scars each one of them bears will be healed, and they will recapture the spirit of childhood stolen from them, and will have the opportunity to grow up into normal men and women.

MORRIS C. TROPER

LEGALITY AND RESISTANCE IN VICHY FRANCE: THE RESCUE OF JEWISH CHILDREN

HILLEL J. KIEVAL

Reprinted from Proceedings of the American Philosophical Society, Volume 124, No. 5, October 1980

American Friends Service Committee Inc.
1501 Cherry Street, Philadelphia, Pennsylvania 19102 • Phone (215) 241-7000

. C. COLLETT
LOUIS W. SCHNEIDER
Executive Secretary

(1)

October 18, 1980

Stephanie Nora
4105 North Brookdale
Apt. B-8
Peoria, Illinois 61614

Dear Stephanie Nora:

I am enclosing a collection of cablegrams, letters, minutes, etc. pertaining to the children's group which came to this country in June 1941. Some of these documents may not specifically refer to that particular group, but give some background information which might be helpful.

The American Friends Service Committee worked on both sides in Spain during the Civil War there, and, when the Loyalist remnant crossed the frontier into France, the Service Committee continued to assist those refugees. Many of these people were placed in concentration camps in southern France, and when Jewish refugees began to arrive a bit later, the AFSC workers already had the organization in place and some experience behind them in regard to the camps. They expanded their work into the camps set up for Jews and other European refugees.

It appears many of the children helped to escape from France were taken from the concentration camp at Gurs. The selection process is discussed to some extent in a few of the enclosed documents. The AFSC obviously worked closely with other groups in relation to assisting the refugee children. The United States Committee for the Care of European Children and the International Commission for the Assistance of Child Refugees were both involved with this effort. The latter group was headed in Europe by Howard Kershner. He previously worked with the AFSC in Spain and later among Spanish refugees in the South of France. The International Commission... was established by Quakers, although it was not under the administration of the AFSC. Howard Kershner wrote a book entitled Quaker Service in Modern War, Prentice-Hall, Inc., New York, copyright 1950. This deals with activities in Spain and France 1939-40. Possibly it might have some useful background material in it. You might also want to peruse Clarence Pickett's book For More Than Bread, Little, Brown and Co., Boston, copyright 1953. This gives some background information on the AFSC's activities in France. Clarence Pickett was the executive secretary of the AFSC from 1929-50.

I am listing on a separate sheet the names of some of the people who appear in the enclosed correspondence to give you information on their whereabouts and whether or not they were AFSC appointees working here in Philadelphia and abroad, etc. I have noted it if they are deceased, and also tried to provide addresses (at least the most recent addresses we have on hand). You might want to be in touch with them, so they can give you their recollection of the events leading to the evacuation of the refugee children.

I hope these items will be of benefit to you. I hesitate to ask, but I wonder if you would be willing to pay for the photocopying of the documents, which amounts to $2.90, and for the postage on the envelope in which all this material has arrived? I'll be appreciative for that assistance.

Best wishes in carrying out your project. If I can be of any additional help please let me know

Sincerely,

Jack Sutters

Jack Sutters
Archives

(2)

Encs.

P.S. Since I see I have sufficient space below, I'll list the names there.

Howard Kershner - Still living, and I believe in California, but I am unable to supply an address for him.

Allen & Dorothy Bonnell - AFSC appointees in Marseilles. I believe the the following address is correct:

11 Single Lane
Wallingford, Pa. 19086

Phillip Conard - AFSC appointee in Lisbon. Now deceased.

Margaret Frawley - Worked/in France and Philadelphia office. Now deceased. for AFSC

Marnie Schauffler - Worked for AFSC in Philadelphia. Spent some time in Lisbon at the time of the evacuation of the children, or before according to the correspondence. Her address is:

Friends House
17300 Quaker Lane
Sandy Spring, Maryland 20860

PROCEEDINGS
of the
American Philosophical Society

Contents of Volume 124, Number 5

Price for complete number $5.00

11/28/83

AMERICAN PHILOSOPHICAL SOCIETY
Independence Square
Philadelphia, Pa. 19106

LEGALITY AND RESISTANCE IN VICHY FRANCE: THE RESCUE OF JEWISH CHILDREN

HILLEL J. KIEVAL

Department of History, University of Washington*

To Georges Garel, b. March 1, 1909, d. January 9, 1979:·

זכר צדיק לברכה

INTRODUCTION

In the course of this essay I hope to investigate a number of specific responses of the French Jewish community to the German occupation and to the implementation of Nazi racial policy in France. I am particularly interested in isolating those actions which might legitimately be described as "resistance," and, more importantly, the process whereby a traditionally conservative, law-abiding community—which has deep emotional ties to the state—consciously decides to abandon the legal framework of its operations.

As it is impossible to consider all aspects of Jewish life in Vichy France, or even all of the activities of official Jewish organizations, I have chosen to focus on one major effort of the Jewish community during the war years: relief work with children and, ultimately, their rescue from the threat of deportation to the death camps. The effort to shield Jewish children from the onslaught of war, homelessness, sickness, and poverty represented a deliberate, although not always well-thought-out, policy of social relief. It was a program carried out by a number of both Jewish and non-Jewish organizations. What makes it fascinating for the student of European resistance is that this work was pursued in conjunction with, and often with the blessings of the administrative agencies of the Vichy government. In the beginning such activity was not at all identified as an expression of opposition to the Vichy regime; nor was it necessarily anti-German. Only after several years did the Jewish organizations come to realize the impossibility of rescuing a segment of the Jewish population while retaining their legal status.

While not ignoring the contributions of other groups in this regard, I plan to concentrate on three of the major organizations which had been caring for Jewish children in France well before the start of the war: the *Oeuvre de Secours aux Enfants*—popularly known as OSE; ORT, the Organization for Rehabilitation through Training; and the *Éclaireurs Israélites de France*—the E.I.F. I shall try to determine how these organizations met the day-to-day demands of the occupation. I shall be asking whether they engaged in resistance activity, and, if so, when; how successful their efforts were to preserve the lives of Jewish children; and to what extent their preoccupations with legal social work inhibited their eventual effectiveness in the area of resistance.

According to what criteria do a group's efforts qualify as organized resistance? Of the hundreds of historical works on the general French resistance to the German occupation that have appeared since the end of the war, few have been helpful in answering this question. The books have often served partisan political purposes, to defend, attack, apologize for, or eulogize some particular group. The more careless among the authors have written of a single, unified, and coordinated resistance effort in France. Some have been so bold as to claim that patriotic Frenchmen began the resistance movement on that fateful June day in 1940 when soldiers of the Third Reich occupied Paris. Neither statement can in fact stand up to a critical examination. There was no single French resistance organization; the groups who opposed the Nazi occupation and Vichy's accommodations to it were as divided as political parties of the Third Republic. And the historical record shows that Frenchmen, by and large, had no stomach for opposition in June, 1940. The dissolution of the Third Republic, the selection of Maréchal Pétain as head of state, and the armistice agreement with Germany all enjoyed tremendous popular approval in the summer of 1940.

A few recent works, however, have demonstrated greater care in achieving a methodological approach to guide the analysis of French resistance movements. Henri Michel has offered a working definition of resistance activity which is both broad and flexible, but critical enough to exclude flagrant examples of mythology and propaganda. He has defined resistance as: "any action or writing, performed or edited, [which was] in violation of the armistice conventions concluded on June 22 between France and Germany, and on June 24 between France and Italy, or in opposition to their application, from whatever place or

* Seattle, Washington 98112.

PROCEEDINGS OF THE AMERICAN PHILOSOPHICAL SOCIETY, VOL. 124, NO. 5, OCTOBER, 1980
Reprint
Printed in U.S.A.

Juives before it was sent along to its destination. One such letter reads in part as follows:

> In the matter of evacuation, our task is almost completed. It was necessary to prepare the way for the systematic and continuous evacuation of the children, to instill in the appropriate agencies the feeling for the need to aid the children in your homes, according to this method, and we are happy to announce that not only have we succeeded, but that it has become a slogan for a large campaign which has now been launched by the United Jewish Appeal and which is directed not only to aiding the children by feeding them, clothing them, instructing them, and assuring medical attention wherever they happen to be, but also by bringing them here and continuing to aid them here. Your task now consists of applying continuous pressure on the interested organizations so that as many children as possible can be brought to your homes. We, on our side, will make use of every occasion to push the matter.[67]

By the middle of April, 1942, only fifty-five children remained at Rivesaltes. OSE was so pleased with the speed with which the liberations were proceeding, that it was able to report in a memo of May 12 to the U.G.I.F. that "the problem of 'children in the camps' can be considered virtually resolved."[68]

It is essential to note that none of this work was either secret or illegal. Even when the French government was not reading the mail of the Jewish organizations, it was constantly being consulted about the complete range of social work in and out of the camps. When the U.G.I.F. finally took full control over Jewish institutional life in the South in March, 1942, cooperation between the state and Jewish organizations like OSE became even closer. Nor is there any indication that the Jewish organizations felt this to be a great detriment to their overall effectiveness. In fact, the evidence points much to the contrary view. OSE reports to the U.G.I.F. at this time were quite complete; nothing that emerges from other sources of the period was omitted from them. In some instances OSE even suggested that the closer affiliation with the state that the U.G.I.F. provided might lead to the growth and improvement of Jewish social work in France.[69] OSE did begin to change its method of operation during late 1941 and early 1942, but it was a change which emphasized the providing of more institutional shelter to victimized children. The work was aimed at removing children from the direct and visible hazards of the internment camps, that is, from sickness, undernourishment, and lack of education. It involved a considerable extension of services within the institutions themselves, and it was pursued in direct conjunction with the delegated authorities of Vichy.

The work was open, free for anyone to see and to inspect, and it seemed to be extremely effective. Ironically, it also resulted in greater and greater concentrations of children in the very establishments which were to become easy targets for future raids and arrests. The liberations from the camps brought the children out of one fire and into another smoldering one.

EMIGRATION TO THE UNITED STATES

Emigration, as a solution to the difficulties of Jewish existence in Vichy France, was certainly not overlooked by the organizations involved in child welfare. In fact, at the moment that the institutional programs for care and relief were at their height, the leadership of OSE clamored to its contacts in the United States to seek ways to facilitate the emigration of large groups of children to that country. But this was an exceedingly complicated thing to arrange. The United States would issue visas only for children under the age of sixteen with relatives or specific institutions to take care of them once they arrived. For every entry visa approved by the United States, exit and transport visas had to be issued by Vichy, and scarce space on transatlantic voyages had to be found.

Negotiations with the United States government were handled by Eleanor Roosevelt's Committee for the Care of European Children. Her contacts with the Jewish community were the Committee to Aid German-Jewish Children and, through it, the Joint Distribution Committee. The Quakers handled the collection and distribution of visas from the American consulates in France, helped to select children to be brought to this country, and accompanied the young emigrants to the port of embarkation. OSE in France provided the general pool of children, and OSE in New York applied pressure on the Joint to try to speed the pace of the negotiations. The machinery, it is clear, was complex, and it moved very slowly. Mid-way through the negotiations the U. S. govern-

---

[67] OSE New York to OSE France (intercepted by the C.G.Q.J.), September 17, 1941 (CDJC, CCCLXVI-6).

[68] OSE memo to the U.G.I.F., May 12, 1942 (YIVO, UGIF-XCVIII, 1).

[69] ". . . grâce aux nouvelles possibilités qui lui ont été offertes, la 3-ème Direction de l'U.G.I.F. (anciennement OSE) a sensiblement accru son activité dan les principales branches pendant la période qui va du début du mois d'avril à mi-mai." (OSE memo, May 12, 1942, YIVO, UGIF-XCVIII, 1). See also OSE France to OSE New York, February 4, 1942 (YIVO, OSE-6): "We cannot, as yet, give you any definite information about the new form of our work here, as the reorganisation has not been achieved yet. We hope to be able to continue our activities, and even develop them. We work now along two lines: (1) to admit as many children as possible from centres d'hébergement into our Homes; only for the month of February we foresee the release and admission of a hundred children, and thus the plan mapped out by our friend Julius [Brutzkus?] is nearly achieved, although not in the way he foresaw it; (2) to extend the network of our social relief and take under our care children of familles affected with T.B. whom we wish to isolate and place in appropriate Nursing Homes."

ment decided to deny entry visas to anyone who was a citizen of Germany or Austria, and confusion reigned thereafter whether or not this edict applied to children under the age of fourteen.

OSE received word from the Quakers in the winter of 1941 that it could submit a list of 500 children whom it would like to send to the United States. As OSE set out to prepare the children's dossiers, permission was granted for an initial group of 111 children to enter the country; seventy of these places were reserved for OSE children. When the first convoy of young émigrés prepared to leave France in May, 1941, it represented eight months of negotiation and work.[70]

Both the United States government and the Quakers proved to be stumbling blocks in the way of achieving greater emigration of children from France. In early July, 1941, L. Gurvic of OSE in France expressed great satisfaction with the way that the Quakers handled the formal relations with the American authorities there. "We were absolutely right in cooperating with them in the close way we did, and this cooperation must be carried on so that the Quakers should take upon them all formalities. Their relationship with the Consul is good and will serve our purpose. . . . Let them assume the direction of the formalities, as it is not a matter of prestige, but of results."[71] Only one week later, however, OSE began to express doubts about the willingness of the Quakers to pursue further emigrations. OSE's French office complained in a letter of July 15 that Quaker officials were worried about the heavy expenses involved in the project. One such person, a Mr. Bonnell, emphasized to OSE that it cost about $500 to send one child to New York, "whereas for the same amount of money a child may be maintained here for a whole year." To this type of argument OSE leaders in France responded:

> Naturally the question must not be put that way and we must endeavour [sic] to bring about the question of the future of the children. If some children may stay here, those on the other hand who have nobody and nothing in France, must be given a chance of making their way through life and emigrate. We explained all this to Mr. Bonnell and he finally agreed with our viewpoint and owned that our opinion was correct, and he promised to write to this affect [sic] to his American Committee.[72]

If the Quakers acquiesced to the OSE point of view with regard to the importance of emigration, the American government acted in the summer of 1941 to complicate the entire procedure. New regulations stiffened the requirements for affidavits and supporting documents from the American side. Biographies, letters of recommendation, character references, and bank or Treasury Department certificates had to accompany each application for entry. Nevertheless, negotiations continued through the summer, and in August, 1941, OSE received another 100 visas. All of the children chosen for this convoy left France by the beginning of September.[73]

OSE leaders in France knew that for many of their children, particularly those whose parents had remained in Central Europe and those whose parents had been deported to the East, emigration to the United States provided the best hope for physical security and psychological well-being. Yet, even as the first convoys of children were being assembled for transport, they expressed grave concerns about the prospect of losing control over these children. Specifically they worried about the fact that the children, once in the United States, would be outside the domain of OSE's institutional supervision, and would either come under the care of some other institution, or would simply be placed with a private family. This tremendous preoccupation with the institutional format of child care caused an extended debate to rage between OSE in France and the New York branch, a debate which highlighted the ideological convictions that helped to prolong the formal structure of relief in France.

The French organization wanted OSE in the United States to build a home for at least 100 children in which it would be able to supervise the lives of some—if not all—of the children who arrived from Europe. Such a project proved to be unfeasible, both because it would have duplicated services which were already available in the American Jewish welfare community and because OSE, in fact, was not the institution which was sponsoring the immigration of the children; that organization was the Committee to Aid German-Jewish Children.

OSE in France grew more and more adamant about the issue of continued supervision over the course of 1941. In July it wrote that it feared that OSE in New York would never become a viable American institution until it extended its functioning beyond fundraising and political pressure to include direct care of children.

> We are afraid that if you remain within the limits and boundaries fixed by the Joint without trying to enlarge your activities . . . you will not be able to live up to your position, and the interest towards your work will weaken, whereas, being a living organization, you might have wider scopes and new groups would gather around you as a nucleus.[74]

[70] OSE France to OSE New York, January 20, 1941, March 26, 1941, and July 2 1941 (YIVO, OSE-1); also OSE report for March, April, and May, 1941 (Consistoire, Uncatalogued-24).

[71] OSE France to OSE New York, July 7, 1941 (YIVO, OSE-1).

[72] OSE France to OSE New York, July 15, 1941 (YIVO, OSE-1).

[73] OSE report for June, July, August, 1941 (CDJC, CCCLXVI-11).

[74] OSE France to OSE New York, July 2, 1941 (YIVO, OSE-1).

More importantly, perhaps, OSE felt that it was committed to a particular type of service, one which stressed moral and educational goals, such as fellowship, cooperation, the practical arts, and Jewish nationalism, as well as practical relief. If OSE were to lose control over the children who emigrated from France, its entire educational program would have been threatened.

> When we commenced work here in France, we were also told that in Western countries it was deemed more normal and convenient to place children in families, that it was less expensive and safer for the children's future. We used to reply to such statements that it might be true in most cases, not in all, and that every possible solution should be carefully studied in all its aspects. According to our opinion a collective life in a Children's Home is a better means of adapting children to new conditions, of ensuring them a better education and training for a life of labour, and besides it is the only way of giving them a feeling of belonging to a group and of being bound to each other by ties of solidarity.[75]

The French leaders urged their American counterparts to "retain control over our children," and pointed to their record of achievement in France as an example of what could be accomplished in the area of child relief.

One would be well-advised to keep in mind written exchanges of this type when one confronts the subsequent immobility of the Jewish relief organizations in France. For bureaucratic inertia was probably not the main cause of their prolonged retention of the legal, institutionalized framework for relief work. Jewish organizations like ORT, OSE, and the E.I.F. brought to their tasks fixed notions—ideological convictions, one might argue—about the proper medium for the delivery of social services. Relief and rescue were only part of an overall system of social work, and virtually no one in France saw the need to sacrifice the greater program for the sake of rescue alone. One distributed food and clothing; one provided medical services; one set up homes and schools; one even liberated children from internment camps or sent them out of the country to avoid particular dangers. No single activity precluded or endangered the performance of another. Each service fell under a great institutional umbrella which provided efficiency, legal protection, and intellectual direction. And the results achieved thus far in France seemed very good.

Although the pace of emigration to the United States was quite slow, the leaders of OSE remained confident through the summer of 1941 that hundreds of additional visas would be forthcoming. By the fall, they grew impatient; emigration loomed before their eyes ever more greatly as a solution toward removing children from the camps and easing the burden on their already packed homes and institutions.

[75] *Ibid.*

The children, themselves, appeared to place a great deal of hope in this means of escaping persecution and misery. In October OSE wrote to New York the following warning: "We could not insist too much on the importance of this problem; emigration occupies such a great place in the spirit of the children and the parents count to such a great extent on their departure, that it would be painful to remove this hope from them, hope which is already quite illusory."[76]

The American government gave permission in principle for the issuance of 500 blanket-visas for destitute children in France. In the end, however, only 100 more were issued after the fall of 1941. OSE in France was furious that more could not be done, but their anger made no headway.[77] The last convoy of children left France for the United States in May, 1942. Only 311 children in all (not including individual families who acted on their own) were removed from France despite the efforts of five organizations.

* * *

A number of relief activities did diverge from the usual pattern of the period. Testimonies have been made, for instance, which show that Jewish children were smuggled illegally across the line of demarcation and given refuge in Catholic homes for the duration of the war.[78] In June, 1942, the Police for Jewish Affairs suspected Abbé Glasberg and Cardinal Gerlier of having camouflaged a new ORT project behind the "front" of a school for the re-education of refugees. The police questioned the existence of the institution, which had received official permission from the prefect of the Hautes-Alpes the previous month because of the fact that its nine staff members and thirteen of its fourteen students were Jews.[79]

In Paris, the *Colonie Scolaire* began to place needy children in the countryside to live with peasant families as early as 1941. The peasant women, called "nourrices," received as much as 800 francs per child per month for their services. In addition, the organization provided clothing and bedding for the child. It is not clear exactly when this activity began, nor how many children were hidden in this way before July, 1942; but notes and letters from several "nourrices" can be found which date from the early part of 1942.[80]

[76] OSE France to OSE New York, October 22, 1941 (YIVO, OSE-1).

[77] See, for example, letter of November 28, 1941 (YIVO, OSE-1).

[78] For example, CDJC, CDLXXVI-3, concerning the clandestine activity of Germaine Ribière.

[79] Police report of June 23, 1942 (CDJC, CCXXXIX-81).

[80] See the uncatalogued documents of the Rue Amelot (*Colonie Scolaire*) at the CDJC. Most of the Rue Amelot materials are located at YIVO.

C. Peter R. Gossels

From:	Nancy Gossels <ngossels@comcast.net>
Sent:	Sunday, June 16, 2013 12:03 PM
To:	Peter Gossels
Subject:	Fwd: found link between Eleanor Roosevelt and USCOM and Pickett and 200 visas

Begin forwarded message:

From: Nancy Gossels <ngossels@comcast.net>
Subject: Re: found link between Eleanor Roosevelt and USCOM and Pickett and 200 visas
Date: June 16, 2013 12:02:08 PM EDT
To: katie hickox <khickox@yahoo.com>
Cc: lisa gossels <lgossels@gmail.com>

Dear Katie,

Congratulations on finding the first independent reference that I know of to USCom's success in bringing 200 Jewish children to the United States in 1941 and for documenting the joint efforts of Clarence Pickett and Eleanor Roosevelt to bring this about. Thank you very much!

Stefan Lewy, who lives in Manchester, New Hampshire, is a good friend of ours. His trip across the Atlantic on the Serpa Pinto, a ship that shuttled between Lisbon and New York during the war years, occurred in 1942, about a year after that same ship brought us to the States.

Peter

On Jun 15, 2013, at 11:42 AM, katie hickox wrote:

HI Peter,

I've asked for an extension to finish writing the article so I have until tomorrow, Monday morning, I'm hoping! (left vm mssg and email for President Joan Simmons of www.dwforum.org. Regardless, I think this article might be able to be published in several different media if I do a good enough job of getting all the source information and writing a good article!

Thanks for the great group photo of you sitting next to Bill Graham. WOW! Thanks for the 2nd document regarding the list of children on the 3rd convoy sent to the US via the Serpa Pinto.

Last night I was up late searching online the Eleanor Roosevelt papers at Hyde park but didn't find anything regarding the 200 visas or Pickett or anything related to her efforts to rescue Jewish refugee children in France in 1941.

However, I finally realized I had to change the search terms, that Quakers was the wrong search term and learned that there are several humanitarian organizations that are sponsored by the Quakers. So presto, this morning finally found what I was looking for.

did you know that another young man on your convoy, Stephan Lewy, says that the Serpa Pinto was stopped and boarded by a German submarine? http://www.holocaustcenterbn.org/steven_lewy_full.html

See here:
My parents and our sponsor provided a new affidavit for me, but a visa was denied even after an attorney pleaded the case in the State Department. Out of desperation, my mother wrote a letter to the President, promising that if a visa were issued, I would be the best American soldier. It worked, a visa was issued. Our family always felt that Eleanor Roosevelt had something to do with it. I left the castle in Chabannes in the spring of 1942, picked up my visa in Lyon, and went to Marseille to await our ship. The waiting period was 6 weeks. We left Marseille, stopped in Barcelona to pick up some Spanish (non-Jewish) refugee children. I was put in charge of them. We continued to Tunisia, disembarked, and continued by bus to Casablanca. We boarded a Portuguese ship, the *Serpa Pinto*, and steamed off to America, 70 Jewish refugees and fifty Spanish children.

Half way across the ocean, we were stopped and boarded by a German submarine. When it left, we expected to be torpedoed, but nothing happened. As we approached Bermuda, we were stopped by the British Navy and taken off the ship. It took them 7 days to inspect the ship and luggage. We then continued on to NY only to drop anchor in the harbor

I just found this webpage:
http://www.gwu.edu/~erpapers/teachinger/glossary/uscom.cfm

The United States Committee for the Care of European Children

The United States Committee for the Care of European Children (USCOM) was founded in the summer of 1940 by Clarence Pickett to help evacuate children from incessant German bombing of English cities, commonly known as the Battle of Britain. The U.S. government wanted to save children by moving them away from areas under attack; therefore, it was receptive to lobbying by humanitarians who argued that British children should be temporarily relocated to the safety of the United States. In June 1940, FDR asked Eleanor Roosevelt to establish USCOM to help transport these children across the Atlantic; however, by the fall of 1940, its evacuation efforts were temporarily suspended after having successfully relocated just over 800 children.

The committee is most often noted for the role it played in trying to evacuate German Jewish refugee children. Although the USCOM could only allow a certain number of refugee children to enter the United States, the committee vigorously lent its support to he Wagner-Rogers Bill which would have expanded the quota significantly. Despite the vocal support that the committee received from prominent humanitarians, particularly Eleanor Roosevelt, the legislation failed to pass. Nonetheless, the support of ER and others enabled the committee to resume and expand upon its work. In 1942 and 1943, USCOM struggled to relocate several hundred Jewish refugee children from Western Europe. The committee continued to function after the war's conclusion, but disbanded completely in 1953.

and this website

http://www.jewishgen.org/databases/holocaust/0171_Hidden_Children_in_France.html

From June through September 1941, three transports managed to bring about 200 children from the OSE homes to the U.S. They were sponsored by the United States Committee for the Care of European Children, The Jewish Children's Aid, and assisted by the American Friends Service Committee (Quakers) in Marseilles.

From: C. Peter R. Gossels <pgossels@socialaw.com>
To: khickox@yahoo.com
Cc: ngossels@comcast.net
Sent: Friday, June 14, 2013 11:36 AM
Subject: Eleanor Roosevelt article

Dear Katie,

I do remember you from the time that we met at Lisa Gossels' showing of "The Children of Chabannes" at Berkley.

Unfortunately, you have not given me enough time to document the statement I made concerning the 200 visas that were given to Jewish kids in Vichy France to admit them to the United States. I do, however, have a list of the 200 kids who arrived in the U.S. with the help of those visas. My brother, Werner Gossels, and I arrived as part of the third of three U.S. convoys of children, sailing on the S.S. Serpa Pinto. Annexed is a list of the names of those children, including the names of Wolodja Grajonza (Bill Graham). Werner Goldschmidt and Al Berg, whose name appears in your e-mail to Lisa Gossels dated June 13, 2013 at 3:45 p.m. You may also enjoy seeing the picture of our younger group at the Chateau de Quincy, showing Werner Goldschmidt and Bill Graham (age 8) sitting next to me in the front row.

The 200 children came to the United States in 1941 under the auspices of the USCOM. USCOM was a subcommittee of the American Friends Service Committee, not OSE or the Joint Distribution Committee, which were both Jewish organizations. Eleanor Roosevelt had been very friendly with Clarence E. Pickett of the AFSC for more than 10 years and enlisted the help of the Quakers to bring us to the United States.

The source of my information is Robert Snyder, who was a Director of Development for the AFSC in New England for many years. He had provided us with a fair amount of information concerning the efforts of the Quakers to help Jews and other people in Germany and France during the 30s and 40s. He had told me that he planned to go to Hyde Park to document Eleanor Roosevelts' role in obtaining those 200 visas, but has not, to my knowledge, done so to date. I tried to reach him this morning, but there was no answer at his house.

So, I can not help you much more with your project before the end of the day, but will send you more information, if you like, when I shall receive it.

Peter

-----Original Message-----

Attached file is scanned image in PDF format.
Use Acrobat(R)Reader4.0 or later version, or Adobe(R)Reader(TM) of Adobe Systems Incorporated to view the document.
ιcrobat(R)Reader4.0 or later version, or Adobe(R)Reader(TM) can be downloaded from the following URL:
Adobe, the Adobe logo, Acrobat, the Adobe PDF logo, and Reader are registered trademarks or trademarks of Adobe Systems Incorporated in the United States and other countries.

http://www.adobe.com/

"Gerda [Schrage] had stayed in Berlin after Hilde's departure and was looking for new support. She lived unrecognized in various apartments, mostly for subtenancy. Like many other illegals, she was often sneaking to friends in the evenings. She went to Gerda Lewinnek, called Gerdi, who at that time still lived in the parents' home. There was cooking for the hidden, sometimes for more than ten people. Gerda, who is a stranger to any fanaticism, who knows no outbursts of emotion and exuberance, has only one word for her friend Gerdi and her mother Emma: "They were angels." She had met the young woman through her brother's mutual friends and was there at once inspired by the energetic, confident girl who also worked in the clothing department. Gerda Lewinnek - she was born in Berlin in 1914 - was the daughter of a Jewish slaughterer and a Christian mother. So she and her brother Norbert were "half-Jews" in Nazi terminology. Her father knew many people at the slaughterhouses in Berlin, so he was able to provide himself, his family and the numerous submerged friends in need again and again with additional rations of meat. In the summer of 1940 he was arrested for a meat smuggling denunciation. He died in October 1941 as a broken man.

Gerdi Lewinnek and her mother Emma, who must have been as courageous as her daughter, set up a network for the needy, which was geared towards daily survival. They cooked meals and distributed fake coupons, because the hidden Jews had no access to rationed food. "They really helped everyone who needed support," Gerda recalls in New York, shaking her head in disbelief and admiration for over sixty years, over people who risked seeing themselves to be there for others. The Lewinneks Gerda owed her fake passport that identified her as a Swiss citizen. Gerdi had organized it over a friend in Switzerland.

Gerdi Lewinnek had to do heavy forced labor for IG Farben six days a week. In the few remaining time, her friend Gerda remembers, she worked at her home as a seamstress, making changes, sewing new clothes from old ones. Qualified seamstresses were in short supply and there was a great demand for a constant reworking of worn items that nobody threw away.

Gerdi's great love was a Jewish boxer, who had even brought it to a Brandenburg championship title: Bully Schott. In the photos, he looks just as you imagine a boxer, small, with a battered nose and protruding ears, the look of self-confidence, almost audacity, a boy from Berlin who can not scare anything.

So he survived three years Sachsenhausen, where it must have been particularly bad in the early years, and Auschwitz, where he had been taken in the fall of 1942 in a cattle car. In both camps, the proletarian boy adapted quickly, saw through the balance of power and was able to assure himself with the sure instinct of supporting various civilian employees. About this helper messages penetrated to his girlfriend Gerdi to Berlin. She was in no way inferior to Bully in her audacity. Several times she went to Sachsenhausen and Auschwitz to see him, even if only remotely, when entering and leaving the work columns.
A "half-Jewish" on a train ride to Auschwitz to meet her lover, which she managed for moments! Gerda tells me this story about her friend in New York, and for a moment, in the joy of this crazy hussar prank, I realize that she, the narrator herself, was once driven by this audacity. Had not she tried again and again to escape the murderers' access, had always thought of escaping, dared her twice and never surrendered to her fate for a second? The two women were similar, young people full of love of life and courage.

After Gerdi Lewinnek's trips to Auschwitz, she and her friends no longer had any doubt about what was going on there. The people on the train closed the windows because of the stench and everyone knew where it came from. Even the illegally living Gerda was having no illusions. She knew, especially through Bully's information, what she would expect in case of arrest and deportation.

Bully is one of the few inmates who escaped from Auschwitz. He escaped in the winter of 1944, made his way to Berlin and contacted his girlfriend. He got a gun on the black market. With that, he shot at a Jewish claw who tried to arrest him and fled again.

A little later Gerdi and her brother Norbert were arrested for "favoring the Jews". For weeks, Gerdi Lewinnek was brutally beaten to divulge Bully's whereabouts. She did not say anything, but cried to her tormentors in the face that she should rather shoot her, because she would betray nothing. In fact, she probably did not know where Bully was at that time.

I would have liked to know Gerdi Lewinnek, this woman who always knew from a safe feeling what was right. In the photos, the slender woman with the shoulder-length dark hair and the unaffected smile looks as familiar as if I had known her for years. Perhaps there are only a few such unperturbed people in every generation like them.

They were angels - but very tangible. Gerdi Lewinnek was not a benefactress who wanted to help all people, she distinguished very accurately and very securely between perpetrators and victims. Like her friend Bully, who defeated a Nazi advocate with his dreaded left after the war and helped the Allied authorities to track down suspects, Gerdi Lewinnek went straight for the people who had made her life hell. Gerda tells me in New York that her friend went to the Jewish community after being released to the imprisoned, notorious Stella. There she would have pulled the hair out of the Jewish grapple, who had tracked down countless hidden people and delivered them to the GESTAPO. Later I read, the blonde hair was Gerdi's scissors fell victim. When I tell Gerda on the phone, she laughs and says, yes, that would be more likely, it probably was more like that. A well-known photograph shows Stella wearing a turban around her bald head, unadorned and robbed of her legendary beauty. Gerdi had put her in that condition.

After the war Gerdi and Bully got married, they converted to Orthodox Judaism. In 1950, both emigrated to Australia, with her son born in Berlin. They named him after Gerdi's father, Martin.

Martin Schott wrote to me that his mother often talked proudly and vividly about her time in Berlin and also about her good friend Gerda.
After a very long illness, Gerdi died in 1993. Her husband Bully, who suffered badly from the loss of his wife, followed her in 2000, at the age of eighty-six.

As a Jewish athlete, an indomitable fighter, and a survivor with an adventurous biography, Bully is the subject of historical research. His life gives substance for books and films. His wife Gerdi also appears in some reports.

Norbert Lewinnek was born in 1916 and managed to survive as a Jew in Berlin during the Deutsches Reich ruled by the Nazis until 1948 when he arrived in Melbourne, Australia. He lived and worked there as a furrier until he died in 2001.

An account of the Lewinnek family's life during the Nazi time translated from a German book by Knut Elstermann entitled "Gerda's Silence", which was produced as a movie in 2008 and directed by Britta Wauer.

Translation

January 4, 1947

Dear Dr. Lewis:

I learned from the Superintendent of 35 Lippehnerstrasse that you wished detailed information concerning the whereabouts of the former owner, Frau Lina Lewy and her daughter, Miss Hilde and Mrs. Charlotte Gossels and I take it as my obligation as a Jew to share with you details concerning the fate of your relatives.

My parents lived in the house of Mr. and Mrs. Lewy and their relatives since 1912 as the oldest tenants and I have lived there since my birth in 1916. Out of the many Jewish families who lived in the house we were the only one that were permitted to survive through a miracle of God, except for my father.

Mrs. Lewy was obliged as the owner of the house to do many things during the time of the Nazis, especially, and she suffered a great deal partly from the governmental authorities but also from the tenants who were not Jewish. From the point of view of the tenants, it was well in the year 1939 as Mrs. Lewy was forced to sell the house for a very low price and she was told in a kindly manner that she also had to live in the house in the future. At the beginning, Mrs. Lewy was also very happy, because she thought she would be left in peace. Unfortunately during the following year, the worst for the Jews, in the year 1941, namely the requirement of the so-called Jewish star, so that each Jew was made to stand out from the Nazi-rabble, even in our house, it was often made obvious.

When the Jews were required to work in the factories, Mrs. Gossels and Miss Hilde were affected as well.

At the end(?) of 1941, the first transports began; the so-called "Evacuation Transports". In 1942, began the forced evacuation of the old Jews who were unable to work and fate overtook Frau Lewy in June 1942.

On the same day Mrs. Gossels received the news that she could travel to Switzerland, but the sudden abduction of her mother caused Mrs. Gossels a nervous breakdown and she lay sick for a long time.

On February 27, 1943 fate overwhelmed all the Jews who worked in the largest factories including Miss Hilde; it was a Saturday and one day later, Mrs. Gossels was taken from her home on February 28 what we first heard in addition. She took luggage for Miss Hilde because most of the Jews went to the transport without luggage; yes, only a very few could still go with a wardrobe and change clothes, as opposed to all of the others who had to go in their workclothes.

-2-

The transport of the women then went to Auschwitz - Monowitz or Birkenau. Mrs. Lewy came to Theresienstadt.

Mrs. Gossels' two children, whom you hopefully know, were brought to safety just in time. I believe to Southern France and I hope the children are still alive. In the event that you have heard nothing from both of the boys, I will search so that I may learn of their whereabouts. I have also published an announcement in the Jewish Newspaper to see if anyone of those who has returned and was together with your relatives on the transport or in the camps has information concerning them.

Concerning the house, I must tell you that the purchaser at the time and current owner of the house is a Nazi. I take it that you can file a claim as a matter of law or to surrender (assign) the claim to the Jewish Community. I am disappointed with our Superintendent, I explained to him, it is such a terrible shame that Jewish property is still in the hands of Nazis. The honorable Superintendent argued, naturally, that the current owner of the house is no Nazi, as everyone knows. But I have sufficient evidence if it is necessary.

I certainly believe that the Jewish Community will represent you well on this occasion and things will get off the ground better if perhaps it is signed by the administrator.

Dear Dr. Lewis, I have a request? of you.

My mother has two sisters and my father a cousin in America; perhaps you can make it possible to get in touch with them in order to help us leave Germany. My father's cousin has already written to us, but we have received no news from my aunts. They went to a lot of trouble in 1938 to help us get out of Germany but their efforts came to nothing because of the war.

It was a great a joy when we were freed by the Allies and all of the Jews should have lived to this day (?) Unfortunately only small things were granted to them and it is now very disappointing, because it is a terrible shame, that we Jews who could not leave at the time and therefore had to remain in Germany and be branded as Jews by Hitler are embattled as outsiders and herewith despite the fact that all of them came out as the victor, just as much as every allied soldier.

But how can the truth be seen we are indeed free men, something that we value greatly, but today it is said we are not Jews, apart from the Germans, and as a result, we must live under the same conditions as the Germans who wanted war and lost it. So begins another battle.

-3-

There is only one objective for us, and that is to get out of Germany as fast as possible, because one can never again be happy in a land where one had to experience such unbearable sufferings and when it is still not going well.

In the hope that it is possible for you to fullfill these requests I shall await your reply sending the best greetings.

Norbert Lewinnek

Norbert Lewinnek
Berlin N.O. 55,
Lippehnerstr. 35.

Berlin d. 4. Januar 1947.

Sehr geehrter Herr Dr. Lewis!

Ich erfuhr [illegible], des Hauses Lippehnerstr. 35,
das Sie näheres über dem Verbleib der früheren Hausbesitzerin Frau Lina Leroy
u. Ihren Töchtern Frl. Hilde u. Frau Charlotte Gossels, Auskunft wünschten,
u. ich halte es als Jude für meine Pflicht, Ihnen näheres über das Schicksal Ihrer
Angehörigen mitzuteilen.
Meine Eltern wohnen seit 1912 im Hause des Herrn u. Frau Leroy, u. gehören
zu den ältesten Mietern, u. ich als Sohn seit meiner Geburt 1926. Von den
vielen jüdischen Familien des Hauses sind wir die Einzigen denen es vergönnt
war, wie durch [illegible] Gottes [illegible] es zu überleben, außer meinem Vater.
Frau Leroy hatte als Hausbesitzerin [illegible] der verruchten Nazi-Zeit, besonders viel
zu leiden, teils von den Behörden, aber auch von den nicht jüdischen Mietern. An
Hand unseres Mietsbuches war es wohl im Jahre 1939 als Frau Leroy gezwungen wurde,
das Haus für einen geringen Preis zu verkaufen, u. man Ihr gütigst versprach,
das Sie auch weiterhin, in dem Hause wohnen darf. Frau Leroy war auch anfang
sehr zufrieden, da Sie glaubte nun Ihre Ruhe zu haben. Leider kam in den nun
folgenden Jahren, das Schwerste über [illegible] im Jahre 1941 nämlich das
tragen des so genannten Judensterns, wo [illegible] nun jeder Jude als Freiwild
dem Nazi-Pöbel ausgeliefert war, auch in unserem Hause machte sich das oft
bemerkbar. Als die Zeit mit dem jüdischen Arbeitseinsatz, in den Fabriken begann
wurden Fr. Gossels u. Frl. Hilde auch davon betroffen. Ende des Jahres 1941, begannen die ersten Transporte, die so genannten „Evakuierungs-Transporte."
1942 begannen die Zwangsverschleppungen von den älteren arbeitsunfähigen
Juden, wo auch im Juni 1942, Frau Leroy das Schicksal ereilte. Am selben Tage bekam Frau Gossels, die Nachricht, Sie könne nach der Schweiz fahren, aber durch

die plötzliche Abholung der Mutter bekam Frau Gossel einen schweren Nerven-
zusammenbruch u. lag längere Zeit krank. Am 27. Februar 1943 ereilte wie alle
Juden, die größtenteils in den Fabriken arbeiteten, so zunächst auch Frl. Hilde das
Schicksal, es war an einem Sonnabend, u. einen Tag später, also am 28. Februar wur
de Frau Gossels aus der Wohnung abgeholt was wir erst nachträglich erfahren habe.
Gepäck hatte Sie für Frl. Hilde mitgenommen, denn die meisten Juden gingen
zum Transport, ohne Gepäck, ja die nur vereinzelte konnten noch zum Garde
robraum gehen u. sich umziehen dagegen fast Alle mußten so gehen, in der Arbeits
kleidung. Die Frauen-Transporte gingen damals nach Auschwitz-Monowitz, u.
Birkenau. Frau Levy kam nach Theresienstadt. Die beiden Kinder, von Frau
Gossels, wie Ihnen hoffentlich bekannt sein wird, waren rechtzeitig in Sicher
heit gebracht, ich glaube nach Süd-Frankreich, u. hoffentlich sind die Kinder
noch am Leben. Sollten Sie von den beiden Jungens noch nichts gehört haben,
so will ich versuchen, näheres über den Verbleib zu erfahren. Auch habe ich in
der „Jüdischen Zeitung" eine Such-Anzeige aufgegeben, ob Jemand von den
Zurückgekommenen, mit Ihren Angehörigen, auf den Transport, o. im
Lager zusammen war u. näheres berichten kann.
Betreffs des Hauses möchte ich Ihnen mitteilen, das der damalige Käufer
u. jetzige Besitzer des Hauses ein Nazi ist. Ich nehme an, das Sie Rechts-
Ansprüche zu stellen können u. veranlassen die Rechts-Ansprüche, der Jüdis
chen Gemeinde in Berlin zu übergeben. Über unseren Verwalter bin ich
enttäuscht, ich erklärte Ihm, daß es eine Schande ist, das Jüdischer Besitz
noch heute in den Händen der Nazis ist. Der Herr Verwalter stritt
natürlich ab, das der jetzige Hausbesitzer kein Nazie sei, wie man heute
allgemein hört. Aber ich habe genügend Beweise, wenn es erforderlich
ist. Ich glaube bestimmt, das die Jüdische Gemeinde, Sie in dieser An
gelegenheit gut vertreten würde, u. der Sache besser auf den Grund ge
we vielleicht der Verwalter es tun würde.

14 d. [illegible] 1947.

Werter Herr Dr. Lewis ich hätte eine Bitte an Sie.

Meine Mütter hat zwei Schwestern, ü. mein Vater einen Cousin in Amerika, vielleicht könnten Sie es möglich machen, sich mit Ihnen in Verbindüng züsetzen, zwecks einer Auswanderüng für üns. Der Cousin von meinem Vater hat üns schon geschrieben, aber von meinen beiden Tanten, haben wir keine Nachricht erhalten. Sie hatten sich im Jahre 1938 für ünsere Aüswanderüng sehr bemüht ü. es scheiterte dürch den Kriegsaüsbrüch.

Es war damals eine Freüde, als wir von den Allierten befreit würden ü. alle Jüden müssten diese Befreiüng erlebt haben. Leider sind es nür wenige, denen es vergönnt war, ü. sind nün sehr enttaüscht, denn es ist eine Schande, das wir Jüden, die damals nicht mehr aüswandern konnten, ü. dadürch in Deütschland bleiben müßten ü. von Hitler als Jüden gebrandmarkt waren, aüfs äüßerte bekämpf würden, ü. hiermit trotz allem als Sieger hervorgegangen sind, wie jeder Allierte Soldat. –

Wie sieht es aber in Wirklichkeit aus: ja wir sind wohl freie Menschen, was wir sehr zü schätzen wissen, aber trotz alledem wir sind nicht Jüden, sondern Deütsche, ü. was ist die Folge, wir müssen ünter denselben Lebensbedingüngen leben als wie die Deütschen, welche den Krieg wollten ü. verloren haben. Somit beginnt ein neüer Kampf. Für üns gibt es nür ein Ziel, so schnell als möglich, aüs Deütschland aüszüwandern, denn in einem Land wo man soviel ünerträgliches Leid erleben müßte, kann man nie wieder froh werden, ü. wenn es üns hier noch so güt ergehen wird.

In der Hoffnüng, das es Ihnen möglich ist mir diese Bitte zü erfüllen, verbleibe ich mit den besten Grüßen, Ihrer Antwort entgegen sehend.

Norbert Lewinnek

Translation

August 14, 1947

Dear Dr. Lewis:

You must have wondered why I could not answer your last letter before now. I did not receive your letter until now, because I had been sent to recuperate near the Harz (mountains) for more than two months by the Joint Distribution Committee.

Now I must impart to you what knowledge I can bring to your concerns:

Mrs. Lewy was forced to sell her house in 1940 after being forced to renovate it from A to Z. The proceeds were not paid to her, but were deposited in a Sperrkonto whence she could withdraw a very small amount each month, only enough needed to sustain a minimum standard of living.

I can report that the entire contents of the household itself were sold at auction at the time and whatever was left behind, like photo albums and books, were burnt in the courtyard. I can now also give you the address of the owner of the house, the one who took over the house at the time, and who even today, is that very same owner. He asserts today that he was a good acquaintance of Mrs. Lewy and that he paid her a very high price for the house and that he really was not a Nazi. I have now assembled sufficient evidence so that if it is necessary I can convince a court to the contrary. I should also let you know that someone has in the meanwhile filed claims against the house. Some days ago a lawyer, who led me to believe that he came on behalf of the Jewish Community sought me out and I gave him all of my information, but, later it turned out to be that he had come from America to investigate the whereabouts of the Lewy family. It had to do with an earlier friend of Mrs. Lewy who wanted to file a claim. The attorney was astonished when he learned from me that both of Mrs. Lewy's grandchildren were alive and that they are the rightful heirs, and he wanted to have the addresses, and I gave him your address and he wanted to get in touch with you.

In connection with this event, I handed the matter over to the Jewish Community because the matters have already cost me a lot of time and trouble.

You can now take these matters in your own hand. If you still need some documents then I will be happy to send them to you so long as I am in a position to do so. You have written me that you will reimburse me for all my expenses, and I would be grateful if you would send me a lebensmittel package as restitution because we need it urgently.

I thank you for writing to my relatives, although we have not received any news from them as yet and we must assume that they changed their address and we must yet wait a little longer.

In the hope that he will receive news from you, greets you

Norbert Lewinnek

Berlin d. 14. August

Sehr geehrter Herr Dr. Lewis!

Sie werden gewiß sehr verwundert sein, das ich erst jetzt, auf Ihren letzten Brief antworten kann. Ich habe Ihren Brief erst jetzt im Empfang nehmen können, da ich über zwei Monate von der Jüdischen Organisation „Joint" zur Erholung nach dem Harz verschickt wurde. - - - - -
Nun möchte ich Ihnen berichten, was ich in Ihrer Angelegenheit bisher in Erfahrung bringen konnte. Frau Levy mußte 1940 Ihr Haus zwangsweise verkaufen, vorher mußte Sie das Haus von A bis Z in Stand setzen lassen. Das Geld fürs Haus, bekam Sie nicht ausgezahlt, sondern es kam auf Sperrkonto, wo Sie monatlich einen geringen Betrag, was Sie gerade zum notdürftigen Lebensunterhalt gebrauchte. Von der Wohnung selbst, kann ich Ihnen mitteilen das das gesammte Inventar damals versteigert wurde, u. was noch

zurückblieb, wie Photo-Bilder u. Bücher würden auf dem Hofe verbrannt. Nun kann ich Ihnen auch die Adresse von dem Hausbesitzer mitteilen, der damals das Haus übernommen hatte u. welcher noch heute der Besitzer desselben ist. Er behauptet jetzt, daß er ein guter Bekannter von Fr. Levy war u. [illegible] einen sehr hohen Preis für das Haus bezahlt hatte, u. er natürlich kein Nazi war. Ich habe nun genügend Beweismaterial gesammelt, um sobald es erforderlich [illegible] zu überzeugen [illegible] Rechtsansprüche betreffs des Hauses stellt. Eines Tages suchte mich ein Rechtsanwalt auf u. bat um Auskunft. da ich in dem Glauben war, das er im Auftrag von der Jüdischen Gemeinde kam, gab ich leider alle meine Informationen preis, aber nachher stellte es sich heraus, das er von Amerika aus beauftragt sei, über den Verbleib von der Familie Levy nachzuforschen. Es handelt sich um eine frühere Freundin von Fr. Levy, u. nun Rechtsansprüche stellen möchte. Der Anwalt war nun

sehr erstaunt als er von mir erfuhr, das die
beiden Enkel-Kinder von Fr. Lonz am
Leben sind, u. Sie die rechtsmäßigen Erben
sind u. er wollte die Adresse haben, dar-
aufhin gab ich Ihm Ihre Adresse u. er
solle sich mit Ihnen in Verbindung setzen.
Nach diesem Vorfall, habe ich die Angelegenheit, der Jüdischen Gemeinde übergeben, da
diese Angelegenheit mir schon viel Zeit u.
Ärger bereitet hatte. Sie können ja nun die
Sache selbst in die Hand nehmen. Sollten
Sie mir noch irgendwelche Unterlagen benötigen, bin ich gern bereit, soweit ich dazu in der Lage bin, es Ihnen zu übermitteln.
Sie schreiben mir das Sie mir all' die Un-
kosten die ich hatte vergüten wollen, u. da
wäre ich Ihnen dankbar, wenn Sie mir als
Entschädigung, ein Lebensmittel-Paket schik-
ken würden, da wir gerade dieses, sehr drin-
gend benötigen. Ich danke Ihnen, das
Sie an meine Angehörigen, gleich geschrieben haben leider haben wir bis heute noch
keine Nachricht erhalten u. muß nun an-
nehmen, das die Adressen sich verändert

3)

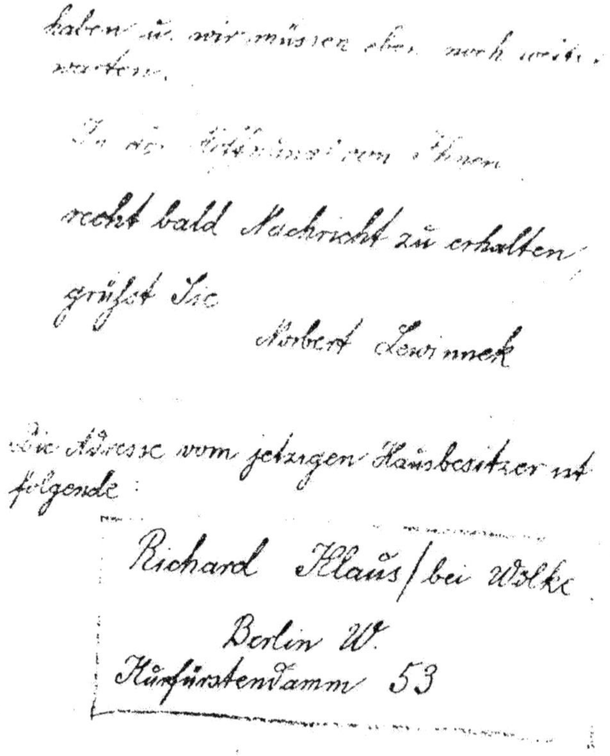

haben zu. wir müssen aber noch weiter warten.

In der Hoffnung von Ihnen recht bald Nachricht zu erhalten, grüßt Sie

Norbert Lewinnek

Die Adresse vom jetzigen Hausbesitzer ist folgende:

Richard Klaus / bei Wolke
Berlin W.
Kurfürstendamm 53

EPILOGUE

On May 12, 2019, Werner, Elaine, Nancy and Peter Gossels as well as their children, Bonnie, Elizabeth, Jon, Warren, Lisa, Amy, Daniel and Jackie, Daniel's wife, returned to Berlin at the invitation of Simon Lütgemeyer and his wife, Britta, to attend the installation of a silent bell board dedicated to the Jewish residents of Lippehnerstrasse 35, who were murdered by the Nazis.

Peter was invited to speak to the current residents and their guests, who had gathered in front of the building to celebrate the unveiling of the commemorative plaque. This is what he said:

"My name is Peter Gossels. My brother, Werner, and I are the grandsons of Isidor and Lina Lewy, who bought this building in or about 1904-1905 as a source of income against the day that he expected to retire. My grandfather died in 1936, but Lina continued as head of the Lewy family. Then, in 1939, Lina was forced to sell this building for a pittance to a Nazi named Klaus.

Lina continued to live in her apartment on the second floor with her two daughters, my Aunt Hilde and my mother, but she had become so poor that she had to rent out space in her apartment to support herself. Then, on October 3, 1942, Lina, a good and innocent woman, if ever there was one, was arrested and deported to the Nazi concentration came at Terezin, Czechoslovakia where she died on November 23, 1942. She was 67 years old.

It took me fifty years to recover this building from the Klaus family. Having accomplished that, my brother, Werner, and I decided that we did not wish to serve as foreign landlords, so we decided to sell this building and donate the proceeds to charity.

As you all know, today is Mother's Day and our family has come to Berlin to honor the life of our courageous and loving mother, Charlotte Lewy Gossels. When it became clear to her that the Nazis would make it impossible for Jewish people to continue to live in Germany, our mother worked for a whole year to obtain visas for her children from the French government so that her sons could escape what proved to be her terrible fate. Thanks to our mother's efforts, Werner and I were put on a train to France on July 3, 1939 and survived to return to Berlin this day. By saving her boys eighty years ago, our mother came to be a grandmother of eight children and a great grandmother of twelve. Seven of her grandchildren are standing here with you today.

Sometime in 1942, our 39 year old mother was forced to work as a slave laborer at a company named Deuta Werke. On February 28, 1943 our mother was arrested, forced into a cattle car with a hundred other innocent people without food, water or heat and deported to Poland, undressed and murdered at Auschwitz on March 2, 1943. That very day, the sixth German Army under General von Paulus surrendered to the Russians at Stalingrad, signaling the beginning of the end of the Nazi regime. Her sister Hilde had been murdered at Auschwitz the day before.

Our mother, grandmother and aunt will always be in our hearts wherever we may be, but that is not why our family has come to Berlin from America:

We feel so fortunate that Simon Lütgemeyer found us and devoted more than a year of his life to research and learn what happened to the Jewish residents of this building during the Nazi regime. We come to honor Simon today. He has provided us an enormous number of documents and information about the Lewy family that we did not have. He even found a series of articles that our father had published in 1936 in the newspaper of the Jewish community. During the course of that year, we have corresponded almost every day and I can say that Simon and Britta have become like family to us. Simon's extraordinary dedication to this project and all that he has accomplished are reflected in the beautiful commemorative plaque that he designed and unveiled today.

Even more important, our family has returned to Berlin to honor you, who stand with us today and are dedicated to making the world and Germany, in particular, a place where everyone can live in peace and harmony with each other. Our mother would be so moved if she could be with us this day.

So, with your permission, I would like to invite you to join our family in reciting an ancient Aramaic prayer that dates back to the time of Jesus, known as the Kaddish, which is included in the daily liturgy of the Jewish people and asks God to grant peace to Israel and to all men and women everywhere throughout the world . . .

Let us now thank God for keeping us alive to enjoy this moment by singing the Shehecheyanu."

June—August 2019 / Iyar — Av 5779

Gossels Family Helps Dedicate Plaque Honoring Family Who Perished in the Holocaust

by Peter Gossels

Eighty years after our mother had taken my brother and me from our home at 35 Lippehnerstrasse in Berlin and put us on a train bound for France on July 3, 1939, I received an invitation from Simon Lütgemeyer, an architect who now lives in that apartment house, to help him dedicate a plaque listing the names of the Jewish residents who had lived there when the Nazis were in power. I had been corresponding with Simon, who is not Jewish, almost every day for a year and we had exchanged information about my family and the other families who had lived in the building.

My grandfather, Isidor, had bought the 42-apartment building in 1905 as a source of income for him and my grandmother, Lina, against the time when he would sell his business manufacturing dresses. Isidor died in 1936. Lina was forced to sell the building to a Nazi for a pittance in 1939, but she continued to live in the building with our mother and her sister, Hilde, until she was deported to the concentration camp at Terezin in Czechoslovakia on October 3, 1942, where she died on November 23, 1942 at 67.

My aunt, Hilde, became a forced laborer and was murdered at Auschwitz on March 1, 1943. Our mother was also forced to work as a forced laborer until she was arrested on February 28, 1943 and murdered upon her arrival at Auschwitz two days later. That day, the Sixth German Army under General von Paulus surrendered at Stalingrad, marking the beginning of the end of Hitler's Third Reich. By saving her sons from her own terrible fate, our mother came to be a grandmother of eight and the great grandmother of 12.

In response to Simon's invitation, my brother, Werner, his wife, Elaine, and four of their five children, as well as Nancy and me, our three children and our daughter-in-law, returned to Berlin on Mother's Day, May 12, 2019, for the dedication of Simon's beautiful brass plaque, a silent bell board, that now graces the outside of the building, opposite the existing bell board. People also came from Australia, Colombia and France in response to Simon's invitation to bear witness.

Simon had decorated the building entrance leading to the courtyard with pictures of our family and other residents who had lived in our building during the Nazi era, as well as a information about each of those families. Simon had also compiled and distributed a 50-page booklet filled with documents about the house, its inhabitants and the sources of information that he had published.

The street where we once lived was closed to traffic on May 12, 2019, and a temporary café on wheels decorated with flowers and filled with drinks and pastry prepared by the residents of the building, was parked in front to provide refreshments as more and more of the residents and those in the neighborhood came to share in the festivities. By the time I was asked to help unveil the plaque and speak, I was surrounded by a semicircle of more than

75 people standing three deep on the sidewalk and street. After concluding my remarks, I asked everyone to join me in reciting the *Kaddish*, the ancient Aramaic prayer that we say when we think of those who have died. We concluded by singing *Shehecheyanu* to thank G-d for allowing us to reach this amazing day.

What had started with formal speeches became a neighborhood block party with lots of kids and adults enjoying a perfect day graced with warm sunshine. Simon then played a recording he had found of *Chanukah* melodies sung by our second cousin, Hanns John (Jacobsohn), who was shot by the Nazis in 1943. Lisa Gossels then showed her film, *The Children of Chabannes*, and Simon showed clips from films made by Fritz Lang featuring our second cousin, Georg John (born Jacobsohn) a well-known actor who died in the Lodz Ghetto, according to Tilmann Korth's *Family History Gossels-Lewy*.

The Gossels family was then invited to visit their former home on the second floor, now occupied by Ms. Gross, an actress, and Mr. Ott, a jazz saxophonist. After bread, cheese, chocolate and wine were served, a jazz concert was presented, as Mr. Ott, on saxophone, accompanied by an impressive bass player and Warren Gossels, drumming on a shoebox, held forth for everyone with their vigorous jazz. The windows were wide-open, the sun was shining and people were dancing in our old living room. Our family home, once filled with fear and darkness, had become a place of light and joy.

The Gossels family, who had suffered so terribly at the hands of the German people, returned to America convinced that the masters of evil who dominated the German mind set 80 years ago have been replaced by decent, caring young people who are committed to making the world, and Germany in particular, a better, more peaceful and generous place to live.

(continued on page 9)

Peter Gossells and his wife, Nancy, with their three children and daughter-in-law, Peter's brother, Werner, and his wife, Elaine, along with four of their five children, returned to Berlin on Mother's Day, May 12, for the dedication of Simon Lütgemeyer's beautiful brass plaque, a silent bell board, that now graces the outside of the building, opposite the existing bell board. The plaque is honoring Gossell's family, who lived in the building prior to perishing in the Holocaust. People also came from Australia, Colombia and France in response to the invitation to bear witness. Simon Lütgemeyer is an architect who now lives in that apartment house.

Live Streaming Shabbat Services

You can view Shabbat services at Temple Shir Tikva via live stream at 6:15 p.m. each Friday and 8:30 a.m. each Saturday. To access the live stream, go to the temple website home page and click on Live Stream in the Welcome box.

Enjoy the live stream and let us know how it works at www.info@ shirtikva.org.

Pearl Street Cupboard and Café Mitzvah Volunteers Needed

First Thursday of Each Month

Temple Shir Tikva provides volunteer servers once a month at Pearl Street Cafe in Framingham. Operated by United Way, Pearl Street Cafe is a warm and welcoming place where those struggling with food insecurity can enjoy a community supper.

Volunteer adults (and children over 10 accompanied by an adult) act as wait-staff, serving guests a freshly prepared, restaurant-style meal. This is a wonderful and rewarding mitzvah opportunity.

Volunteers arrive at 5 p.m. to assist with set-up and receive assignments. We serve clients from 5:30 -7:30 and then assist with cafe and kitchen clean-up. With everyone's help, the evening ends around 7:30 - 8.

Contact Carrie Morenberg at cpmorenberg@gmail.com for more information.

AFTERWORD

Our grandmother, Charlotte ("Lotte") Lewy Gossels was a hero. She saved her two sons, Peter and Werner, who were just 5 and 8 years old, when she entrusted them to the care of strangers in order to help them escape from Nazi Germany. We cannot begin to imagine the pain and anguish she lived with once she put her boys on a train bound for France on July 3, 1939. It is heartbreaking that they were never reunited. When her mother, Lina, was deported to a concentration camp at Terezin, Czechoslovakia, Lotte may have sacrificed her own chance to escape to Switzerland from Germany. Her letters to her sons reveal her love, courage, bravery and selflessness as well as her work ethic, deep commitment to family and Judaism, sense of humor and positive outlook on life. These are all attributes she fostered in Peter and Werner.

When he boarded that train at the age of eight, Peter was forced into a parental role: He shouldered the responsibility to take care of himself and his little brother – comforting him and communicating back to their Mutti and Vati, as they moved from place to place and faced threats to their lives. Peter has continued to be a caring big brother to this day.

Lotte's letters subtly reveal how conditions worsened in Germany – the omissions tell much of her story. At first she could write directly to France; later she had to route her letters through intermediaries in Amsterdam. When, in September of 1941, she knew that the boys were emigrating to America, she wrote to "innumerable people in different parts of the United States, in an effort to obtain from them some kind of indirect statement about the boys." When he arrived in New York, Peter wanted to shield his Mutti from worrying about his being ill, needing a cast for his leg, and being in the hospital. Charlotte's final letter shows that Aunt Lucy had let her know that her boys had made it safely to the United States and that Peter was recovering and about to be placed with a family. We hope that Lotte took comfort in knowing that her efforts had saved them.

Tremendous credit is due to the courageous and kind-hearted people who sheltered, nurtured and educated them in France, and to those in Europe and the United States who arranged for their safe passage from France through Spain to Portugal where they boarded the Serpa Pinto, a ship that brought them to New York. In particular, the Joint Distribution Committee, the Comite Israelite Pour Les Enfants, the Oeuvre de Secour aux Enfants (OSE), the Hebrew Immigrant Aid Society (HIAS), the American Society of Friends (Quakers), and the Jewish Child Welfare Association cared for and rescued Peter, Werner as well as other refugee children.

Peter and Werner have always expressed gratitude to the families that took them in so they could live safely in the United States. Werner became part of the extended Glaser/Gordon clan. Peter's homelife was far less stable, but he considered Arnold Singal, who shared his bedroom with Peter, to be a lifelong friend. Peter and Werner did visit their father, Max, and Melanie Gossels in Venezuela, and it was again Peter who managed to work through all the difficult complications of travel outside and the uncertainty of re-entry to the United States for himself and his younger brother. Peter excelled academically at Boston Latin School and received a scholarship to study at Harvard and later at Harvard Law School. Acting on Peter's advice, Werner received a scholarship to study at Yale after he graduated from Brookline High. They both became naturalized citizens of the United States. Peter married Nancy Lee Tuber and Werner married Elaine Ruth Furman; both wives share a deep friendship and embody so many of Lotte's characteristics: intelligence, beauty inside and outside, Jewish values, leadership and love for family.

Peter devoted five decades of work to regain ownership of the property in Berlin where they had lived and that Lina Lewy, his grandmother, was forced to sign over to a Nazi. When his long efforts finally succeeded, Peter and Werner sold the building and donated the proceeds to charity to honor the memory of Charlotte Lewy Gossels, her sister Hilde, mother Lina, and the other innocent victims of the Nazi Holocaust. Their memory lives on through funds for scholarships, academic excellence, aiding Jews and others in need and teaching about human dignity.

Many, with such a difficult start in life, would think of themselves as victims – but not Peter and not Werner. Charlotte Lewy Gossels' legacy is her sons, her eight grandchildren and twelve great-grandchildren. We know she would be proud of the men her sons became and the example they have set for their family and community. We are grateful to our grandmother for her courage and her perseverance against such odds and the love, nurturing and support of her sons that led them to freedom. Our only regret is that we never had the opportunity to sit by her side and know her as the loving grandmother she would surely have been.

May her memory be for a blessing.

Lotte Gossels' Grandchildren

THANK YOU

This book would not have been composed without the help of my brother, Werner, and our wonderful families.

Much of the information and documentation of my grandfather's life has been contributed by Simon Lütgemeyer, an architect who lives at 35 Käthe-Niederkirchner Strasse and has researched the history of the Jewish residents of the building who were deported by the Nazis to concentration camps. Additional information about the Lewy family was gleaned from the remarkable "Family History Gossels Lewy" published by Dr. Ing Tilmann Korth in 2018.

The fine translation of our mother's letters came from Anneliese Hall of Cape Porpoise, Maine, and Cornelia Sittel of Arlington, Massachusetts.

A major contribution to this book came from my assistant, Cheryl Cant, her daughter, Jennifer Brennan, and Andrea Reider of Andrea Reider Books.

And how can I thank my amazing bride of 61 years, Nancy Lee Gossels, for her love, wisdom and editorial contributions to this project.

C. Peter R. Gossels

ABOUT THE AUTHOR

C. Peter R. Gossels is a retired attorney, who lives in Wayland, Massachusetts, with his wife, Nancy, a poet, artist and liturgist, who is our family's loving soul.

Made in the
USA
Middletown, DE

77397985R00210